SQL:
A Beginner's Guide

Forrest Houlette

Osborne/**McGraw-Hill**

Berkeley New York St. Louis San Francisco
Auckland Bogotá Hamburg London Madrid
Mexico City Milan Montreal New Delhi Panama City
Paris São Paulo Singapore Sydney Tokyo Toronto

Osborne/**McGraw-Hill**
2600 Tenth Street
Berkeley, California 94710
U.S.A.

For information on translations or book distributors outside the U.S.A., or to arrange
bulk purchase discounts for sales promotions, premiums, or fund-raisers, please contact
Osborne/**McGraw-Hill** at the above address.

SQL: A Beginner's Guide

1234567890 2CUS 2CUS 01987654321

ISBN 0-07-213096-2

Publisher   Brandon A. Nordin
Vice President and Associate Publisher   Scott Rogers
Editorial Director   Wendy Rinaldi
Project Editor   Monika Faltiss
Acquisitions Coordinator   Timothy Madrid
Tech Editor   Chris Herring
Copy Editor   Bob Campbell
Proofreader   Brian Galloway
Indexer   Jack Lewis
Computer Designers   Roberta Steele, Tara Davis, Lauren McCarthy
Illustrator   Michael Mueller
Series Design   Gary Corrigan
Cover Design   Greg Scott
Cover Illustration   Kevin Curry

This book was composed with Corel VENTURA™ Publisher.

To my wife, Judy, and my daughter, Alex,
who rib me because my home office glows
at night when the lights are out due to
the LEDs on all the equipment.

About the Author

Forrest Houlette is a computer writer and consultant who lives in Louisville, Kentucky. He is president of Write Environment, Inc., a consulting firm that specializes in Visual Basic software development, custom documentation, training, and software for both education and business. He is also a consultant with Ajilon, an international provider of information technology services. Forrest holds a Ph.D. in Linguistics and Rhetoric from the University of Louisville. He began working with computers when he took a course in FORTRAN in 1979. Since then, he has programmed in BASIC, the Digital Authoring Language, C, C++, WordBasic, SQL, SQLWindows, and Visual Basic. During his career as a university professor, he taught linguistics and focused on using artificial intelligence techniques to improve software for writing. He has written computer-based education programs for the teaching of writing, one of which, Write Environment, won the Zenith Masters of Innovation competition. Forrest now focuses on writing about computers and creating custom software. He has taught courses on Windows 95, Windows NT, Office 97, and Visual Basic for Learning Tree International. He has authored or co-authored books for IDG, New Riders Publishing, Que, and Sybex. He is also a Microsoft Certified Product Specialist. His current placement with Ajilon is with Vencor, a healthcare provider headquartered in Louisville.

Contents

Acknowledgments

A number of people have worked hard on this project to make it a success. Timothy Madrid, Monika Faltiss, and Wendy Rinaldi at Osborne/ McGraw-Hill put forth a lot of effort, and have been superb to work with. The technical editor for this book, whose name I have never actually seen, has been outstanding at catching the misstatements and confusions that arise when you try to accommodate all SQL dialects in a single book. His comments have been invaluable. My agent, David Fugate, as always, has been greatly appreciated. There are lots of people behind the scenes that I never get to meet who do the layout, indexing, and design on the book. Many thanks to all of them.

Introduction

Everything I've done with computers I've done by accident. Well, maybe it was serendipity. Learning SQL, the topic of this book, was no different. I started my career in another field. In that respect, I am a little like Clifford Stoll, author of *Cuckoo's Egg: Tracking a Spy Through the Maze of Computer Espionage*. He was an astronomer whose grant ran out, so he started running the UNIX boxes that other astronomers used. I started out my career as a linguist who specialized in English discourse, and got involved in computing because I had to deal with statistics. When I started, I took a freshman-level course in FORTRAN so that I could understand how to interact with the IBM 370 that the university used on a time-sharing basis with a regional consortium of businesses and academic institutions. I learned how to punch my cards, format my output, and write simple formulae. Then I graduated to SAS and SPSS so that I could crunch numbers. I had achieved my goal of facilitating my work as a linguist, and I was very comfortable with my level of computing skills. I had no plans to be anything other than a linguist. And Cliff Stoll had no plans to be involved in one of the most publicized hacker cases when he started.

However, in 1982 I bought a Franklin Ace 1000 because I needed a word processor, and I took a course in BASIC that was offered free to educators at Radio Shack. In my spare time, I started developing educational software. That experience led me down a path that eventually led to this book, and I really never intended to take that path. My experience with educational software led me to participate in a Digital Equipment Corporation Special Investment Grant in the mid 1980s, for which I developed a system for teaching writing in the Digital Authoring Language. I developed some pretty cool stuff for that grant, but the university I worked for owned it all. Unfortunately, the university had no concept of how to be in the software business. We developed some pretty serious disagreements. But I was hooked on writing software.

Recognizing that mainframe computer-assisted instruction was not the future of computer-aided learning, and accepting that the university and I could not resolve our differences, I leased my own equipment and bought the Microsoft C compiler. My software needed multitasking, and at that time the only multitasking available for a PC was this thing called Windows, which not too many people had heard about. I bought the Windows 2.11 Software Development Kit, and I started writing Windows software for the PC. I thought my stuff was pretty cool, but no one else in my area took much notice. But I was happy just working with my toys and advancing my research into computer-aided learning. I really enjoyed being a linguist who worked in this area.

In the late 1980s, however, I did two foolish things. I got a paper accepted at the International Conference on Technology in Education, and I submitted some software to some contest called Masters of Innovation that Zenith Data Systems sponsored. I went to Brussels to the conference, had a great time, and came back home to find out that disagreements within the university were surfacing again and I really hated dealing with them. Down at the bottom of my stack of mail, about two feet high after the trip, was a letter from Zenith. Figuring that it was a letter politely telling me that my entry had not won the competition, I tossed it into the low priority pile, and dealt with all the university hassles, righting the wrongs as best I could and starting work on an ulcer in the process. About a week later, I finally opened the letter from Zenith. I had won, and my winning only aggravated the conflicts within the university. One day I reached the point where I was reading the want ads for solace.

Under the E's there was an ad for an editor. I could do that, I said to myself, so I sent in a résumé. I got the call, I went for the interview, I didn't get the job, but they asked me to try writing a book for them. And they offered to pay me. I had long had a dream of being a professional writer, so I took the contract. This experience was cooler than writing the software. I had Windows 3.1 in beta form, people liked what I was writing, and I felt good about what I was doing. I was hooked. I stayed with the university for a couple more years. I even ran a Novell network for them during that time. However, the disagreements got to be too aggravating. I decided to become a consultant. So I bought a fax machine (you can't be a consultant without one of those), and I took a leave of absence. I went to Tech Ed to score some connections, and I stepped out on my own.

Now, if you haven't done it, working for yourself is a real rush. I spent two years writing books, doing contract training, and developing educational software. I learned more about the Windows NT operating system during that time than anyone should. I was on the ground floor of Windows 95 publishing. I wrote an article for the *Windows Tech Journal*. And then I had an experience that forced me to learn SQL.

The training contracts grew farther and farther apart, and I could not replace the business fast enough to stay on my own. I took a job at a real estate investment trust writing programs in SQL Windows. I was programming against an Oracle database, and I had no choice but to learn SQL. This was a strange time in my life. I wrote programs that no one ever actually used, and the handwriting was writ large upon the wall that after the company finished merging with the company it had just bought, pink slips would be in the pay envelopes for many on the IT staff. I found another job, this time in textile manufacturing, and learned to program against SQL Server in Visual Basic. Then I returned to being a consultant, this time with Ajilon, and I continue to program in Visual Basic for SQL Server. And I obviously still write books. Which brings us to introducing this one.

Who Should Read This Book

So welcome to Osborne's *SQL: A Beginner's Guide*. As the name suggests, this book is for everyone from raw programming trainees to programming professionals learning to use SQL for the first time. If, like me, you found that your training in programming left you unprepared to communicate with databases, do not feel alone. Most practicing programmers learned SQL on the fly because somebody bought an Oracle database, the database that introduced SQL as a database programming language. Therefore, they had to learn SQL to work with Oracle. As SQL went through the standardization process, other databases supported it, and SQL became the standard way of talking to a database.

We hope you'll find the material interesting, well-rounded, clear and concise, and just plain fun. We've focused on avoiding using sample databases. We use one sample to practice some basics, but as soon as you are ready to do some real work, you create and work with a database that eventually will find its way into production. You participate in building the prototype of a system that eventually will be offered to the educational software marketplace.

What This Book Covers

This book is broken into 17 modules and 2 appendices. The modules contain pretty much all you need to know to immediately begin querying databases, from selecting data from tables to creating tables and databases. All along the way you work both with standard SQL, using a query editor to submit queries, and embedded SQL, using Visual Basic as the example programming language. We begin at the point where most programmers begin working with databases: how to connect. Then we explore basic select, insert, update, and delete operations. Next we take on functions, building tables, creating databases, and writing stored procedures. In addition to creating a real-world database, you write the prototype of the administrative tool that administrators will use to manage the database. You learn how to run basic queries interactively with the database, you learn how to write stored procedures, and you learn how to embed all the SQL you write inside of another program that functions as the client to the database.

At the back of the book there are two appendices. The first is an answer guide, giving you the correct answers to the Mastery Check questions which are at the end of each module. The second provides some background theory about the Structured Query Language. Our goal in the modules is to focus on SQL from the practical, how-to point of view. In the second appendix, we bring you up to speed on relational database theory and how SQL is structured.

This book also has a Web site, where all the code is available for easy download and use in your own query tool or development environment. If you follow along with the examples used in this book and download the code, you have basic templates for any type of query that you need to write.

Module 1, "Accessing the Database"—In this module, we cover how to connect to a database. We cover using query tools to connect, using ODBC, using DAO, and using ADO. We make the argument that ADO is the most advantageous method to use currently, but show you how to connect using all these methods.

Module 2, "Retrieving Data"—SELECT is the most frequent verb in SQL, and this module shows you how to use SELECT queries to retrieve data from a database. We cover not only basic SELECT statements, but joins, the use of WHERE, grouping, and similar topics. You learn all there is to know about using SELECT right away. We examine using data controls to retrieve data using embedded SQL.

Module 3, "Inserting Data"—One goal of most front-end database programs is to provide for data entry. In this module, we focus on inserting data using the INSERT statement. We show you how to use embedded insert statements in Visual Basic to create a simple database data entry program.

Module 4, "Updating Data"—Changing data is another common SQL task. In this module, we use the UPDATE statement to change data already stored in the database. You will learn some of the headaches associated with using INSERT and UPDATE to manage data from a Visual Basic program.

Module 5, "Deleting Data"—This module covers the use of the DELETE statement to remove data from the database. You are cautioned about its perils, and you practice using it from both a query tool and a Visual Basic program.

Module 6, "Creating Tables"—Before you do much SQL programming at all, you discover the need for temporary tables. This module shows you how to create both temporary and permanent tables, and how to manage them. We cover data normalization here to help you build efficient tables.

Module 7, "Creating Databases"—Most programmers don't create databases; database administrators do. But just in case you need to, we show you how to create a database, and we walk you through the thinking process of creating the Portfolio database, one that will eventually see release as a product.

Module 8, "Using Operators"—Now that you have a database, you will want to do more complex things in your queries. This module focuses on the variety of logical and mathematical operators SQL provides, and shows you basic techniques for using them. We also practice fixing bugs in the programming we have done so far. The only way to build debugging skills with SQL is to experience a few bugs and fix them.

Module 9, "Using Functions"—Every programming language has functions, and this module serves as your quick reference to SQL functions. You get practice using selected functions to build useful queries.

Module 10, "Building Subqueries"—A subquery is a query within a query, and they can perform especially useful work in SQL statements. This module shows you how to build and use them in a query tool, and how to embed them in an application.

Module 11, "Building Views"—Views are like tables that are built on demand. They allow users access to data, but they also allow you to limit what users can do with the data. We show you how to create views and use them to your advantage as a SQL programmer.

Module 12, "Building Stored Procedures"—Stored procedures are queries that you build and store on the database server. They run at the server, saving you the overhead of processing queries at the client. They are typically faster than client-based queries, and you can use flow control within them to perform complex programming. This module shows you how to build basic stored procedures.

Module 13, "Programming in Stored Procedures"—Most databases extend SQL to allow you to write programs within stored procedures. This module shows you how to build programming steps into your stored procedures.

Module 14, "Using Parameters"—Like functions in a programming language, stored procedures can accept parameters. You can pass values to your stored procedures that are used in processing the queries. This module shows you how to add parameters to your stored procedures.

Module 15, "Using Cursors"—Cursors allow you to receive and manipulate a recordset in SQL. Some programmers see them as performance hogs. This module shows you when to use them and how to create and use them efficiently.

Module 16, "Building Unions"—Unions are a type of query that allows you to unite data sets into a single dataset. Typically they are used with temporary tables. However, some databases let you use unions to build views on the data. We show you not only how to build a union, but practical scenarios in which to use them.

Module 17, "Winding Down the Portfolio Project"—The Portfolio database is a database we have built and programmed against throughout the book. It is the prototype of a production system that eventually will be released. In this module, we take a look at several issues relating to this database that we brought up along the way but have not explored. We ask you to use your SQL skills to solve several programming problems.

Appendix A, "Answers to Mastery Checks"—Each module contains questions at the end (called Mastery Checks) that check to make sure you've absorbed the basics, and Appendix A provides the answers to these questions.

Appendix B, "A Little SQL Theory"—Since we focus on practical SQL throughout the book, we provide this appendix to allow you to explore the basic theory behind SQL and relational databases.

How To Read This Book

This book can be read from beginning to end, starting with the first module, but you can also open any module for an easy-to-follow introduction to the specific SQL topics or capabilities you are interested in. Each module explains in detail the topics it covers, and includes many working examples demonstrating the capabilities of SQL. In addition, at the end of most of the modules is a project that illustrates, step-by-step, the creation of a working application using the most important parts of the material discussed in the module.

Special Features

Throughout each module are **_Hints and Notes_**, as well as **_detailed code listings._** The code all works fine and the source code can be downloaded in zip files from the Web site in full, at **www.osborne.com** and then the name of the project file (in the Module01 folder you'll find the zip files for Module 1 projects). There are **_1-Minute Drills_** that check to make sure you're retaining what you've read (and help focus your attention on the more important points). There are **_Ask The Expert_** question-and-answer sections that give in-depth explanations about the current subject. Included with the book and on the Web site are **_Projects_** that take what you've learned and put it into working applications. At the end of each module are **_Mastery Checks_** to give you another opportunity for review, and the answers are contained in **_Appendix A_**. Overall, our objective is to get you up to speed quickly, without a lot of obtuse, abstract, and dry reference to formal coding practices.

So let's get started. You won't believe how easy and fun it is to write SQL queries. Good luck!!

Part I

Learning the Essentials

Module 1

Accessing the Database

Goals

- Learn how to connect to a database
- Create a connection using ODBC and OLE DB
- Create a connection from a program using DAO and ADO
- Create a connection from a program using a connection library

Welcome to *SQL: A Beginner's Guide,* a guide to programming databases using the Structured Query Language. You'll find that this guide is organized the way most programmers have to learn SQL, by the seat of their pants in the midst of a project. As a result, we are beginning at the beginning from the programmer's point of view. This module covers connecting to a database, the first thing your program must do before you can execute any SQL statements. Don't worry, if you've never done any SQL before, much less programming, you should be able to follow along. We aim to show you the exact steps to follow.

Before we connect, however, we need to define just what databases we will be using in this guide. You can use Structured Query Language to communicate with many different databases. SQL made its appearance as a part of Oracle in 1979. Since that time, it has appeared in IBM's DB2, Sybase, SQL6, Microsoft's SQL Server, and many end-user databases like Borland's Paradox, Microsoft's Access, and dBase. The language was first standardized in 1986, giving each implementation a common core that allows a programmer an easy time of communicating with different database products. You can use a given vendor's tool or third-party products, such as Watcom's SQL Engine, to connect to databases produced by different manufacturers and issue SQL queries. You have lots of options in the market for using SQL to manage data.

For this book, we will frame all the exercises and examples using databases constructed in Microsoft SQL Server. SQL Server is a relatively common database. In addition, you can download the Microsoft Data Engine (MSDE) from http://msdn.microsoft.com/vstudio/msde/download.asp free of charge, so long as you own one of Microsoft's Visual Studio development tools. It is also a part of Office 2000 Premium and Developer editions, and those who develop applications on MSDE can distribute MSDE with the applications royalty free. As a result, the databases we develop for this book are available on the book's Web site, and they include MSDE as a royalty-free component in the distribution package.

MSDE is not an industrial-strength SQL database. It cannot handle more than five user connections, significant amounts of traffic, or advanced database operations like replication. As a result, you can't use MSDE for significant business databases; however, it works just fine for a single user practicing with SQL, or for limited database applications. Microsoft sees it as a marketing teaser that you can use to interest clients in SQL Server's database technology. That client's logical migration path as the data storage needs increase is to SQL Server.

Hint

SQL has been standardized by the American National Standards Institute (ANSI), and the standard has been through several revisions. The current standard is ANSI SQL-92. The current revision in process is called ANSI SQL-98, or SQL 3.

Relying on MSDE in our examples requires a note of caution. The implementation of standard SQL (also known as ANSI SQL) is common to all SQL databases. However, each database manufacturer extends SQL a little bit with proprietary functionality. That extra functionality means that Microsoft has its own SQL dialect, and Oracle has its own, and Sybase has its own. Even Microsoft's implementations on Access and SQL Server are different. As a result, we will focus on writing ANSI SQL that should run on any database. Notes and hints will keep you aware of the differences among the databases available on the market.

Enough of these preliminaries, however. If you are going to learn SQL, you have to connect to your database. So let's get on to building that connection.

Connecting to the Database

In a typical business database installation, you won't ever see the computer where the database is running. The database will reside on a server in a server room, and you will work on a desktop computer elsewhere. To communicate with the database, you will connect to it over the network. In fact, any computer that receives data from the database or adds data to the database connects over a network of some kind.

Typically your connection takes place over a local area network (LAN) or a wide area network (WAN). Your computer has a network interface card installed, and the networking cable plugs into this card. The most common type of card is an Ethernet adapter; however, you could be using a Token Ring adapter. The network interface card transmits requests to distant servers over the network cable and receives responses to those requests over the same cable. The transmissions take place according to a set of agreements called protocols, the most common of which is the Transmission Control Protocol/Internet Protocol (TCP/IP).

Protocols allow two types of names on the network that allow you to communicate with another computer. Each computer can be given a name, a string of characters that identifies it on the network. To communicate with a computer on the network, therefore, you can simply type its name into the Run dialog box and click OK. If you try this, however, you will get the error that the file or one of its components could not be found, and you will not communicate with the computer. You have to use a special convention to inform your operating system that you are not looking for a file, but rather another computer on the network. This convention is to precede the name with two backslashes (\\), as shown here. When two backslashes begin the name, Windows looks not on the local drive, but on the network, for the resource.

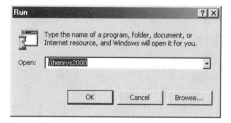

Hint

The naming convention that uses two backslashes to denote network communication is called the Uniform Naming Convention. As a result, names like \\Henrys2000 are often called UNC names. The UNC name without the backslashes (Henrys2000) is often called the NetBIOS name, since it is used by the NetBIOS networking protocol, a protocol created by Microsoft and used by Windows up through Windows 98, as the network address.

To communicate with a database on a server, therefore, one piece of information you need to know is the server's name. For this book, we have set up a Windows 2000 server named Henrys2000 to contain our databases. Microsoft SQL Server runs on Henrys2000. To connect to Henrys2000's databases, we need only to supply the server's name when requested.

However, there is another piece of information you will also want to know about your server. To communicate on the network, you actually communicate with network addresses, unique numbers assigned to each computer, rather than with computer names. Networks run special services on their servers that match names to addresses. Some of the most common of such services are the Domain Name System (DNS) used on the Internet, and the Windows Internet Name Service (WINS) that runs under Windows. No matter how the process of resolving names to addresses takes place, it can fail. And it can leave you unable to communicate with your database for long periods of time. As a result, you will want to know the address of your database server. Typically, you will need the IP address, since most networks use the TCP/IP protocol. However, you may need the address physically burned into a ROM chip on the network card (called the Media Access Control, or MAC, address) on some networks. On the network used for this book, Henrys2000 resides at the IP address 192.168.42.252.

Armed with these pieces of information, we are ready to try a connection. All we need is a tool that will allow us to create the connection.

Ask the Expert

Question: Okay, I bought this book to learn SQL, and we aren't doing SQL yet. Why all these preliminaries?

Answer: Actually, these aren't preliminaries. Everyone I know who had to learn SQL had to pick it up on the job. Connecting to the database is the first task of the job prior to learning SQL. If you can't connect, you can't learn. I am approaching this task of teaching SQL by starting with the first principles.

Question: Why is SQL such a back-burner topic for programmers?

Answer: I think the answer to that question is that people who teach programming think that the goal of a program is to cause a computer to execute instructions in ways appropriate to the task at hand. The tasks have changed significantly since I started programming. I started out building programs that controlled the computer sitting in front of me. Now I am mainly working to control data that is stored on another computer. As this role has changed, I had to acquire the skill of manipulating data. I needed

SQL to do that. Programmers often see SQL as the database administrator's problem. Now that programs focus more on controlling data, SQL has become everybody's problem.

Question: **Why SQL? Aren't there other ways to address databases?**

Answer: Actually, there are probably lots of more efficient ways to access data. However, proprietary methods are not in favor any longer. We need to access data stored on disparate devices with some reasonable efficiency. Like it or not, SQL happens to have been a way of accessing data that became popular, and then standardized. Once it had become a standard, lots of vendors supported it. Look at the issue from the point of view of rendering text and graphics on a page. HTML is one way to do it. It is not efficient from the programmer's point of view, but it is popular and widely supported. As a result, all of us use it daily on the World Wide Web. SQL has pretty much had the same fate.

Using a Query Tool

Every database on the market offers some type of query tool, and some independent software vendors sell query tools that will connect with any database. All the tools that run under Windows have some common features. First, when they start, they present a connection dialog box that connects you with a database. Second, these tools offer a multiple document interface, so that you can have several connections active at once, each represented by a child window in the query tool. Finally, each connection window typically has two panes. In one, you type your SQL query. In the other, the results of your query appear.

The following illustration shows the connection dialog box for SQL Server's Query Analyzer, the query tool distributed with SQL Server. As you can see, it requests three types of information. First, it asks for the name of the server. (The address of the server can be used as well.)

1

Second, it wants to know whether the Query Analyzer should start the server if it is currently stopped. Normally when the server is unavailable, it is unavailable for a reason, and the administrators who have stopped it probably won't appreciate you starting the server. On a production network, you normally would not check this box. However, if you are working on a development server over which you have control, you may want to check it. Developers can easily forget to restart the database, so having the Query Analyzer start a stopped database is a real convenience.

Finally, the connection dialog box asks for a username and password to authenticate you. Databases typically offer two security schemes. Under one, your domain username and password are used. Since SQL Server runs on Windows NT or Windows 2000, the first option button, Windows NT Authentication, represents this possibility. Under the second scheme, the database itself maintains its own list of usernames and passwords. The second option button allows you to use this type of security scheme.

Hint

Query tools typically do not know which security scheme is in place at the time you make these choices. As a result, if you make the wrong choice, your connection will fail. Retry the connection with the other security scheme selected before you panic about whether the database server is down.

Type in the server name, select a security option, and click OK. What happens depends on the tool you are using and how you have configured the names of databases on your network for data access. In general, under Windows you have two means of connecting to a database, using ODBC or using OLE DB. Some query tools may require one of the methods and disallow the other. SQL Server Query Analyzer allows both, so you should get your connection the first time with just the information we entered. However, with other tools, you may have some setup work to do.

1-Minute Drill

● **Give two ways to name a server when you connect using a query tool.**

● **Name the two most common technologies for connecting to a database.**

Using ODBC

Soon after Windows made its appearance as version 2.11, Microsoft wanted to provide a means for Windows users to connect to databases easily. At this point in the history of the operating system, Windows really was a program that ran on top of another operating system, MS-DOS. If you wanted to connect to a database, you needed to use the operating system's services to connect. Making such a connection was not a problem as long as the database resided on the PC you were using. DOS knew how to handle files stored

---

● Name a server either by its NetBIOS name (the text name that shows in the Network Neighborhood properties) or by its IP address.
● The two technologies are ODBC and OLE DB.

on its local drives, and a database was just another type of file. However, when you added a network into the picture, making a connection became a significantly larger problem. DOS had no means of using networked resources. DOS by itself did not know how to talk to a network.

Communicating with a network was not just an issue of installing a device driver like you used to communicate with your printer. Networking required a driver to allow DOS to communicate with the network interface card, but also a series of programs called *protocols* that allowed communication between two computers that contained network interface cards. The network adapter was a transmitter-receiver. The driver for it allowed DOS to transmit and receive using the card and a cable. The protocols were agreements about how to transmit and receive.

Even with protocols in place to allow efficient transmitting and receiving, DOS still had no means of communicating with a database. Each database vendor had its own means of contacting the database, logging in, and submitting queries. Recognizing that order was significantly better for business than chaos, Microsoft and the major database vendors formulated a strategy called Open Database Connectivity, abbreviated ODBC. ODBC put in place a set of protocols for uniformly addressing databases. The specification covered issues like uniform ways of addressing the server, logging in, and submitting queries. ODBC became a layer of software that, on the user end, provided a standard way to communicate with a database and, on the operating system end, allowed each vendor to translate information provided by the user to meet the requirements of the database.

You are probably most familiar with ODBC as an icon in the Windows Control Panel, whether you have used it or not. This icon opens a Control Panel applet that permits you to define a database connection. The early versions of this applet were somewhat arcane in their structure. Users had to know a great deal in advance of opening the applet in order to make the connection, and the advance knowledge was not often information that users easily retained. As a result, ODBC had a reputation for being difficult for end users to use. The latest version, however, has a comparatively easy wizard interface.

In most versions of Windows currently on the market, the ODBC icon appears in the Control Panel as soon as you select Start | Settings | Control Panel. However, in Windows 2000, the icon hides underneath the Administrative Tools icon. Opening Administrative tools reveals an icon named Data Sources (ODBC). This is the icon you use to build database connections (see Figure 1-1).

Once you have opened the ODBC applet, for the most part, you need only to focus on one of the first three tabs of the dialog box that appears, shown in the following illustration. Each of these tabs lists connections to databases, and you can readily see that several are provided for you. Almost any application that can use an ODBC connection installs one for you during its setup program. This practice harks back to the days when ODBC was a

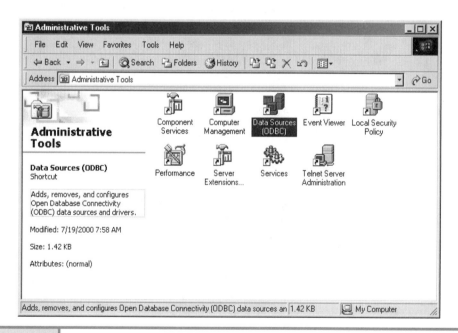

Figure 1-1   Open the Administrative Tools icon to locate the ODBC applet

mystery to the average user. So if, for example, you want to use an Excel spreadsheet on your local computer as a database, you can easily do so.

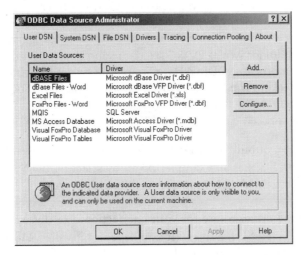

Your first question in building a connection to your database is which of the first three tabs to use. To connect, you need to create a Data Source Name, or DSN. If you create a User DSN, that DSN is tied to the user who is logged in. If you are logged in, you have access to your database connection. If I am logged in, I don't have access to the user DSN that you created. User DSNs are good for a situation where different users must share the same computer but must have access to different data sources.

A System DSN, by contrast, provides a data source tied to the system. Whenever the system is up, the data source is available. Systems used on a factory floor, for example, to record production data for a shift are good candidates for use of System DSNs. You don't want to worry that someone might have logged in under their own username instead of the shift's login, for example. You want to make sure that the database is available for work however the user has logged in.

File DSNs are stored in files, and as a result are portable across systems. Moving a file DSN to another system is a matter of copying the file. What is most useful about File DSNs, however, is that you can open them in Notepad and examine all the parts of the connection string. Such a tactic is useful if you are trying to connect to the database from a programming environment and need to know specific parameters and settings in order to build a connection string to pass to the ODBC driver.

Hint

The default folder where ODBC file data sources are stored is Program Files\Common Files\ODBC\Data Sources. If a user has changed this location, clicking the Set Directory button on the File DSN tab will reveal the currently active location.

The process of building a DSN is similar in all three cases. We will build a System DSN as an example. Begin by selecting the System DSN tab and clicking the Add button. Then follow these steps:

1. Select the driver to use for your connection. For this example, we have selected SQL Server. (If you have not installed MSDE or SQL Server client tools or a similar package that installs the SQL Server driver, you may not see this option. In this case, select an option for another database, such as Access, a file for which is likely to appear on your drive somewhere.) Click Finish.

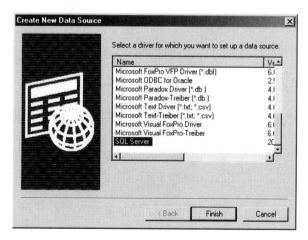

2. In the Create New Data Source dialog box, enter a name for the connection. You will use the name to connect to the data source in the future.

3. Enter a description if you like. The description appears when you view the connection using the ODBC Control Panel applet.

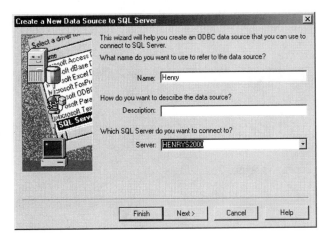

4. Select the server to connect to. You can type in the name or choose from the drop-down list. Click Next.

5. Select the security scheme you want to use. Windows NT security, the default, allows you to attach using your Windows NT username. Basically, once you have logged into your domain, you do not need to log into the SQL Server. Pass-through authentication takes place in the background. If you use SQL Server authentication, you need to supply a username and password provided by the database administrator. Click Next.

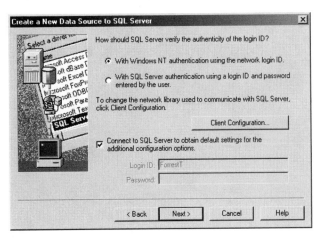

6. The next dialog box allows you to set up some special parameters. For most, accept the defaults unless a database administrator tells you otherwise. The one you may want to change is the default database. You can choose from a list of those on the server, and you want your default to be the database you will be using. Click Next.

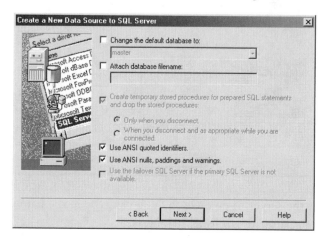

7. The last dialog box offers you a chance to change more specialized settings. You can set up log files for your database sessions, override default encryption schemes, or change the language used for system messages. In most cases, you do not need to change these settings. Click Finish.

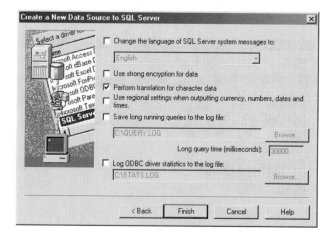

8. The last dialog box presents a summary of the settings that will be used for the connection. The most critical control here is the Test Data Source button. Click it to make certain you can connect. If you can't, click Cancel, back up, and verify settings. If you fail, click Test Data Source again just to be sure. At least one SQL Server in my acquaintance has been known to time out on the first attempt to connect for no known reason. Click OK to finish setting up the connection, and OK again to close the ODBC Control Panel applet.

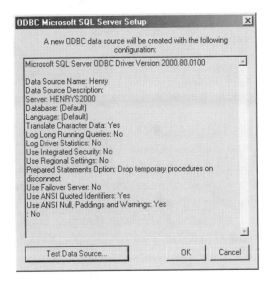

At this point, congratulate yourself on having connected to a database using ODBC. Keep in mind that almost every database vendor supports this method of connection. Connecting, however, is one thing. Features of the connection are another. The vendor determines what features the connection supports.

Do not be surprised, for example, if you cannot scroll through a recordset backward in later exercises. Oracle ODBC drivers have been known, for example, not to support this feature. Take heart, however, if you find that the vendor's driver is somewhat lame. Companies like InterSolv manufacture full-featured ODBC drivers that can replace the vendor's driver and supply the functionality you may crave.

What is behind the ODBC connection? Here is what appears in a file DSN set up to connect to a local Access database:

```
[ODBC]
DRIVER=Microsoft Access Driver (*.mdb)
UID=admin
UserCommitSync=Yes
Threads=3
SafeTransactions=0
PageTimeout=5
MaxScanRows=8
MaxBufferSize=2048
FIL=MS Access
DriverId=25
DefaultDir=D:\My Documents
DBQ=D:\My Documents\db1.mdb
```

Notice that this looks remarkably like any ordinary INI file, which is exactly what it is. You can recognize the database location and default directory in the last two lines, the driver name in the first line, and various settings in the remaining lines. What you must realize from this examination is that an ODBC connection involves a general driver that picks up a specific add-on driver for the given manufacturer's database. This pair of cooperating drivers then needs some configuration information. Some of the information, like UID (for User ID) is reasonably transparent. Other settings, like DriverId, depend on the manufacturer, as well as on the graces of the ODBC Connection Wizard, for their values. (You can also find recommended values in the technical documentation provided by the vendor.) In general, however, the main ODBC driver gets hints from the vendor's driver about how to connect, and a set of INI values are passed along to both values to tell them how to behave. These INI values can be concatenated into a single string variable, and when they are so concatenated, they are called the *connection string*. When you program a database connection, you may be asked to provide parts of the connection string to the driver.

1-Minute Drill

- **Explain when to use a File DSN.**
- **Explain when you should use a System DSN.**
- **Name two important features that must be in a DSN in order to make a connection.**

Using OLE DB

ODBC was the computer industry's first stab at providing universal access to databases. If you have an ODBC driver for your operating system, you can connect to a database. However, you have to set up the connection using the services of the operating system. Which means, of course, you have to set up a connection on each machine. Which in turn means, of course, that for every machine on your 2,000-node network to connect to the database, you have to set up connections on 2,000 machines. Your network administrator knows the pain that these revelations lead to in configuring networked computers.

To help avoid the complexity of having to set up per-computer connections, Microsoft settled on a strategy of Universal Database Access. Microsoft decided to provide connectionless connections (don't be concerned about the oxymoron) to any data source as a part of its Distributed Internetworking Architecture (also known as DNA). The concept behind Universal Data Access for DNA is an installable driver known as a provider. Any computer on which a provider has

---

- **Use a File DSN when you want the data source name to be portable to several computers.**
- **Use a System DSN when you want any user who logs into the machine to be able to use it.**
- **There are several important pairs: Driver and server name, userid and password, server name and database name, for example.**

been installed can connect to the database for that provider. Microsoft as an operating system manufacturer provides providers for the major database vendors. As a result, if Windows is installed, you can connect to a database.

Actually, you as a user can't connect directly except through the ODBC Control Panel applet. However, you as a programmer can connect, and you do not have to set up an ODBC connection to do it. You use a connection string that is handed off to a provider to make the connection. The connection string contains all the information necessary for the provider to initiate the connection to the database. The name Microsoft chose to apply to this technology is OLE DB. OLE is the moniker associated with Object Linking and Embedding, which got such a bad name as Microsoft evolved the technology that Microsoft changed the name to ActiveX. The programming technology for making an OLE DB connection is called ActiveX data objects.

So what is the value of this "connectionless" technology? First, it does allow universal data access. Any data that can be read using a provider can be accessed as a database. Second, Microsoft provides lots of providers. Imagine wanting to move data from an Excel spreadsheet to an Access database. Microsoft provides the providers to get the job done. Fine, you say, Microsoft manufactures all of these products. They also manufacture text file providers for OLE DB. If you can dump data to standard text file formats, you can move it to any common database in use at present, even if neither Microsoft nor the vendor supply the OLE DB provider. When Microsoft called it Universal Data Access, they were serious about the Universal. They meant for there to be a means of moving the data from point A to point B even under adverse circumstances. The value of this technology is that it does accomplish this goal. However, to access OLE DB, you have to be using development software that allows you to work with it.

Because this technology focuses on programming connections to databases, we really cannot investigate it further until we are ready to connect to a database from a program. The next few sections explain how to do so.

Connecting from a Program

Connecting to a database from a tool like Query Analyzer allows you to frame queries and submit them to the database. After query processing is complete, tools like Query Analyzer allow you to see the data returned in a list format with each database record representing a line on the screen. While such tools are useful, the form in which they return data is not especially useful. You can't use it to write a report unless you want to cut and paste the data as text into a program like a word processor or a spreadsheet. Any calculations you want to do with the returned data, you must complete by hand.

ODBC and OLE DB allow you to make connections to databases, but they do not provide you with a means of working with the databases. You need a tool at least as sophisticated as Query Analyzer to take advantage of the connection. In fact, many such tools require that you establish an ODBC connection before you can use their interface to frame and submit queries. As a result, to do any useful work with a database, you need to learn how to connect to it from a program. You need to see how to establish the connection, retrieve data, and manipulate data using code that you write yourself.

To establish a connection, you need to use an interface to the database. At the lowest level, machine language instructions establish the connection and provide data services to your program. Writing in machine language or assembler, however, is not an elegant job. For this reason, higher-level languages have been devised to abstract the complex formalisms of writing programs into simpler constructs. Instead of managing addresses and registers to store data in memory, we write the following:

```
strMyVariable = "Hello World!"
```

The hard work of encoding the data and placing it in particular memory registers with known addresses is hidden behind the scenes. A compiler undertakes most of this complex translation for us.

To communicate with a database, however, we need a specialized interface. Vendors supply these and typically call them Application Programming Interfaces, or APIs. APIs can be relatively low level, such as a group of C language functions that you can link to your program and call to access data. APIs can be fairly high level, such as the object-oriented interfaces that Microsoft has popularized. Low-level interfaces offer speed. High-level interfaces offer convenience.

Using a Connection Library

An example of a low-level interface is the ODBC API written in C and stored in a set of dynamic-link libraries (DLLs) that include the acronym ODBC in their filenames. You can find these files by searching your drive for files that include ODBC in the name. Depending on what software you have installed, you will find at least an ODBC16 file that allows connections between 16-bit programs and a database and an ODBC32 file that allows connections between 32-bit programs and a database. You may find other, vendor-specific ODBC DLLs as well. Typically, these libraries are associated with a particular database access program, such as Crystal Reports or the Watcom SQL Engine.

Note

Microsoft packages a Data Access software development kit with its Visual Studio suite of application development tools. Its setup program is located on CD 2 in a folder named DASDK. This kit contains all the files necessary for writing direct database access applications using any of the Microsoft tools. Other vendors, Watcom and InterSolv among them, offer similar tools.

The functions contained in these files are not many. The easiest way to see them is to open the file ODBCAPI.BAS included with the Visual Studio development environment. The function definitions are the following:

```
Public Declare Function SQLAllocHandle Lib "odbc32.dll"
(ByVal iHandleType As Integer, ByVal lInputHandle As Long,
lOutputHandlePtr As Long) As Integer

Public Declare Function SQLFreeHandle Lib "odbc32.dll"
(ByVal iHandleType As Integer, ByVal lHandle As Long) As Integer
```

```
Public Declare Function SQLDriverConnect Lib "odbc32.dll"
(ByVal hConnection As Long, ByVal hWnd As Long,
ByVal sInConnectionString As String, ByVal iStringLength1 As Integer,
ByVal sOutConnectionString As String, ByVal iBufferLength As Integer,
iStringLength2Ptr As Integer, ByVal iDriverCompletion As Integer)
As Integer

Public Declare Function SQLDisconnect Lib "odbc32.dll" (
ByVal hdbc As Long) As Integer

Public Declare Function SQLSetEnvAttr Lib "odbc32.dll" (ByVal hEnv As Long,
ByVal lAttribute As Long, ByVal sValuePtr As String, ByVal lStringLength
As Long) As Integer

Public Declare Function SQLSetEnvAttrLong Lib "odbc32.dll"
Alias "SQLSetEnvAttr" (ByVal hEnv As Long, ByVal lAttribute As Long,
ByVal lValue As Long, ByVal lStringLength As Long) As Integer

Public Declare Function SQLExecDirect Lib "odbc32.dll"
(ByVal hstmt As Long, ByVal szSqlStr As String, ByVal cbSqlStr As Long)
As Integer

Public Declare Function SQLEndTran Lib "odbc32.dll"
(ByVal iHandleType As Integer, ByVal hConnection As Long,
ByVal iCompletionType As Integer) As Integer

Public Declare Function SQLFetch Lib "odbc32.dll" (ByVal hstmt As Long)
As Integer

Public Declare Function SQLFetchScroll Lib "odbc32.dll"
(ByVal hStatement As Long, ByVal iFetchOrientation As Integer,
ByVal FetchOffset As Long) As Integer

Public Declare Function SQLSetStmtAttrLong Lib "odbc32.dll"
Alias "SQLSetStmtAttr" (ByVal hStatement As Long, ByVal lAttribute As Long,
ByVal lValue As Long, ByVal lStringLength As Long) As Integer

Public Declare Function SQLCloseCursor Lib "odbc32.dll"
(ByVal hStatement As Long) As Integer

Public Declare Function SQLGetDataLong Lib "odbc32.dll" Alias "SQLGetData"
(ByVal hStatement As Long, ByVal iColumn As Integer,
ByVal iTargetType As Integer, lValue As Long, ByVal lValueLength As Long,
lActualLen As Long) As Integer

Public Declare Function SQLGetDiagRec Lib "odbc32.dll"
(ByVal iHandleType As Integer, ByVal hHandle As Long,
ByVal iRecNumber As Integer, ByVal sSQLState As String,
lNativeErrorPtr As Long, ByVal sMessageText As String,
ByVal iBufferLength As Integer, iTextLengthPtr As Integer) As Integer
```

Whether you are used to C, Pascal, or Basic syntax, you can get a sense of what these functions do. In order to connect to a database, you need a pointer, or handle, to the database. Getting a handle is a two-step process. First you call SQLDriverConnect to establish the connection, then you call SQLAllocHandle to get the handle. To execute a query, you call SQLExecDirect. Other functions allow you to manage cursors, fetch recordsets, and so forth.

To use the API, first you link the library into your program. In Visual Basic, the language we will use for our coding examples, you add the ODBCAPI.BAS to your project. Select Project | Add Module from the menu, navigate to the file using the Existing tab of the Add Module dialog box, and click the Open button. In other languages and development environments, you might follow other procedures. In C, for example, you include a header file in your code file by using a #include directive. After you compile the program, you run a linker, which binds your object code and any libraries it uses into a single executable file.

Once you have followed the appropriate inclusion process, you can call the functions to access your data. The easiest way to connect to a database using ODBC calls directly is to use the SQLDriverConnect function. Because it is the easiest, we will use it here as our example of connecting to a database in this fashion. To use this function, you must have a valid connection string to use to connect to the data source. Connection strings take two basic formats with ODBC. In the first, you specify the driver name and the server name explicitly, as follows:

```
"DRIVER={SQL Server};SERVER=MyServer;UID=sa;PWD=MyPassWord;DATABASE=pubs;"
```

In this form of the connection string, the driver name goes in curly brackets. The server name and additional connection information are in plain text, as is the name of the database that you plan to use on the server. In the other form, you use the name of a DSN that you established using the ODBC Control Panel applet. This form looks like the following:

```
"DSN=MyRemote;UID=sa;PWD=;"
```

In this case, the name of the database server and the default database are included in the DSN. You add the UID and PWD parameters to the string to inform the ODBC driver what username and password it should use in making this connection via the DSN.

To make the actual connection, you will want to store your connection
string in a string variable. Then you call the SQLDriverConnect function and
pass it several important parameters. The following code fragment illustrates
what is necessary:

```
Dim strConnectionString As String

strConnectionString = "DRIVER={SQL Server};
    SERVER=MyServer;UID=sa;PWD=MyPassWord;DATABASE=pubs;"

Call SQLDriverConnect(SQL_NULL_HANDLE, Null, strConnectionString,
LenB(strConnectionString), vbNullString, 0, 0, SQL_DRIVER_NOPROMPT)
```

Connection string

Length of connection string

Special settings for driver

These three statements are all that is required to make the connection.
The first allocates a string variable. The second assigns the connection string
to the variable. And the third makes the connection.

SQLDriverConnect requires several mysterious parameters. The first is
a handle to the existing connection. Since we have not allocated an existing
connection, we provide the value SQL_NULL_HANDLE, which essentially
tells SQLDriverConnect to cope with the fact that we have not given it an
existing connection. The second is the handle of the window making the call.
We can pass a value here if we want the connection to be associated with the
window we are using. We are passing Null because we don't have the need
to associate this connection with a window. The third parameter is the
connection string itself. The fourth parameter is the length of the connection
string. Parameters five, six, and seven are a receive string buffer, its length,
and the address at which the buffer is located. Receive buffers are common
in low-level C programming. SQLDriverConnect places return information
in this variable, and we can check it afterward to see what the function has
communicated to us. In this case, we are not using the buffer, so we pass it

a null string. The final parameter is a value that tells SQLDriverConnect whether to prompt the user for any missing connection information as it tries to make the connection.

Note

All of the constants used in this function call are defined in the ODBCAPI.BAS file. All represent integer values. They are provided descriptive names to make reading the code easier.

So now you know how to connect using ODBC. If the connection process seems complicated, you are perceptive. The ODBC API is a very flexible set of C language functions. To use them, you have to play by C programming rules, and you have to play by the rules associated with system-level programming in Windows. Often those rules are counterintuitive, and you are required to think in ways that don't seem directly related to accessing data with SQL. As a result, there are more appropriate ways for you to create database connections as a SQL programmer. Microsoft provides two of them, and database vendors like Oracle and Sybase provide others. In each case, these connection methods wrap the low-level ODBC API in an interface that is oriented toward the work you do. As a result, these methods provide SQL programmers with the methods most used in database programming today.

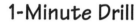

1-Minute Drill

● **Explain the difference between the two types of DSN strings you can create.**

● **Name the software development kit that Microsoft sells for building database access into programs.**

● **Name the function that allows you to create a connection even if you have not previously created one.**

● One type references the driver name and the server name; the other type references only the data source name.
● The kit is the Microsoft Data Access Software Development Kit.
● The function is SQLDriverConnect.

Ask the Expert

Question: I've looked at the ODBC function calls, and they are tough going. When should I choose this technology?

Answer: The only time to use the ODBC API is when speed is absolutely of the essence. I once worked in a manufacturing environment where every box produced traveled a conveyer to its inventory location. Each box had a bar code, and each box passed a scanner that read the bar code and recorded the items produced in a database. The program that was originally created under Windows 95 to record the scans used the ODBC API because DAO was too slow. My job, however, was to update the programs, and I updated them to ADO. ADO had all the speed required. As a result, I find it hard to imagine the need to use ODBC function calls directly.

Question: Is there an API that underlies ADO?

Answer: For any set of objects that Microsoft creates, there is an underlying C API. If you want, you can look into the Data Access SDK to find the API behind OLE DB, ADO, and universal data access. You will find it as complex as the ODBC API, and you will not find much speed advantage in using the API. The object interfaces are more intuitive and, as a result, more useful to you.

Question: Are there any quirks to the new ADO interface? Microsoft is known for releasing products earlier than the world thinks they are ready.

Answer: Yes, there are. ADO provides several methods of opening both connections and recordsets, a couple of which save several lines of code. I have run into circumstances where using the shorthand way of opening the connection blocks you from using some features. As a result, I recommend managing ADO objects explicitly yourself. If you need a connection, build it yourself. Don't let a call to create a recordset build your connection in the background. Objects created in the background sometimes have behavior that you might not expect.

Question: If you had your choice, would you use an API, DAO, or ADO?

Answer: I prefer ADO, hands down. Its speed has been more than adequate. I have found few bugs that don't have clear workarounds. And you can take advantage of some of the latest technologies, such as Extensible Markup Language, when you are ready to do so. I have also found that computer manufacturers who are changing their direction orphan the old technology far sooner than I am ready to abandon it. I like to stay toward the cutting edge, and I think ADO is that edge right now.

Using DAO

The interface Microsoft first provided to database programmers was called Data Access Objects (DAO), and they first became popular in association with writing applications to get at data stored in Microsoft Access. They became popular because of their ease of use. As a result, most development environments started to support them. DAO allows you to add a reference to your project that defines the object interface. In Visual Basic, you select Project | References from the menu, scroll down the list of references available until you find DAO, check the box next to the reference name, and click OK. In other programming environments, you add the type library to the project in a similar way.

The DAO interface is defined in a type library file, which has the standard extension TLB. When you add a reference in Visual Basic, you are adding the information in the type library to your project. A type library defines objects, that is, conceptual entities that enable you to work with resources on the computer. Each object has properties, which you can set to values and thereby define the object's behavior. Each object has methods as well, which allow you to take action with the object.

All of this discussion is fairly abstract until you apply objects to a problem. If you want to access data, it would make sense to use a database object. You ought to be able to set the connection string as an object property, and to tell the database object to connect to the database using the connect method. In this way, objects provide logical ways for you to define your interaction with resources on the computer.

In Microsoft languages, you create objects by declaring them like variables. DAO provides a database object. To declare a database object in Visual Basic, you use the Dim statement, just as in declaring a variable. Declaring the object allocates storage for it and initializes the storage area to receive object properties and to use object methods. To declare a database object under DAO, use the following statement:

```
Dim dbMyDatabase As DAO.Database
```

Note a couple of things in this declaration. First, we are providing the name of the object. We can make it be anything that we like. Second, we are using the object type defined by DAO to declare our object. DAO.Database invokes the information in the type library that allows the compiler to create the object.

Having declared the object, however, we are not ready to use it. We must instantiate it in order to be able to use it. Instantiating gives the abstract object a physical presence. Its properties are filled in, it is connected to its database, and we can then use the object for actual work. To instantiate a DAO database object, we use one of the methods defined in the DAO type library. DAO provides an object called DBEngine that is ready for us to use immediately without further definition. This object has an OpenDatabase method that instantiates the database object for us. To instantiate any object in Visual Basic, you use the Set statement. To create a DAO connection to a database, use this Set statement:

```
Set dbMyDatabase = DBEngine.OpenDatabase ("c:\NorthWind.mdb")
```

This presentation of the OpenDatabase method presents its minimal form, the form you use to connect to a database stored as a local file. OpenDatabase actually can take up to four parameters. The first, shown here, is the database name. When the database resides in a file, often the name is the only parameter required. However, when you reach out to database servers, you need more information. As a result, you can provide the following information as a part of the method call:

- **Database Name**   A string that either names the file or represents the connection string for the database.

- **Options** A constant value that defines whether users are prompted for missing information in the connection string. The possible values are dbDriverNoprompt (no prompt allowed), dbDriverPrompt (show the dialog box for each connection attempt), dbDriverComplete (show the dialog box only if necessary), and dbDriverCompleteRequired (show the dialog box only if necessary, and disable options already provided). These values are defined in the DAO type library and DLLs.

- **Read-Only** The value of True to make the database connection read-only, the value of false to make it read/write.

- **Connection** This is a string value that you can use to pass additional connection information not provided in the Database Name parameter.

A connection statement using DAO with all the information provided might look like the following:

```
Set dbMyDatabase = DBEngine.OpenDatabase ("Pubs", dbDriverPrompt, False,
"DRIVER={SQL Server};SERVER=MyServer;UID=sa;PWD=MyPassWord;")
```

In any case, after you execute this statement in your program, you are connected to the database and ready to work.

Using ADO

ActiveX Data Objects (ADO) are Microsoft's new data access strategy designed to accompany its OLE DB approach to universal data access. ADO objects provide a different hierarchy of objects for accessing databases. They rely on a different underlying technology rather than the ODBC API to provide access to data. (However, there is an OLE DB provider for ODBC databases. If you cannot connect using straight OLE DB, OLE DB talks to ODBC to get you connected.) The structure of the objects is much less oriented toward Microsoft Access, which is the database program and the core database engine that gave rise to DAO. As a result, many find ADO more intuitive for interacting with databases than DAO. As Microsoft focuses on Extensible

Markup Language (XML) as a means for accessing databases through firewalls over the Internet, ADO supports the feature set that is future-oriented for Microsoft as a company.

To connect to a database using ADO, you need to add references to your development project for the ActiveX Data Objects and the ActiveX Data Objects Recordset Library. After you do so, if you want a database connection, you create a connection object. The connection object has one property that you need to set, the ConnectionString property. It has an Open method that you call to open the connection. To establish a connection under ADO, here is the code you need to execute:

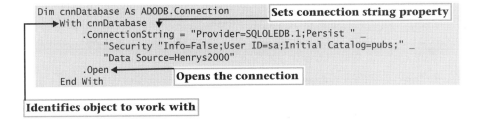

```
Dim cnnDatabase As ADODB.Connection        Sets connection string property
With cnnDatabase
    .ConnectionString = "Provider=SQLOLEDB.1;Persist " _
        "Security "Info=False;User ID=sa;Initial Catalog=pubs;" _
        "Data Source=Henrys2000"
    .Open                    Opens the connection
End With

Identifies object to work with
```

Setting the connection string is very straightforward. All the information goes in the same property, not in two possible parameters, as in DAO. In addition, the connection string is slightly different. Notice that you must name a provider rather than a driver or a DSN. Providers are the drivers that OLE DB uses in making connections, and their names are not well documented. You would think that somewhere Microsoft would present a list of them. However, this documentation has yet to be created. If you are looking for even a common database provider name, you might have to search TechNet, the Microsoft Developer's Network, or Microsoft's Web site for several minutes before finding it.

In any case, after this code executes, you are connected to your database. Our entire purpose in this chapter is to show you how to make such connections. In subsequent chapters, we will show you how to write and execute SQL commands against the database you are connected to. Let's get on with that task now.

Project 1-1: Create a Connection

You won't be able to learn any SQL if you are not connected to a database. As a result, in this project, we are going to focus on making the choice. How you learn SQL ultimately depends on what tools you have to use to learn SQL. Most commonly, programmers practice with SQL using a query tool. But most of the work they do, they do from a programming environment. So this project aims at getting you connected.

Step-by-Step

Download the Microsoft Data Engine from this book's Web site. Run the installation program to set up the database engine and related tools. This installation gives you the Enterprise Manager, which allows you to configure databases graphically, and the Query Analyzer, which allows you to practice with your database.

1. Open the Query Analyzer. It presents you with a dialog box that prompts you to make a connection. Fill in the information for your local server, which MSDE set up on one of your local drives.

2. Verify that the connection took place. You should see a window into which you can type text.

3. Set up your preferred programming environment. If you have Visual Studio, make sure that you have Visual Basic installed. We will use VB for our examples in this book. If you are programming in C or another language, you should be able to translate the VB examples into your syntax with ease.

4. Create a DAO connection in your programming environment to your MSDE database. The two example databases provided are Pubs and Northwind.

5. Create an ADO connection in your programming environment to your MSDE database.

☑️ *Mastery Check*

1. When should you use a User DSN to create an ODBC database connection?

2. When is ADO the best database object technology to use for making connections?

3. Which methods can be used to create connections to SQL databases?

    a. Data Access Objects

    b. Open Database Connectivity Objects

    c. Query Analyzer Objects

    d. None of the above

4. Give the practical use for a tool like Microsoft's Query Analyzer for programmers who are developing SQL database programs.

Module 2

Retrieving Data

Goals

- Learn how to select data from a database
- Practice creating select conditions
- Learn how to join tables
- Learn how to embed SQL in a host language
- Create basic programs that present data

Having learned how to connect to a database, you are probably wondering how to do something with that database. This module focuses on the most basic activity you engage in with a database: retrieving data that has been stored in the tables. To prepare you to retrieve data, we need to review some database fundamentals.

The databases that support SQL are all *relational databases*. The definition of a relational database is a collection of related information. That is, you can assume that because two items of information, names and addresses, for example, appear in the database, they have some relationship to one another. The names and addresses do not appear randomly. The pairing of a name and an address in the database implies a relationship of "belongs to." The person by that name receives mail at that address, for instance, and the address belongs to that person.

In order to capture these relationships, data in a relational database is not structured randomly. A basic unit called a *table* organizes the data. Each table contains *rows* and *columns*. Data items that appear in a single row are related. In our example, related names and addresses appear on a single row. Fred and One Bedrock Place appear in a row together, and by virtue of their appearance in this row, we assume that One Bedrock Place is Fred's address, and not someone else's address.

The columns in the table classify the nature of the data items that are related by virtue of row membership. The Name column identifies that whatever appears at this position in any row is a person's name. The Address column identifies that whatever appears in this position is an address. Membership in a row that has columns makes the data items in the row belong to a set. In fact, a database table is a conceptual representation of the set theory we all struggled with in grade school mathematics.

Hint

Special terms are associated with tables. The number of rows in a table is called its *cardinality*. The number of columns is called the table's *degree*. If two columns can be converted to the same data type, they are called *domain compatible*. If two tables have the same degree, they are said to be *union compatible*.

2

Columns also play a special classificatory role in a database; they identify the type of the data stored in them. Data type is the means by which data storage is interpreted. At the lowest level, data is always stored as binary digits. How those bits are grouped and interpreted, however, is a function of their data type. Eight bits make a byte, but if that byte is an integer in data type, then those eight bits represent a counting number between 0 and 256. If they represent character data, those bits represent a code that corresponds to an alphabetic character or a symbol. Several data types are available, and their exact interpretation depends on the database vendor. SQL defines many data types, however, that are common across databases that implement SQL.

Let's take a quick review and then get to work. Data is stored in tables. Tables have rows that group related data items together, and columns that classify the data as to its type and its role in the world. Our goal in this module is to retrieve data from the database, so this goal translates into retrieving data from tables. SQL provides a verb that allows us to undertake this operation: SELECT. To retrieve data from tables, you use some form of a SELECT statement.

Using Select

SQL is a language that, like any other computer language, is structured around a series of command verbs. The verb that retrieves data from a database is SELECT. This verb by itself accomplishes nothing, except to throw an error on your screen when you try to run the command. To retrieve data using SELECT, you must use it with additional objects, phrases, and clauses.

The required object is a list of column names. You may list the columns one by one, separated by commas, or you may use the wildcard * (pronounced "star" in SQL) to indicate all columns. In addition to the object, you need a FROM phrase. The object of this phrase is a table name, or a list of table names separated by commas. To give you a sense of what a SELECT statement looks like with all of its parts, here is the simplest SELECT statement you can create:

```
SELECT * FROM MyTable
```

The result of this statement is to return all of the columns from the table MyTable in whatever database you have attached to. This statement also returns all of the rows.

Let's attach to a database and make this statement less abstract. Open the Query Analyzer and attach to the SQL Server. SQL Server ships with two sample databases, Northwind and Pubs. We will work with Pubs this time. Don't forget that you choose your database in Query Analyzer using the drop-down list on the toolbar of the document window that represents your database attachment. But to make things even simpler, we are going to learn some good habits. When working in Query Analyzer, put this command on the top line of your window:

```
USE Pubs
```

This statement tells the database server you are attached to which database to use, in this case Pubs.

On another line, enter this statement:

```
SELECT * from authors
```

Run this command by clicking the button with the green triangle in the toolbar. The results will be that a table of data appears in the lower pane of your connection window. This table will have the columns au_id, au_lname, au_fname, phone, address, city, state, zip, and contract, as shown in Figure 2-1. Every row has returned from the table as well.

Now, at this point, let's review some of what you have seen for best practices. Eventually you are going to be using SQL to build databases as well as to extract data from them, so we need to reinforce best practices as we work. You have just had a great success executing your first SQL statement. Its results have a lot to teach you.

First, notice that the column names have no spaces in them. Most databases allow you to use spaces in the column names, but these columns don't. They don't for a good reason. Spaces in column names require you to enclose the column name in square brackets if you want to use it in a SQL statement. Using spaces therefore requires additional typing in each SQL statement, but it also introduces multiple possibilities for errors. Forget the brackets where they are required, and you won't get the results you expect. You will get an error, or you may get the wrong

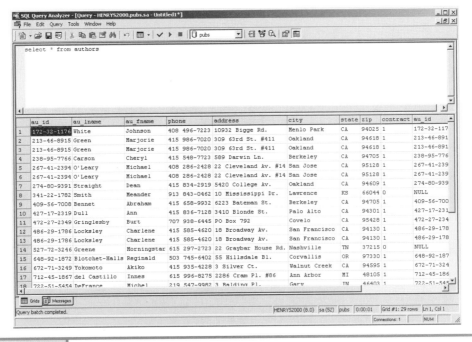

Figure 2-1 | **The results of your first SELECT statement represent the entire contents of the authors table**

column. Imagine someone naming a series of columns [author], [author two], [author three], etc. Leaving the brackets off [author two] and accidentally inserting a comma between the two elements of the correct column name will cause data to return with some SQL databases. The [author] column will return, and another column named [two] will also return. It will contain no data, but it will return. Do not use blank spaces in column names as a general rule.

Second, notice that each author has a unique number assigned in the au_id column. Such columns are often called *identity columns*. They guarantee that each row in the table is unique. Remember those grade school classrooms where the teacher had to keep three Steves and two Julies straight? A database has the same problem. Identity columns resolve this issue with data that may itself contain no unique combination of fields in a row to provide unique identification for that row. Unique identification of rows is important to SQL databases. If you SELECT some data, you want to be able to tell John Smith number one from John Smith number two in the authors table, especially if you owe one a royalty of $10,000 and the other owes you a payment for labor incurred indexing his book.

Third, notice the use of the underscore character to substitute for a space to help with readability. Au_id is easier to read than auid. You should adopt a convention for maintaining readability. Capitalizing the first letter of word units in a column name is another good convention. It makes no difference which you use, but make your column names readable. Make them descriptive as well. Zip is highly preferable to Z as a column name. When you look at zip, you have a sense of what data the column contains, and a reasonable guess as to its data type (a string of 5 or ten characters). When you look at Z, you have only guesses as to what the data is, and no clue about its data type.

So, you have returned your first table from the Pubs database using a SQL SELECT statement. You may be wondering whether all you can do is return complete tables. In fact, if returning tables was all you could do, SQL would be rather boring and inflexible. After you got the data back from the database, you would have a lot of work to do to make the data fit your purposes. SELECT actually morphs in a variety of ways to make the data returned fit your purposes.

To demonstrate this flexibility, let's see how to return a limited number of columns. Remember that the objects following SELECT and preceding FROM can be a list of columns. If you wanted to return only the names of the authors in your database, because you needed to build a document in a word processor that simply listed all the authors, you could do so. You simply ask for the columns that contain the information you need by listing the columns explicitly, separated by columns. Here is the SELECT statement to use:

```
SELECT au_fname, au_lname FROM authors
```

The listing returned appears in Figure 2-2. As you can see, you got only the names you requested.

Hint

The order of columns returned by a SELECT is determined by the order in which you list the columns in the SELECT statement, not the order in which the columns appear in the table. You can retrieve the data, therefore, in the order you want to see it.

The basic SELECT statement also allows one further permutation that is important to know about. You might perhaps want to format the names into last name first order, separated by commas, for inclusion in your document. SQL allows you to perform such basic formatting with the concatenation operator, the plus sign (+). An example shows this feature best. Try the following statement in your query analyzer:

```
SELECT au_lname + ', ' + au_fname AS full_name FROM authors
```

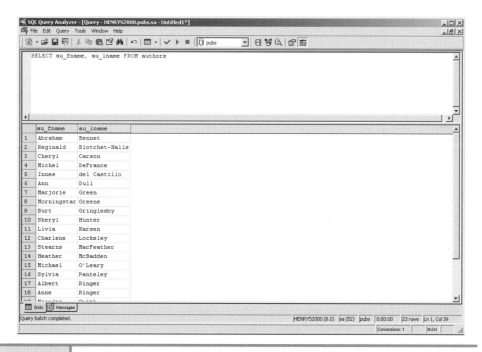

Figure 2-2   Providing a list of column names allows you to select a subset of the data in the table

This technique returns the formatted output shown in Figure 2-3. Note a couple of tricks. We concatenated a string of characters, which is delimited by single quotes, into the name string. The plus signs accomplished the act of joining the text of the last name to the comma and space to the text of the first name. We also named the result using the AS keyword. AS simply treated the output as if it were a column, and made the name following AS the column name. Using AS, you can make any set of values returned with formatting into a column in your data set. Once you have the data set (also called a recordset) accessible within a program, you can access the concatenated names by referring to the column name full_name. In essence, you just created a column on the fly.

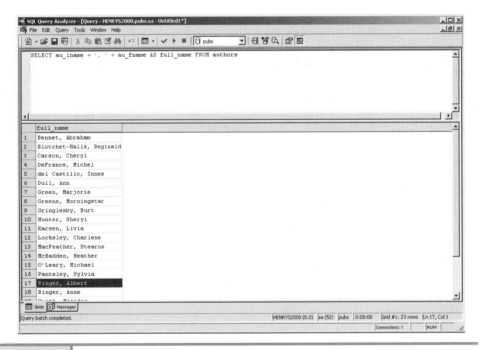

Figure 2-3   You can use AS and the plus operator to apply special formatting to data returned using SELECT

2

┤*Note*

You may notice that all of the SQL keywords appear in all capitals in the text, but they are often in lowercase in the Query Analyzer figures. When formally presenting SQL statements, the usual practice is to capitalize all the keywords. When working in the Query Analyzer, following this convention wastes time. You can use lowercase without causing problems. When you include SQL statements in a program, the best practice is to type the keywords in all capitals as an aid to debugging. Lowercase statements, however, will still run from your program.

┤*Hint*

Be aware as well that some databases require that you terminate SQL statements with a semicolon (;). SQL Server does not, but Access, Oracle, and Sybase are examples of those that do.

1-Minute Drill

- **Explain how to list columns in a different order from how they appear in a table.**

- **Explain when you use a semicolon in a SQL statement.**

- **Explain what the * character does.**

- List the columns in the order you want them to appear in the SELECT statement.
- Use a semicolon to terminate your SQL statement if the database you are using requires it. If you need it and it's not there, you will get an error message.
- The * character stands for "all the columns." It returns all the columns in the table or tables you are selecting from.

Adding a Where Clause

So far, we have looked at using a SQL SELECT statement to return an entire table, or to return a subset of the columns in a table. If you want to limit the number of rows that return, you have to add another keyword, or you have to add a WHERE clause to your SELECT statement.

The keyword approach is to use TOP in your SELECT statement. For example, you can use the following statement to get 10 authors from the authors table:

```
SELECT TOP 10 au_lname + ', ' + au_fname AS full_name FROM authors
```

The TOP keyword indicates that you are to get the first x rows from the table. The number following TOP indicates how many rows to get. This approach is useful when you are sampling the data in the table, or you just need some authors as examples of the total set of authors in the table. But for most working interactions with a database, you don't want the authors that just happen to float to the top. You want authors you chose for a reason. In most cases, you extract data for a reason.

The WHERE clause allows you to express the reason explicitly as a part of your SELECT statement. The words that follow WHERE express a condition that the authors must meet in order to return from the database. For example, if you need to find out which authors live in Utah, you can use the following WHERE clause:

```
SELECT * FROM authors WHERE state = 'UT'
```

Using this statement allows you to find out that Anne Ringer and Albert Ringer are the only two authors living in Utah.

To use WHERE effectively, you need a brief introduction to data types. Each column has a data type associated with it, which defines how the bits that make up the data in the column are interpreted. Table 2-1 identifies the data types commonly associated with SQL databases.

Hint

While these data types are typically associated with SQL databases, some databases may not support all the types or may vary in their naming conventions slightly. Microsoft implemented the Unicode extensions of char and varchar, for example, in SQL Server 7.0, and these were not supported by other SQL databases in release at the time.

Name	Storage	Reference
binary	Up to 8,000 bytes of binary data	"column_name =" & variable_containing_data
bit	Integers 0 or 1	column_name = 1
char	A fixed-length string of characters not encoded as Unicode	column_name = 'string'
datetime	Date and time values from 1/1/1753 to 12/31/9999	column_name = convert(datetime, "1/1/1753", 101) [use 108 for times]
decimal	Numbers containing decimal fractions from $-10^{38}-1$ to $10^{38}-1$	column_name = 31.2
float	Floating point decimals from $-1.79E+308$ to $1.79E+308$	column_name = 1.234
image	A variable length string of bits (binary data) with a maximum size of 2^{31}	"column_name =" & variable_containing_data
int	Integers from $-2^{31}-1$ to $2^{31}-1$	column_name = 31
money	Numbers representing monetary values from -2^{63} to $2^{63}-1$	column_name = 10.68
nchar	A fixed-length string of characters encoded as Unicode	column_name = 'string'
ntext	A variable-length string of characters not encoded as Unicode with a maximum size of $2^{31}-1$	column_name = 'string'
nvarchar	A variable-length string of characters encoded as Unicode	column_name = 'string'
numeric	Same as decimal	column_name = 31.2
real	Floating-point decimals from $-3.40E+38$ to $3.40E+38$	column_name = 1.234
smalldatetime	Date and time values from 1/1/1900 to 6/6/2079	column_name = convert(datetime, "6/6/2079", 101) [use 108 for times]
smallint	Integers from $-2^{15}-1$ to $2^{15}-1$	column_name = 31
smallmoney	Numbers representing monetary values from $-214,748.3648$ to $214,748.3647$	column_name = 10.68
sysname	nvarchar(128)	column_name = 'string'

Table 2-1   SQL data types and methods of referring to them in SQL statements

Name	Storage	Reference
text	A variable-length string of characters not encoded as Unicode with a maximum size of 2^31–1	column_name = 'string'
timestamp	A unique number in the database	column_name = 1234 (Normally, you would not select data on the basis of this number)
tinyint	Integers from 0 to 255	column_name = 31
varbinary	A variable-length string of bits (binary data) with a maximum size of 8,000 bytes	"column_name =" & variable_containing_data
varchar	A variable-length string of characters not encoded as unicode	column_name = 'string'
uniqueidentifier	a globally unique identifier (GUID), that is, a number unique in the world	column_name = 1234 (Normally, you would not select data on the basis of this number)

Table 2-1   SQL data types and methods of referring to them in SQL statements *(continued)*

Table 2-1 shows you the name of each data type, what type of data it encodes, and how you might reference that data type in a SELECT statement. You need to know this information now, but not because you need to worry about how to store data. You can worry about that later when you start creating columns in tables. Right now, you need to focus on how to refer to data in a WHERE clause.

For example, our last SELECT statement included the following WHERE clause:

```
WHERE state = 'UT'
```

In this case, state is a column that contains char data that has a fixed length of two characters, abbreviated char(2) when you see a description of the data type. Because state represents character data, we had to place the value in single quotes. In Table 2-1, the Reference column lists this type of reference as "column_name = 'string'." What you see in the Reference column is, therefore, exactly what you should place in your WHERE clause.

In order to extract all the authors from the authors table who currently have contracts, for example, we need to change the way we reference data stored in the contract column. This column is of the bit data type and stores only a 0 or a 1. As a result, to pull the authors who have contracts from the table, you need to use the following SELECT statement:

```
SELECT * FROM authors WHERE contract = 1
```

Ask the Expert

Question: You need to know a lot of information to write a SELECT statement. How do I find out what data type a column is?

Answer: Your database administrator should provide you with a list of columns and data types. If you can attach to the database with a valid login, each database provides some sort of tool like Microsoft's Enterprise Manager that allows you to view table definitions. You can also use the sp_help stored procedure to view information about any table. Use this syntax:

```
EXEC sp_help tablename
```

Question: How can I be certain that my WHERE clause gets all the data I need?

Answer: When you execute queries against a database, you can never be 100 percent certain that you have retrieved all the relevant cases that you intended to retrieve. You can be certain that you collected all the records you asked for, but what you asked for might not be what you intended. SQL syntax, like that of any computer language, sometimes plays tricks on even the best programmers.

Getting the right data means keeping your cases clear. You need to start when you design the database. Make sure your columns contain unambiguous data. Usually, columns that contain data that comes from the world, like names and addresses, are unambiguous. If you ask for all the names spelled "SMITH," you will get them. It's the columns that contain codes that describe the nature of other columns that can trip you up. An example in Pubs is the contract column in the authors table. Does this mean that the author currently has a contract? Once had a contract? Or perhaps has a contract that has yet to be signed? We don't know for sure. You need to be certain when you design the column, and you need to make certain all users use the column correctly.

Question: **How can I test SELECT statements that retrieve critical data, say financial data that has to be right?**

Answer: You need to have a few cases that have been worked out by hand to known and well-reviewed results. For the financial example, you should have a period of time from which, say, the company knows how many deposits it made and how many checks it wrote. You should be able to match your query results against the paper results. The query is right when the two match.

The alternative is to create a test database that contains a limited number of records that you insert. You should know from the records you put in how many records should return under each query circumstance. Your queries can be certified as correct when your predictions match your results.

Question: **Is it really necessary to test queries?**

Answer: Yes. Especially when making mistakes has large consequences. If you miscalculate a checkbook reconciliation, clients will have less money or more money than anticipated. One case will result in a nice surprise at audit time; the other case results in penalties and fees.

Question: **Are most queries adequately tested?**

Answer: Probably not. Many companies fly by the seat of their pants when dealing with database queries. Under most circumstances, testing for completeness and accuracy of queries degenerates to "Oh yeah, we got some data back." You can rely on SQL to be accurate under most circumstances. The more complicated the queries, however, the greater the need for testing.

2

Adding Order By

So far, we have not been concerned about the order of our data. It appears in our table listing exactly as it is stored in the database. As a result, we see the data in the order it was added to the database. We can change that order if we want, and to do so we need to add an ORDER BY phrase to our SELECT statement. This phrase has the following syntax:

```
ORDER BY column_name [sort_order]
```

Note that the sort order designator is optional.

To get a list of authors with contracts sorted by last name in ascending order, we can use either of the following SQL statements:

```
SELECT * FROM authors WHERE contract = 1 ORDER BY au_lname
SELECT * FROM authors WHERE contract = 1 ORDER BY au_lname ASC
```

As you might guess, ascending sort order is the default order applied by SQL unless you specify a sort order. If you want descending sort order, you must remember to supply the DESC sort order tag; otherwise, your results will not be as you expect. To sort this same list in descending order, you must use this statement:

```
SELECT * FROM authors WHERE contract = 1 ORDER BY au_lname DESC
```

You can use multiple columns for sorting. A common name sort is to sort by last name in ascending order, and to sort by first name. Since we have stored the two parts of the author name in two separate columns, we can sort in this way. The SQL statement that performs the sort is written in the following way:

```
SELECT * FROM authors WHERE contract = 1 ORDER BY au_lname, au_fname
```

Note that we relied on default sort order in performing this sort.

Hint

A good principle to apply in designing a database is to store information you want to be able to sort in separate columns. You can always recombine the columns in your queries using the concatenation operator.

1-Minute Drill

● **What do you need to include character data within in the WHERE clause?**

● **What is the default sort order for ORDER BY?**

Adding Summaries

Sometimes you want to use a select statement to return more than the data stored in the columns. If you are working with financial data, for example, you might want to return a region and an average sales figure for the region. If you are working with authors, you might want the count of all the authors who live in a given state. Perhaps you would like the lowest price a product has ever been sold for, or the highest price a product has been sold for. Or perhaps you need the total number of authors who have contracts currently in force.

So far, we have not shown you a way to answer such questions with a SELECT statement. However, SQL offers you aggregate functions that can allow you to answer these questions. The common aggregate functions are the following:

AVG   Calculates the mean value of the values returned in the selected field

COUNT   Calculates the number of rows returned, or the number of nonnull values returned by a field

MAX   Calculates the maximum value returned in a field

MIN   Calculates the minimum value returned in a field

SUM   Calculates the sum of the values returned in a field

● **Single quotation marks**
● **Ascending**

For a value to participate in any of these functions, it must first be returned as part of a rowset. In other words, if you want the aggregate function to apply to all values stored in the table, the function must be in a SELECT statement with no WHERE clause. If you want the function to apply to only some of the values in a table, you must select those rows from the table using a WHERE clause.

Let's try some example queries against the Pubs database. First, in the sales table, the quantity of items is recorded in a column named qty. Let's find out what the average quantity is for a sale. Use this query:

```
SELECT AVG(qty) FROM sales
```

Running this query returns the result 23. We can get the largest quantity ordered using the MAX function:

```
SELECT MAX(qty) FROM sales
```

Running this query returns the result 75. Similarly, we can get the smallest order using the MIN function:

```
SELECT MIN(qty) FROM sales
```

Running this query returns the value 3.

If we want to count the number of orders with a quantity greater than 30, we need a WHERE clause that will help us to limit the rowset. We also need the COUNT function. This statement will accomplish the task:

```
SELECT COUNT(ord_num) FROM sales WHERE qty > 30
```

This query returns the result 4. If we want to know the total quantity involved in those orders, we can use the SUM function:

```
SELECT SUM(qty) FROM sales WHERE qty > 30
```

This query returns the result 200.

If you add other column names to these queries, as you may want to do, SQL will produce an interesting error, as shown in Figure 2-4. The full text of the error is "Column 'sales.ord_num' is invalid in the select list because it is not contained in an aggregate function and there is no

GROUP BY clause." What is happening behind the scenes to produce this error? In order to aggregate data, SQL must first group it. When we collected the entire group of orders from the table, we secretly created a single group behind the scenes, the group of all orders where qty exceeded 30. However, when we throw an additional column name in the SELECT statement, SQL tries to match the sum with the other column name, and it has no way to do so. It needs to group the data by ord_num, as shown by the results in Figure 2-4, in order to compute the sum by order number.

Take a look at the results of this query, shown in Figure 2-5, to see what is happening:

```
SELECT ord_num, SUM(qty) FROM sales WHERE qty > 30 GROUP BY ord_num
```

The result is a table that contains the order numbers where qty is greater than 30 and the sums where qty is greater than 30. In effect, we have

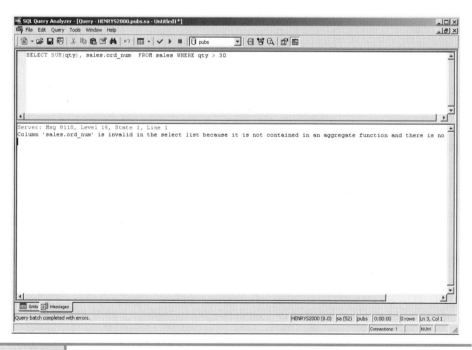

Figure 2-4   You must use a GROUP BY phrase with columns that do not appear in an aggregate function

2

Figure 2-5 The result of summing quantities grouped by order number

partitioned the sum we created with the previous query, which summed
all the order numbers where qty was greater than 30, back into its individual
components. In processing this query, SQL first orders all the records into
groups by order numbers. Since there are four order numbers that match the
WHERE clause, we have four groups of records. We then compute the sum
for each group. For the group defined by order number A2976, for example,
the sum was 50.

Now it is true that by grouping according to order number, we placed
exactly one record in each group, and the SUM function added one number
to nothing to create the SUM. This was not a vacuous exercise, however.
First, it shows how GROUP BY works, and, second, it shows that you ought
to be careful what you group by. Grouping by a field that uniquely identifies
each record renders aggregation a waste of time, because there is nothing to
aggregate. Instead, you want to group by columns that produce interesting
groups to aggregate, such as title_id, so that you can find out how many of
each title you have sold.

However, unique identifiers can sneak into queries when you least expect they will cause problems. SQL requires that any column name in a query where aggregate functions are present either participate in an aggregate function or be included in a GROUP BY phrase. For this reason, you want to include only the fields that are relevant to the query, and you want to check your results against a data set with known answers available. If you are not careful, you can accidentally compromise your calculations using aggregate functions.

Adding a Having Clause

WHERE works very nicely for selecting rows from a table. However, you cannot use aggregate functions in a WHERE clause of the type that we have been creating. For that reason, SQL provides another keyword that allows you to limit the size of a rowset by using aggregate functions. This keyword is HAVING, and it is most commonly used only with grouped data.

Hint

You can use aggregate functions in a WHERE clause only if you are using a subquery (see Module 8) in the WHERE clause.

HAVING appears following the GROUP BY phrase. You must group your data in order to use HAVING, unless every other column name is included in an aggregate function, a feat that you are unlikely to accomplish, but that probably is not impossible. Here is an example of a query that returns four title IDs that meet the condition of having total quantities greater than 30:

```
SELECT title_id FROM sales GROUP BY title_id HAVING SUM(qty) > 30
```

If you want to prove that you don't need a GROUP BY phrase in every query containing a HAVING, try this query in the Query Analyzer:

```
SELECT COUNT(title_id) FROM sales HAVING SUM(qty) > 30
```

This query returns the value 21. On the face of things, it would seem that these are the 21 titles that had total sales greater than 30. Look carefully at the table, however. First, the table contains only 21 rows, and only 16 unique title IDs. The following query gets only the unique title IDs from the database:

```
SELECT DISTINCT title_id FROM sales
```

The DISTINCT keyword prevents the return of duplicate values from the title_id column. Ten of these title IDs have a total quantity of less than 30. The following query proves this point:

```
SELECT  title_id, SUM(qty) FROM sales GROUP BY title_id
```

What has happened in our HAVING with no GROUP BY? First, we returned the total count of fields with a valid value for title_id in the rowset returned by our query. We returned all 21 rows, so we had 21 valid values for title_id. Second, HAVING sought to apply to a group. It applied to the group defined by COUNT(title_id), which is the group of all the rows that can be counted in the table. We got a valid return. There are 21 rows in the table that, when grouped as a single group, have a total qty that is greater than 30.

The moral of the story is to be careful how you define your groups. SQL will do exactly what you ask it to, not what you intend for it to do. You may be expecting errors in this situation, but your expectation is based on your intention. SQL is concerned only with valid set operations, and this set operation was valid.

1-Minute Drill

- **If a column name is not included in an aggregate function, what must it appear in?**
- **When can you use HAVING without a GROUP BY?**
- **What does GROUP BY do?**

- The column name must appear in a GROUP BY phrase.
- You can use HAVING without GROUP BY when all column names are included in aggregate functions.
- GROUP BY orders data into groups defined by the values in the column(s) placed in the GROUP BY phrase.

Joining Tables

Up to this point, we have used two tables in the Pubs database, authors and sales. We have confined our SELECT statements to retrieving data from a single table. However, retrieving data from single tables only can be extremely inefficient. We might want to relate authors to sales information so that we can understand who our best-selling authors are, or so that we can determine how much we owe each author in royalties. To do so, we must retrieve data from multiple tables at once.

SQL allows you to join tables together in an operation known as a *join*. Having said so, we need to clarify that join syntax varies, depending on the implementation of the SQL standard you are using. The classic SQL syntax for building a join is the following:

```
SELECT * FROM table1, table2 WHERE table1.identity = table2.identity
```

First, let's describe what this syntax returns. It returns all columns and rows from both table1 and table2 where the value of a column in table1 equals the value of a column in table2. Keep in mind that this query is not guaranteed to return all the rows in both tables. There may be rows where the column in table1 does not equal the column in table2. Or there may be more rows in one table than the other. This query returns only those rows where the two column values are equal. This type of join is called an *inner join*.

Note

You can always use a table identifier to uniquely identify a column name. Simply attach the table name and the column name using a period, as you see in this query. The complete name of each column can be specified as *databasename.ownername.tablename.columnname.* You could refer to the au_fname column as pubs.dbo.authors.au_fname, for example. You can leave off any single leftmost element, so you can use pubs.authors.au_fname or authors.au_fname. If you leave out an intervening element, you need to use multiple periods to hold the place of the missing element, as in pubs...au_fname.

The syntax for building an inner join has changed in the SQL 92 standard. An inner join is built using the following syntax:

```
SELECT * FROM table1 INNER JOIN table2 ON table1.au_id =
table2.au_id
```

Microsoft implemented this syntax in SQL Server 7.0, and you may find other databases that support it as they are updated to implement the latest features defined in the evolving new SQL standard. The advantage of this syntax is that it explicitly identifies the type of join. With inner joins, knowing the type is not so much of an issue. There are two other types of joins, however, where seeing an explicit representation of the join type is extremely useful.

Hint

Special terminology is often associated with joins. Joins of this type that rely on an equality in the ON clause are called *equi joins*. Joins that use another operator in the join condition are called *nonequi joins*. Taken together, both equi joins and nonequi joins are called *theta joins*. A join without a condition is called a *cross join,* and it produces a result set that has a row for every possible combination of the rows in a table, a result set that is also known as a *Cartesian product*.

Generically, these two join types are called *outer joins*. They return all the rows from at least one of the tables involved in the join. In early SQL syntax, you specified an outer join by placing a plus sign after the name of the table all of whose rows should be included, and sometimes you were limited to one outer join per query. With the new syntax, you can see much more clearly what happens with the outer join.

To clarify what happens in an outer join, you need to visualize the tables sitting side by side. You have a table on the left, and a table on the right. You have two types of join operations available; one is a left outer join, in which all rows from the table on the left are returned, even if there are no matching rows in the table on the right. Where there is a missing row, null fields are inserted in the rowset returned. You can also have a right outer join, in which all rows from the table on the right are returned.

Fortunately in the syntax, the tables appear to the left and right of each other in the SELECT statement. Here is the syntax for a left join:

```
SELECT  * FROM table1 LEFT JOIN table2 ON table1.au_id =
table2.au_id
```

In this case, all the rows from table1 come back, even if there is no matching row in table2. Where there is no match in table2, null fields are inserted into the row set. The syntax for a right join is similar:

```
SELECT  * FROM table1 RIGHT JOIN table2 ON table1.au_id =
table2.au_id
```

In this case, all the rows from table2 return, and null fields are inserted where there is no matching row in table1.

To demonstrate what happens in joins, let's look at some data returned from Pubs. Let's do an inner join between the employee table and the job table. Here is the query for the inner join:

```
SELECT * FROM employee INNER JOIN jobs ON employee.job_id = jobs.job_id
```

This query returns 43 rows containing the employee information from the employee table and the job descriptions for each employee from the jobs table, as shown in Figure 2-6.

To convert this query to a left join, replace "INNER" with "LEFT" and run the query string again. You return the same 43 rows. This should be no surprise, because you would expect each employee to have a job description assigned to him or her. Convert the query into a right join by replacing "LEFT" with "RIGHT." When you run the query, you will see a different result. The query returns 44 rows, and the employee information for one of these rows is null. Obviously, there is one job description that has not been assigned to an employee in the database. In our right join, all the job description rows have to return, even if there is no matching row in the left-hand table.

Typically, you use inner joins to link tables in queries. Normally you want to return rows with data rather than rows with no data. In the case of the job description not assigned to an employee, we normally do not need to know about it in data operations involving employees. We want the job description assigned to the employee to show up, not an unassigned job description.

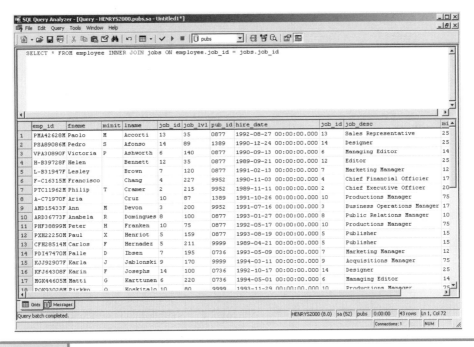

Figure 2-6 The inner join returns 43 rows with no null fields

Right and left joins are useful, however, when you are asking a question that requires all the rows of one table in the answer. For example, when you want a chart of all the patients in a nursing facility that shows which ones have required treatment for medical events that occur during a twenty-four hour period (a common report in nursing facilities), you need to have all the rows in the residents table show up in the rowset returned from the database. You need only the treatments that have been applied, but you need all the residents regardless of whether they received treatment. A left join of the residents table to the treatments table produces this result.

Sometimes you need to build tables that bridge between other tables. Pubs contains such a table, the one named titleauthor. The purpose of this table is to facilitate joins among tables that hold related information, but that have no reason to include the unique identifiers associated with each other. For example, the authors table contains the list of authors. The titles table contains the list of titles. For each author, you have many titles, a so-called one to many relationship. To link each author with all his or her titles, you would have to include an unknown number of title fields if you embedded the links in the authors table. When you face the need to link from one element to many, you need such a bridge table so that a join can provide an efficient link for you.

Let's look at the SELECT statements to see how this relationship works. The following statement gets a list of authors:

```
SELECT  * FROM authors
```

Once we have a list of authors, we need to link the authors to a list of title IDs. This we can get from the titleauthor table, since it contains rows that have an author ID column (au_id) and a title ID column (title_id). We use an inner join because we want no null title IDs or author fields to appear. We want only the data rows that have a full match on the join criteria. Here is the SELECT statement that performs this work:

```
SELECT  * from authors inner join titleauthor on authors.au_id =
titleauthor.au_id
```

Now we have a set of rows that pair each author with a title ID. To attach actual titles to title IDs, we need an inner join to the titles table. Here is the SELECT statement that does the work:

```
SELECT  * from authors inner join titleauthor on authors.au_id =
titleauthor.au_id inner join titles on titleauthor.title_id =
titles.title_id
```

The result set is shown in Figure 2-7. As you can see, we have a set of rows, one for each author/title pairing, that we can use to identify who has written which titles. If we want to see them organized by author, we can add a GROUP BY phrase to group the rows by author. We can also use ORDER BY to sort them in an appropriate order, perhaps by title, so that all the titles for a given author would be in alphabetical order.

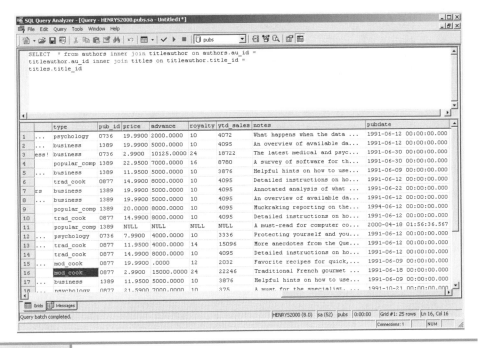

Figure 2-7   This result set returns rows that link authors and titles using a bridging table

Ask the Expert

Question: How can you keep right and left joins separate?

Answer: Draw a diagram. You can't make mistakes easily if you draw the diagram and make reference to the diagram when you write the SQL statement.

Question: Can you combine left and right outer joins?

Answer: Yes, you can, in which case you create a full outer join. Substitute the word "FULL" for "LEFT" or "RIGHT." The following statement shows the syntax:

```
select * from authors full join titleauthor on authors.au_id =
titleauthor.au_id
```

Question: When would you use a full join?

Answer: There really are not many occasions for this type of join. You use it when you need one row in the result set that represents each row in both tables. Since many lines will have null values for the columns from one table, processing the result set in a program is difficult. Typically a program will iterate through the data looking for certain values. For at least some of the rows, the value you seek will be null. You have to have an action to undertake when the value is null; otherwise, using the full join is simply a waste of processing time.

Question: Is there an easy way to avoid the problem we had when we let COUNT create the groups for HAVING?

Answer: There are two ways. One, the easiest, is to make sure that you use an explicit GROUP BY with HAVING, even if you don't have to. Then you know how the data will be grouped. The second is to recognize that aggregate functions create only a single group, the group of rows that participated in the aggregation. Any group to the left of HAVING feeds into the HAVING predicate. If you always check to make sure that all groups to the left of HAVING are the ones that the HAVING predicate will act on, and if you always write out a definition of what the group is, you won't fall into the trap.

Combining Fields and Creating Columns

We have already seen that you can combine fields together in queries. We formatted names by concatenating string data types together using the concatenation operator (+). You can combine fields in many ways. There is only one rule to follow: use the AS keyword to name whatever combination you have created so that you have a means of accessing the combination later on. If you use a reporting package like Crystal Reports to present data, you need a name for the combination; otherwise, you cannot present the resulting value in the report. If you use DAO or ADO to collect a recordset, you need a means of accessing the combination in the recordset. The name you give the combination is the means you have.

Just to review, here is how to concatenate character data to create a formatted string:

```
SELECT au_lname + ', ' + au_fname AS full_name FROM authors
```

In addition to basic concatenation, you can perform math on fields as well. If you wanted to calculate the total dollar value of sales, you could use the following query:

```
SELECT  qty * price as total_sale FROM sales INNER JOIN titles ON
sales.title_id = titles.title_id
```

The math operators are the standard +, −, /, and * familiar in most programming languages. Exponentiation is done using the carat (^) character.

In addition, you may wish to select a constant value into a column, or a constant value when a WHERE condition is true. For example, you might want to have a field that identifies the month for which any query is valid. You can place the month name in a column returned by your query using syntax like the following:

```
SELECT *, 'July' AS the_month FROM titles
```

This query returns all the columns from the titles table and one more column named "the_month" that contains the month name "July."

Hint

Any name created using AS is called a *correlation name.*

1-Minute Drill

● **What is the most frequent join type and why?**

● **What operator do you use to multiply field values?**

● **Why should you name computations with AS?**

● **If table1 has 20 rows and table2 has 30 rows, what kind of join between table1 (left-hand) and table2 (right-hand) returns at least 30 rows?**

PresentingData.vbp

Project 2-1: Presenting Data

Getting data into the Query Analyzer is useful, but data becomes even more useful when it becomes part of a program that allows users to interact with the data. When you use SQL from within a program, those SQL commands are called *embedded SQL*, because they are embedded within another programming language. In this section, we are going to create a quick Visual Basic program that extracts data from the Pubs database and presents it to a user for viewing only.

Step-by-Step

1. Open Visual Basic and create a new standard project. This action leaves you with a project containing a standard VB form, as seen in Figure 2-8. To this project, we need to add an ADO data control.

2. Select Project | Components and check the box next to Microsoft ADO Data Control (SP4) (OLEDB). Click OK.

3. Select the new data control icon from the toolbox and draw the control on the form.

● An inner join, because normally you do not need to return null values for rows.
● The asterisk operator.
● You need to name computations so that you can refer to the resulting value when you want to present data.
● A right join.

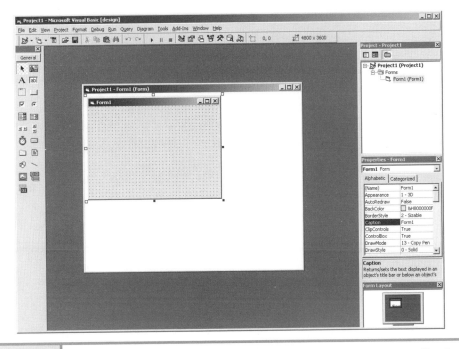

Figure 2-8   The VB project you need to start building a data access application

4. Right-click the control and select ADODC Properties from the context menu.

5. In the Property Pages dialog box, select Use Connection String and click Build.

6. In the Data Link Properties dialog box, select the SQL Server driver from the list in the Provider tab.

7. Fill in the server information in the Connection tab (see Figure 2-9). Click OK. You have just created a connection to the server.

Hint

If you ever need help creating a connection string, the Build button in the ADO data control ADODC Properties option helps tremendously. It properly formats the string with the provider name, connection information, and any additional properties that the server might need. Since the documentation on connection strings is so weak, you might find yourself using this little wizard frequently.

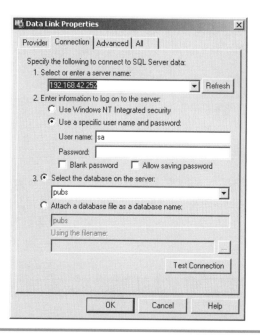

Figure 2-9   Use this configuration information to connect to the server

8. Select the RecordSource tab in the Property Pages dialog box, select the command type 1-adCmdText, and enter the SQL statement "SELECT * FROM authors" in the Command Text (SQL) text box. Click OK. You have embedded SQL in your program.

9. Select the text box on the toolbox and draw seven text boxes on the form.

10. For each text box, set the Data Source property to Adodc1 (the name of the data control) and the Data Field property to the name of one of the columns in the authors table. These names should automatically be listed after you set the Data Source property. If they are not, try opening the ADODC properties as you did in step 3 and use the Test Connection button to activate the connection.

11. Run your application. You now have a viewer that shows you the names, addresses, and phone numbers of the authors in the Pubs database (see Figure 2-10).

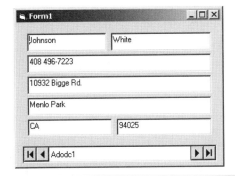

| **Figure 2-10** | This program presents the name and address information of authors in the Pubs database |

 Mastery Check

1. A SELECT statement can have the following parts

    a. SELECT, FROM, INSERT

    b. SELECT, GROUP BY, INSERT

    c. SELECT, ORDER BY, UPDATE

    d. ORDER BY, HAVING, GROUP BY

2. Use a join to accomplish which of the following tasks:

    a. Linking two tables so that rows return from both tables for a query

    b. Linking the value of one unique identifier to another

    c. Preparing two tables for data entry

    d. Permanently tying two tables together for data input

3. Explain what embedded SQL is.

4. What is the older syntax for creating an outer join?

☑ Mastery Check

5. What is the concatenation operator?

6. Explain what the AS keyword does.

7. What type of join returns the fewest rows?

8. The distinguishing characteristic of an outer join is

    a. It returns at least all the rows from one of the joined tables.

    b. It can be classified as one of at least six types of outer join.

    c. It uses the JOIN keyword alone to specify the nature of the join.

    d. None of the above

9. What is a join that does not rely on an equality in the WHERE or ON clause called?

10. What does GROUP BY do?

Module 3

Inserting Data

Goals

- Understand how to insert data into tables
- Learn how to use a SELECT statement with INSERT
- Understand the use of the VALUES clause
- Have built a data entry application using an embedded INSERT statement

In Module 2, we saw how to exploit a connection to the database to retrieve data previously stored in the database. In this module, we focus on how to put data into the database. The verb that SQL provides for undertaking data insertion is INSERT. In some respects, INSERT statements are very flexible. They allow you to put complete records into existing tables, to place partial records into tables, and to create tables. In some respects, however, INSERT statements can be tricky. If you are building ad hoc queries using Query Analyzer, you can work with minimal forms of INSERT. If you are embedding SQL in a program, you need to use a particular form of the INSERT statement so that changes in the database do not break your program.

We are going to approach learning about INSERT by starting with its minimal forms. Then we will examine its different forms, pointing out the possible contexts for using each form. Along the way, we will note the problems associated with each form. By the end of this module, you should be well versed in all the subtleties of using SQL INSERT statements.

Using Insert

The purpose of an INSERT statement is to place data in a table. Therefore, in its minimal form, INSERT requires the following basic elements:

- The verb INSERT, which begins the statement

- A destination for the INSERT operation

- A list of values for the INSERT operation, marked by the VALUES keyword

Thus, the minimal syntax for an INSERT into pubs.titleauthor is the following:

```
INSERT authors VALUES('010-10-1012', 'lname', 'fname', '5551212', NULL,
NULL, NULL, NULL, 0)
```

This statement, so long as you enter it exactly as you see it, will work. It has a number of subtleties to it, however. For example, replace 'lname' with null and you will get a constraint error. Delete the dashes in '010-10-1012' and you will receive a constraint error. We have much to explore here, so let's get on with the issues.

First, the minimal syntax for INSERT uses the keyword followed by the table name followed by the VALUES keyword, followed in turn by the list of values in parentheses, with each value correctly marked for its data type. String values are enclosed in single quotes. Numeric values are not enclosed in quotes. In this case, the sole numeric value is the last one. Actually, it is of the bit data type, so the only numeric values it can take are 0 and 1.

Hint

In some databases, you will not need the VALUES keyword. VALUES was added as a requirement in the SQL 3 standard.

Next, note that we used NULL for some of the fields. The basic purpose behind using NULL in these fields was to demonstrate that we could. We can because these fields are explicitly marked in the definition of the table as allowing NULL values. The other fields are marked not to allow NULL as a value. As a result, using NULL instead of a string value for 'lname' results in an error. The last name field (au_lname) cannot be NULL. It must contain a data value. The database checks this constraint when you attempt an INSERT, and it throws an error if you attempt to place NULL in a column that cannot accept NULL as a value.

Note

NULL means that there is no data present in the field. It is not the equivalent of 0. Zero is actually a numeric data value that has meaning within the number system. NULL has no meaning as a value.

How are you as a SQL programmer supposed to know what columns can be NULL and what columns cannot be NULL? If you have no access to database administration tools, you have to ask your database administrator to tell you. If you do have access to database administration tools, one of your tools will tell you. For example, in the SQL Server Enterprise Manager, right-click the table name and select Properties from the context menu. The Table Properties dialog box has a check mark in the Nulls column for any column that can accept NULL as a value.

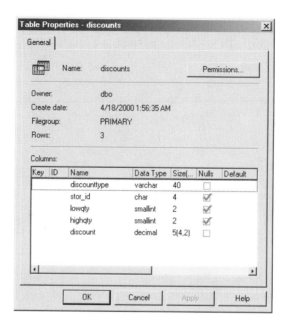

Next, you must be concerned about other constraints that may apply to a table during an INSERT operation. The primary constraint that can interfere with an INSERT is a key constraint. (We will cover what keys are in Module 6. For now, just accept that they do exist and can interfere with INSERT.) Tables contain values known as *keys,* and keys serve to uniquely identify rows. The key for pubs.authors is au_id. This column appears in other tables, most notably pubs.titleauthors. When a key appears in multiple tables, normally a *key constraint* applies.

Key constraints typically require that the value of the key be defined and inserted in one and only one table. In actual implementation, the key value can be inserted in any table with a column for it, but it must be inserted in one and only one table before it can be inserted in any other table. The key for the authors table is the first column value, '010-10-1012'. We can insert this value in pubs.authors without difficulty, because pubs.authors is is defined as being the table that must first possess a value for au_id before any other table can possess the value. Pubs.titleauthor also contains the column au_id. If you try to place '010-10-1012' in titleauthor before you place it in authors, you receive an error. The database checks the key constraint, discovers that the value must first be in pubs.authors.au_id, and checks this column to see if the value is present. If the value is present in pubs.authors.au_id, the insertion succeeds. If the value is not present in pubs.authors.au_id, the insertion fails and the database returns an error.

3

Hint

You can easily identify keys in most graphical representations of a table's structure. Database management tools typically mark them with an icon. SQL Server and Access, for example, use a small key to indicate that a column serves as a key.

To learn what constraints are in place on keys, you need to see a database diagram. To create a database diagram in SQL Server, follow these steps:

1. In the Enterprise Manager tree view, open the server, then open the Databases list, then open the database, and select Diagrams.

2. Right–click the right pane of the Enterprise Manager. Select New Database Diagram from the context menu.

3. In the Create Database Diagram Wizard, click Next.

4. Select the tables to be added by clicking each one (see the following illustration). Multiple selection with SHIFT+click (for contiguous multiple selection) and CTRL+click (for noncontiguous multiple selection) works in this list box. Click Add, and then click Next.

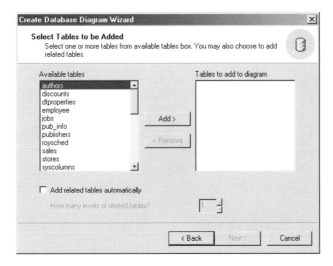

5. Click Finish to build the diagram. The open diagram appears in a child window.

6. Click the Save icon to save the diagram.

7. Click the Close button on the child window to close the diagram.

8. Double-click the diagram's icon to open the diagram.

Once you have the diagram open, you can see the key constraints easily. They are represented as lines among the tables. The location that defines the key has a key icon terminating the line. The location that checks the constraint before allowing the insertion terminates the line with an infinity symbol. Formally, these icons represent the one to many relationship that typically exists among tables that share a key. Where the key is defined, there may be one and only one row that contains the key. The key's purpose is to identify rows uniquely in that table. In the other tables, the key links rows in that table to the data uniquely identified in the table where the key is defined.

For example, the authors table uniquely identifies the authors who write for this publisher. The titleauthors table serves to link an author to the titles the author has written. Authors may, but are not required to, write more than one title. As a result, titleauthors must be able to contain multiple rows in which the same author ID can appear, because linking the author ID to the title ID in a row in titleauthors is our way of bridging between the unique authors and the unique titles. Were we to SELECT all the titles for a given author, as we did in Module 2, we would need to join authors to titles in order to find all the titles associated with a single author. The join operation builds one row per title-author combination.

To get complete information about a key constraint, right-click the line that represents it and select Properties from the context menu. The Properties dialog box shows you the name of the constraint, which is a useful item of information, since a key constraint error refers to the constraint violated by this name. You also see the two tables involved, and the field names involved. The Selected Relationship drop-down list allows you to navigate among the constraints associated with the tables linked by the line.

Hint

While it is good database design to name all instances of a key column the same, you will find databases where this practice has been ignored. As a result, you may need to view this constraint information.

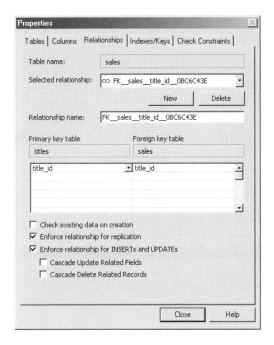

3

Yet another type of constraint can interfere with your INSERT statements. This type of constraint is called a *check constraint*. It tells the database to check the value entering the field for a pattern match. If the data matches the pattern, the INSERT can take place. If the data does not match the pattern, the INSERT fails.

The au_id field has a check constraint on it. To see this constraint definition, right-click the authors table title bar in the diagram and select Check Constraints from the context menu. In the Properties dialog box, the definition of the constraint appears in the Constraint Expression text box. In this case, the expression is as follows:

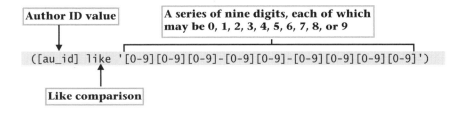

You can readily identify the column name au_id in the leftmost position. The LIKE keyword means that au_id must match the following pattern. The pattern appears between the single quotes. Each bracketed item represents one of the characters that must appear in the pattern. These bracketed elements indicate that the character in this position must represent a 0, 1, 2, 3, 4, 5, 6, 7, 8, or 9. Where you see a character, such as a dash, not enclosed in brackets, then that character must appear at that position. This constraint effectively defines the pattern commonly associated with the social security number. Any author ID must match this pattern, or the INSERT will fail.

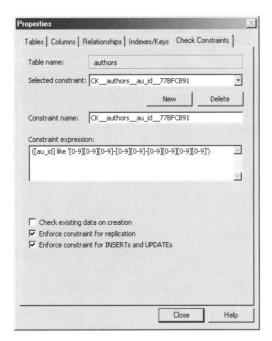

After examining these issues, you can appreciate the complexities associated with the INSERT operation. And so far, we have ignored complexities associated with the syntax of the statement. You can use more than the minimal syntax, and in most cases you are wise to do so. The minimal syntax works well for adding complete rows (that is, where you specify an explicit value for each field) using the Query Analyzer. The reason is simply that you have less to type and can work more efficiently. Other forms of the statement are more appropriate in other contexts.

INSERT allows you to use the INTO keyword. The form of the statement using this keyword is as follows:

```
INSERT INTO authors VALUES('010-10-1012', 'lname', 'fname', '5551212',
NULL, NULL, NULL, NULL, 0)
```

INTO explicitly indicates that the INSERT destination follows, and it provides greater readability for the statement. Readability is a factor you will greatly appreciate when you have to take over maintenance of someone else's code, so use INTO in writing your INSERT statements.

Another syntax variation allows you to explicitly mention column names. This variation is as follows:

```
INSERT INTO authors (au_id, au_lname, au_fname, phone, contract)
VALUES('010-10-1013', 'lname', 'fname', '5551212', 0)
```

Note that we did not supply a complete list of columns for the table. We could, but we do not have to. We are required, however, to supply a column name and a value for each column that cannot be NULL. In this way, you can insert into only the columns where you need to place data and let the database supply default values for the others. The default value will either be NULL or a value defined as the default when the table was created. The Table Properties dialog box shows default values in the Default column. Note that pubs.authors implements the default value of '(UNKNOWN)' for the phone column.

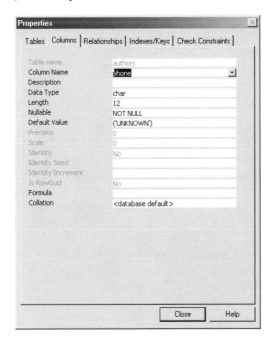

INSERT has some default behaviors that you need to know about. If you provide no list of column names, INSERT takes the first value in the values list and matches it with the first column in the table definition, takes the second value in the values list and matches it with the second column in the table definition, and so forth until all values have been matched with columns. If you have your values listed in an order that does not match the order of columns in the table definition, you will either put the wrong value in a column or experience a data type mismatch error. The latter problem is much less severe than the former. If you insert the wrong value in a column, you may have great difficulty discovering the error.

In addition, this default column matching requires values for all columns in the table. You cannot omit a column from the list. The database is using the order in the VALUES list to determine which column to use. If the database finds fewer values than it has columns, it generates an error. This behavior is particularly important when you embed SQL statements in a program. These statements are effectively masked from view, and no one in the organization at any given time is guaranteed to know the exact form of the statement. If a database administrator has to add a column to a table, for example, she is not guaranteed to know that some program somewhere uses an abbreviated form of INSERT. However, if such a form of INSERT is in use, adding a column will cause the program to generate an error. If you use the form of INSERT with a column list, adding a column to a table will not cause the SQL statement to generate an error. As a result, you should use column lists in all embedded SQL INSERTS.

Note

If you must add a column to an existing table against which programs insert data, you should either make the column nullable or design it to insert a default value if it is not included in an INSERT statement. Adding a nonnullable column with no default value requires that the column be added to all INSERT statements, or the statements will generate errors.

You may be wondering, having seen that keys can appear in multiple tables, if you can use a JOIN to insert the key in more than one table. The answer, frankly, is that we all wish we could, but we can't. Inserting the same value in multiple tables requires multiple INSERTS.

Hint

You can work around this constraint by using INSERT against a view. See Module 11 for more information.

1-Minute Drill

● **Describe what value NULL has.**

● **Is the INTO keyword required in an INSERT statement?**

● **Why should you use a column list and a values list?**

Ask the Expert

Question: What do I most need to keep in mind when I am using INSERT?

Answer: The most common mistake in inserting data is forgetting about which constraints are operating on a table. If your INSERT statement fails for mysterious reasons, investigate the constraints immediately. Someone probably has applied a formatting constraint or a key constraint to one of the columns.

Question: What do I do if the data I need to insert is of the wrong data type?

Answer: You have two options for converting data, the Convert function and the Cast function. Cast has the following syntax:

```
CAST(DataAsYouHaveIT AS DataTypeYouWantItToBe)
```

Convert has the following syntax:

```
CONVERT(DataTypeYouWantItToBe, DataAsYouHaveIt, (OptionalStyleDescriptor))
```

● **NULL is the absence of a data value. It has no value.**
● **INTO is not required, but it improves readability.**
● **To keep your code from breaking if someone changes the table definition.**

I tend to prefer Convert, because it has more options. Many data types, such as datetime, allow you to use a number as the style descriptor to select an appropriate international date format.

Question: **Should I check the data in any way before I insert it?**

Answer: There is one cardinal rule of database programming: Thou shalt not put junk in the database. When you collect a value from a user, you should check to make certain that it is in range, of the correct data type, and in the right format before you undertake the INSERT operation. In Visual Basic and similar event-driven programming languages, the Change event on any control is an excellent location for data validation code. If you know that data will always come from a control in the wrong format, use CAST or CONVERT to correct the data format. Having multiple redundant checks for data correctness is not a bad idea, especially in complex programs. There is always one more path through the program, especially Windows programs, of which you are not aware. It may be the path that thwarts all the checks and puts bad data in the database. Of course, don't redundantly validate data to the point where performance suffers. Just remember that bad data complicates every database user's life if it gets into the database.

Question: **What do I do if bad data has gotten into the database?**

Answer: I have worked a number of contracts where I have followed a crew that did not validate data prior to insertion. You have two choices. You can either find and correct all the bad data, or you can correct for it afterward. If the correction is one of data type (for example, "two" where "2" should appear), you can usually use UPDATE statements to locate and correct each bad case.

Sometimes, however, you will not know what the correct data should be. Some databases accept the year 100 as a valid year. If a data entry error on a four-digit year leaves you with a three-digit year, you have no way of

3

predicting which character was accidentally deleted. In such cases, you can only live with the problem, and correct for it when you experience it.

Correcting for bad data after it enters the database means that you have to know a bad value when you see it. Our date case is simple to correct for. If all years are supposed to be four characters long, check for anything less, and correct for it when the case appears. Sometimes, however, you will either not be able to predict bad values or be able to develop a definitive list of the problems. In these situations, you must develop your coping strategies as each case appears.

Using Select with Insert

INSERT offers you great flexibility in choosing what to insert into a table. For example, assume that you have just entered a number of authors and a number of titles in the authors table and the titles table. You have also created an entry for each pairing in the titleauthor table. (Don't worry, the programming exercise in this module will show you how to create just such a data entry application using either ADO or DAO.) Now assume that you want to build a table that contains the unique pairing of all title and author records. You want one row in the table for each author–title pair in the database.

Note

We want not to worry about why you would create such a temporary table at this moment. Instead, we want to stay focused on exploring the nature of the INSERT statement. Such statements are often used to populate temporary tables or views. You will learn a bit more about temporary tables in a later section in this module. You will learn much more about temporary tables in Module 6. You will learn all about views in Module 11.

To insert data in such a table, you would use an INSERT statement that contains a SELECT statement. The basic form of such a statement is as follows:

```
INSERT into temptable SELECT authors.au_id, au_lname, au_fname, phone,
address, city, state, zip, contract, au_ord, royaltyper, titles.title_id,
title, type, pub_id, price, advance, royalty, ytd_sales, notes, pubdate
from authors inner join titleauthor on authors.au_id = titleauthor.au_id
inner join titles on titles.title_id = titleauthor.title_id
```

If you run this query in the Query Analyzer, it produces an error. We need to first create the table in the database if we expect this data to load into the table. (If you are comfortable with using Enterprise Manager to create tables, note that Figure 3-1 shows the table definition for temptable.) There is another factor that we must also pay attention to. First, you cannot use SELECT * in this query with impunity. All SQL databases will complain about ambiguous column names. What ambiguous column names, you ask?

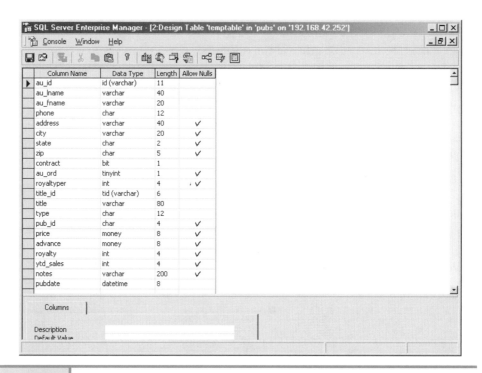

Figure 3-1 Use this table definition to create temptable using Enterprise Manager

Technically, the SELECT * form of this query selects au_id twice and title_id twice. Because we are getting all columns, we get au_id from authors and au_id from titleauthor. The same happens with title_id. If you examine the result set in the Query Analyzer when you run the SELECT * version of the query, you will see both pairs of columns present.

To avoid the ambiguity, you can attach the table name to each column, selecting authors.au_id and titleauthor.au_id, for example. If you resolve the ambiguity, you have to name all the other columns in the statement. You can SELECT *, or you can name the columns. So in creating our INSERT . . . INTO . . . SELECT statement, we named all the columns we wanted to see. You will notice, of course, that we chose not to duplicate au_id and title_id. There is no point in selecting these values twice, unless we are dead set on proving to ourselves that the values are identical.

Adding a Where Clause

Suppose you only need to work with a subset of the records this query produces. You can easily use a WHERE clause to restrict the output. An example follows:

```
INSERT into temptable SELECT authors.au_id, au_lname, au_fname, phone,
address, city, state, zip, contract, au_ord, royaltyper, titles.title_id,
title, type, pub_id, price, advance, royalty, ytd_sales, notes, pubdate
from authors inner join titleauthor on authors.au_id = titleauthor.au_id
inner join titles on titles.title_id = titleauthor.title_id WHERE pubdate <
GETDATE()
```

Hint

Getdate() is a SQL function that returns the current system date and time. To rely on such functions implies that you are keeping your system date and time properly set. Most operating systems include some sort of time package that will contact the Naval Observatory either by modem or via an Internet connection to set your system clock to the current time with one of the observatory's atomic clocks.

This query returns all title–author pairings that are published prior to today. We exclude titles that we intend to release in the future but have already entered into the system because they are in process.

Adding a Having Clause

You may also group your data and use a HAVING clause to select the relevant records. In this case, you use GROUP BY to create the grouping, an aggregate function to calculate a relevant criterion, and a HAVING clause to enforce the criterion, for example:

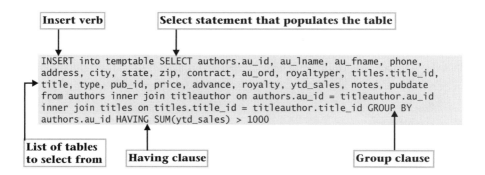

Insert verb

Select statement that populates the table

```
INSERT into temptable SELECT authors.au_id, au_lname, au_fname, phone,
address, city, state, zip, contract, au_ord, royaltyper, titles.title_id,
title, type, pub_id, price, advance, royalty, ytd_sales, notes, pubdate
from authors inner join titleauthor on authors.au_id = titleauthor.au_id
inner join titles on titles.title_id = titleauthor.title_id GROUP BY
authors.au_id HAVING SUM(ytd_sales) > 1000
```

List of tables to select from

Having clause

Group clause

Here we select only the authors whose combined ytd_sales on all their books exceeds 1000. How did we make sure that we summed the ytd_sales for all books? We grouped by au_id. Each author, therefore, forms a group. Any aggregate function will calculate for all the items in a given author's group of titles. SUM takes care of the addition for each group, and HAVING enforces the condition we have set.

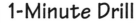

1-Minute Drill

● **What does a SELECT within an INSERT do?**

● **When are you most likely to use a WHERE clause in a SELECT inside an INSERT?**

● **When are you most likely to use a HAVING clause in a SELECT inside an INSERT?**

● A SELECT provides the list of values to insert into the table columns identified in the INSERT.
● When building a temporary table or view.
● When building a temporary table or view with additional columns for summarized (or aggregated) data.

Using Select Into

Someone in the audience has to be grumbling about having been told that we need to create tables but not being shown how as of yet. We will remedy this complaint right now. You don't have to know anything about creating tables to create a table. You simply need to know a trick, and a very useful trick it is. There is a form of the SELECT statement that functions to select records, create a table, and insert the records into the table, all in one SQL statement. This statement is the SELECT . . . INTO statement. To create a table for all of our data and enter the data in one fell step, you use this statement:

```
SELECT authors.au_id, au_lname, au_fname, phone, address, city, state, zip,
contract, au_ord, royaltyper, titles.title_id, title, type, pub_id, price,
advance, royalty, ytd_sales, notes, pubdate INTO temptable FROM authors
INNER JOIN titleauthor ON authors.au_id = titleauthor.au_id INNER JOIN
titles ON titles.title_id = titleauthor.title_id
```

You have to admit that this is a useful trick. The SELECT part of the statement can either be SELECT * or SELECT plus a list of column names. Keep in mind that column ambiguity will haunt you with such statements. The INTO phrase acts like an abbreviation for INSERT INTO, except that it creates the table. The FROM clause allows you to do any acceptable set of joins that you would like to undertake. You can add WHERE and HAVING clauses if you wish. The net result is a new table in the database, with your data in it, ready for use. You can also use AS to create additional columns that you might need later but do not have data for at the time you create the table. The following three examples demonstrate each of these options:

```
SELECT authors.au_id, au_lname, au_fname, phone, address, city, state, zip,
contract, au_ord, royaltyper, titles.title_id, title, type, pub_id, price,
advance, royalty, ytd_sales, notes, pubdate INTO temptable FROM authors
INNER JOIN titleauthor ON authors.au_id = titleauthor.au_id INNER JOIN
titles ON titles.title_id = titleauthor.title_id id WHERE pubdate <
GETDATE()

SELECT authors.au_id, au_lname, au_fname, phone, address, city, state, zip,
contract, au_ord, royaltyper, titles.title_id, title, type, pub_id, price,
advance, royalty, ytd_sales, notes, pubdate INTO temptable FROM authors
INNER JOIN titleauthor ON authors.au_id = titleauthor.au_id INNER JOIN
titles ON titles.title_id = titleauthor.title_id id GROUP BY authors.au_id
HAVING SUM(ytd_sales) > 1000
```

```
SELECT authors.au_id, au_lname, au_fname, phone, address, city, state, zip,
contract, au_ord, royaltyper, titles.title_id, title, type, pub_id, price,
advance, royalty, ytd_sales, notes, pubdate INTO temptable, 1 AS NewColumn
FROM authors INNER JOIN titleauthor ON authors.au_id = titleauthor.au_id
INNER JOIN titles ON titles.title_id = titleauthor.title_id
```

Hint

The phrase "1 as NewColumn" selects the value 1 into a column named NewColumn for each record created in the table. You can then use an UPDATE statement (see Module 4) to change the value to a more appropriate value in later manipulations of the information in the table.

When would you use this statement? When you need a temporary table to avoid having to create a gigantic, complex single query. You can select the data you need into the table, perform additional manipulations and changes on the data in the table, and then use the information in the table for reports or further queries. Keep in mind that temporary tables are intended to be temporary. Typically, you create them and then either delete all data and reuse them or delete them from the database when their usefulness ends. Typically you would pair the use of this statement with an appropriate DROP statement (see Module 6) to delete the table.

1-Minute Drill

● **What does a SELECT INTO do?**

● **How can you create an additional column with a constant value as its default value?**

● SELECT INTO creates a table using the columns and rows identified in the statement.
● Use a phrase like "1 as NewColumn" in the column list in the statement. This creates a column named NewColumn and inserts 1 as the value for each row in the table.

DataEntry.vbp

Project 3-1: Data Entry

In the last module, our programming exercise caused you to embed SQL using the ADO Data Control provided with Visual Basic. While the data control is great for allowing a view of a table, when it comes to inserting data, another way of embedding SQL is better. You can set the properties of the data control to allow an insert to take place whenever the user scrolls past the last record, but you can insert only to the recordset you have open in the data control. We have laid out a scenario in this table where you have to undertake insertions into three tables, authors, titles, and titleauthor, when you add author and title information to the system. Such an INSERT is awkward using the data control. In this project, we will see how to undertake such an insertion using both ADO and DAO.

Step-by-Step

1. Open the PresentingData project from Module 2.

2. Click the ADO Data Control and press the Delete button.

3. Select File | Save Project As and save the project as InsertingData.vbp.

4. Right-click Form1 in the Project Explorer and select Save PresentingData.frm As. Save the form as InsertingData.frm.

5. Add ten text boxes to accommodate the fields in the titles table, and two more text boxes to accommodate additional fields in the authors table.

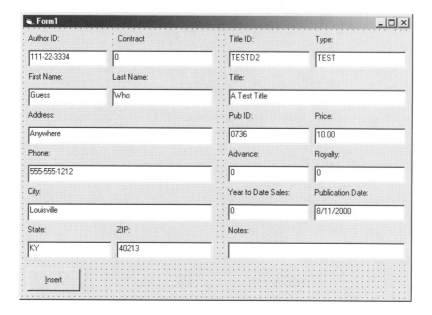

6. Rename the text boxes so that their names consist of "txt" + the field name. This makes working with them in the SQL statement much easier. Set the Text property to provide default data settings.

Hint

Be sure to use an existing value of pub_id from the publishers table; otherwise, you will violate a key constraint.

7. Add the following declaration in the General section of the code window:

```
Const USING_DAO As Boolean = False
```

8. Add a button to the form and name it "cmdInsert." Its caption should be "&Insert."

9. Add references to the DAO 3.6 library, the ActiveX Data Objects 2.6 library, and the ActiveX Data Objects 2.6 Recordset Library.

10. Double-click cmdInsert to open the code window.

11. Enter the following code for establishing connections:

```
'For the DAO connection

    Dim dbMyDatabase As DAO.Database
    'For the ADO connection

    Dim cnnMyDatabase As New ADODB.Connection

    Dim cmdMyDatabase As New ADODB.Command

    Dim rstMyDatabase As New ADODB.Recordset
```

> **Define database connection objects**

12. Enter the following code to create the INSERT statements:

```
If USING_DAO Then

Set dbMyDatabase = DBEngine.OpenDatabase("Pubs",
    dbDriverPrompt, False,
  "DRIVER={SQL Serve r};SERVER=MyServer;UID=sa;")

    dbMyDatabase.Execute ("insert into authors (au_id,
      au_lname, au_fname, phone, address, city, state, zip,
      contract) " & _

      "values('" & txtAUID.Text & "', '" & txtLName.Text &
          "', '" &
       txtFName.Text & "', '" & txtPhone.Text & "', '" &
          txtAddress.Text &
       "', '" & txtCity.Text & "', '" & txtSta te.Text & "',
          '" &
        txtZIP.Text & "', " & txtContract.Text & ")")

    dbMyDatabase.Execute ("insert into titles (title_id,
      title, type,
        pub_id, price, advance, royalty, ytd_sales, notes,
          pubdate) " & _
        "values('" & txtTitleID.Text & "', '"
          & txtTitle.Text      & "', '" &
        txtType.Text & "', '" & txtPubID.Text & "', " &
          txtPrice.Text &
        ", " & txtAdvance.Text & ", " & txtRoyalty.Text & ",
          " &
        txtYTDSales.Text & ", '" & txtNotes.Text & "', '" &
          txtPubDate &
          "')")

     dbMyDatabase.Execute ("insert into titleauthor (au_id,
       title_id) " & _
         "values('" & txtAUID.Text & "', '" & txtTitleID.Text
           & "')")
```

> **If we are using DAO**

> **Create DAO connection**

> **Execute SQL statement**

3

```
Else ◄──────  [If we are using ADO]

    With cnnMyDatabase

[Create ADO    .ConnectionString = "Provider=SQLOLEDB.1;Persist
connection]       Security
                   Info=False;User ID=sa;Initial Catalog=pubs;Data
                  Source=Henrys2000"

        .Open

    End With
                                              [Execute SQL
    With cmdMyDatabase                         statement]

        .ActiveConnection = cnnMyDatabase

        .CommandType = adCmdText

        .CommandText = "insert into authors (au_id,
            au_lname,   au_fname,
            phone, address, city, state, zip, contract) " & _
            "values('" & txtAUID.Text & "', '" &
             txtLName.Text & "', '" &
            txtFName.Text & "', '" & txtPhone.Text & "', '" &
            txtAddress.Text & "', '" & txtCity.Text & "', '" &


            txtState.Text & "', '" & txtZIP.Text & "', " &
             txtContract.Text
            & ")"

    End With

    Set rstMyDatabase = cmdMyDatabase.Execute

    With cmdMyDatabase                  [Set up and execute
                                         next SQL statement]
        .CommandType = adCmdText

        .CommandText = "insert into titles (title_id, title,
            type, pub_id,
            price, advance, royalty, ytd_sales, notes,
             pubdate) " & _
            "values('" & txtTitleID.Text & "', '" &
             txtTitle.Text & "', '"
            & txtType.Text & "', '" & txtPubID.Text & "', " &

            txtPrice.Text & ", " & txtAdvance.Text & ", " &
```

```
             txtRoyalty.Text & ", " & txtYTDSales.Text & ", '" &

             txtNotes.Text & "', '" & txtPubDate & "')"

    End With

    Set rstMyDatabase = cmdMyDatabase.Execute

    With cmdMyDatabase

        .CommandType = adCmdText

        .CommandText = "insert into titleauthor (au_id,
            title_id) " & _
                "values('" & txtAUID.Text & "', '" &
                    txtTitleID.Text & "')"
    End With

    Set rstMyDatabase = cmdMyDatabase.Execute

End If
```

13. Enter a value in each field, then run your program and try inserting data.

┼Note

You may have noticed that this is a bare-bones program. It will insert data, but it does not check the integrity of data before inserting it. You can use the Masked Edit Control with a mask template to force appropriate data entry. You can also add code to the Change event for each text control to verify that the value is appropriate. In addition, we have no error handling. Future projects will show you how to add these features as we study more about SQL.

☑ *Mastery Check*

1. An INSERT statement can have the following parts:

    a. INSERT, FROM, SELECT

    b. SELECT, GROUP BY, INSERT

    c. INSERT, INTO, VALUES

    d. Both a and c

2. A SELECT INTO statement can have the following parts:

    a. Table name, list of columns, list of joins

    b. SELECT, FROM, INSERT

    c. INSERT, INTO, FROM

    d. Both b and c

3. Explain when to use SELECT INTO.

4. Explain when to use a SELECT inside an INSERT.

5. How can constraints cause problems for an INSERT?

6. Can you insert NULL into a key value?

7. How do you check to see whether constraints operate on a table?

8. What does the GetDate() function do?

9. If you modify a table after some programmer has been working with the table for some time, what should you take care to do?

10. If you use a key column in multiple tables, what should you take care to do?

Module 4

Updating Data

Goals

- Understand how to change data that has already been inserted into a table
- Learn how to use a WHERE clause with UPDATE
- Understand the use of the HAVING clause in an UPDATE statement
- Learn how to use UPDATE with a join
- Have practiced using data validation with your embedded SQL application
- Have built a data entry application using an embedded UPDATE statement

In the last module, we focused on inserting data into a table. This module focuses on changing data once you already have it in the table. The SQL verb for changing data already placed in the database is UPDATE. It allows you to alter anything from none to all of the records present, depending on how you define WHERE or HAVING conditions. Typically, you use UPDATE in one of two contexts: one where data has legitimately changed, as when an author changes her address and phone number due to relocation; the other where data must be corrected, either because of data entry errors or because someone has revised the coding scheme for entering data. While UPDATE provides great flexibility to change data, it is also a dangerous SQL command, because it has the power to change every record in a table. Accordingly, right up front, we need to emphasize a critical point: Don't forget to use WHERE or HAVING! If you do, you will always update all the records in the table. Having issued this reminder, we should proceed to working with UPDATE.

Using Update

Let's imagine a scenario with Pubs in which you might want to update every record in a table. Say you discover one day that all your authors have signed contracts, and you need to flip the Contracts column from 0 to 1 for every author. You can go through Enterprise Manager and manually check the box in the column for each author, but this method cannot be used from a program. Instead, you can use the UPDATE statement in its most minimal form to accomplish the task, as follows:

```
UPDATE authors SET Contract = 1
```

The UPDATE statement begins with the UPDATE verb, followed by the name of the table to update, followed by the SET keyword, followed by the name of the column to update, followed by an assignment operator, followed by the value to insert into the column. This statement therefore can be paraphrased as the following: In the authors table, set the column Contract to the value 1 in each row of the table. You may have only one table identified for update. However, you may have multiple columns following SET. Simply separate the assignment statements with a comma, as in the following:

```
UPDATE authors SET Contract = 1, Phone = ''
```

If you execute this statement in the Query Analyzer, not only will all the rows in the table have a Contract value of 1, but all the Phone values will also be set to blank.

1-Minute Drill

- **What are the most critical keywords associated with UPDATE?**
- **How would you update multiple tables using UPDATE?**
- **Is a column containing a blank string the same as a column containing NULL?**

DataValidation.vbp

Project 4-1: Data Validation

In the last module, the programming exercise focused on inserting data. This exercise focuses on data validation. Our goal is to learn how not to have to use UPDATE to correct data entry errors. We will take a look at how to check each text box in our data insertion program for correct values before we execute the insert. Proper data validation obviates the need to make corrections after the fact, and it guarantees that all data values represent the proper coding schemes for each column.

- **WHERE and HAVING. If you forget to use them, you may change more records than you intended to.**
- **Use multiple UPDATE statements.**
- **No. A blank string represents a data value. NULL represents the absence of a data value.**

Step-by-Step

1. Open the InsertingData.vbp project and save it as DataValidation.vpb. Be sure to save the form as DataValidation.frm.

2. Start by selecting each text box that stores char or varchar data and setting its MaxLength property to the length allowed by its data type specification. A varchar(6), for example, would have a MaxLength of 6. Setting MaxLength prevents entry of data that is longer than it should be.

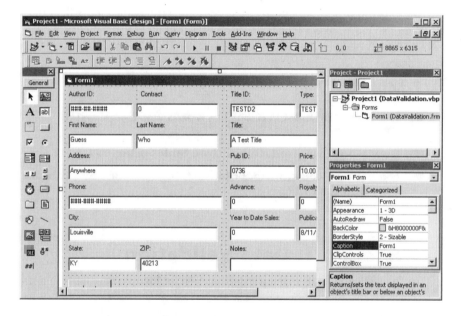

3. Open the Project menu and select the Components item. In the dialog box, check Microsoft Masked Edit Control. Click Apply to make sure the control appears in the toolbox. Then click OK.

4. Replace the text boxes for Author ID and Phone with masked edit controls.

5. Set the MaxLength property on these controls to the appropriate values, 11 for Author ID and 12 for Phone.

6. Set the mask property to ###-##-#### for Author ID and ### ###-#### for Phone. The pound signs (#) represent a numeric character, and the dashes represent characters that should appear in the string. You are forcing users to enter the correct kinds of characters in these boxes.

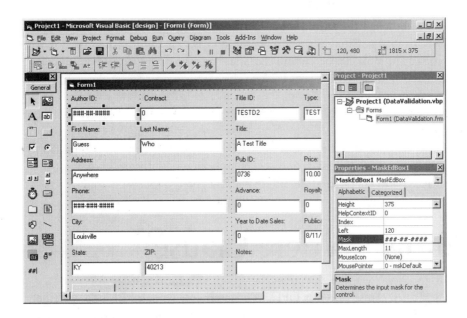

7. For each control that could represent a numeric value, add code like the following to its Change event:

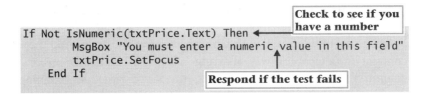

Check to see if you have a number

```
If Not IsNumeric(txtPrice.Text) Then
        MsgBox "You must enter a numeric value in this field"
        txtPrice.SetFocus
    End If
```

Respond if the test fails

8. For each text control that could represent a date value, add code like the following to its Change event:

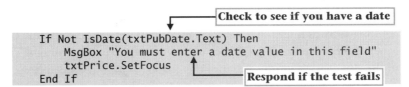

Check to see if you have a date

```
If Not IsDate(txtPubDate.Text) Then
        MsgBox "You must enter a date value in this field"
        txtPrice.SetFocus
    End If
```

Respond if the test fails

After you have added all these checks, you can rest assured that you have prevented your users from entering most kinds of incorrect data. You still cannot prevent someone from entering Zaphod Beelblebrox as an author, because you can never predict what a valid author's name might look like. But you can at least be assured that the name cannot exceed the maximum allowed. You are certain that if a number entry cannot be evaluated as a number, the user is sent back to the text box to correct it. You can be certain that if a date value cannot be evaluated as a date, then the user is sent back to the text box to correct the entry.

You can add two additional factors in evaluating dates, if you like. One would be to check the year portion using DatePart( ) to see if it is a four-digit year. The other would be to check the range of the date. Databases have ranges of dates that they deem valid. SQL Server, for example, accepts January 1, 1753, as its first valid date. If you are working with historical data, you may wish to check to make sure that a date entered meets the minimum acceptable value.

Adding a Where Clause

If you don't want to update every record in your database, you need a WHERE clause on your UPDATE statement. As in a SELECT statement, the WHERE clause limits the number of rows involved in the statement's operation. The basic format of an UPDATE statement with a WHERE clause is as follows:

```
UPDATE authors SET Contract = 1 WHERE Zip = '40205'
```

This statement should look familiar by now. We are setting the contract bit (a technical way of saying "placing a 1 in the Contract column") for each author who lives in the 40205 zip code. Running this statement in the Query Analyzer will actually accomplish nothing, unless you have added an author with the zip code of 40205. Pubs, as it ships with SQL Server or the Microsoft Data Engine, does not include this zip code on any of the author records.

Since we are now working with a statement where precision of defining records is extremely important, we ought to look at some of the other choices for the WHERE clause. With UPDATE, accidental changes to the data can go unnoticed until the change is long divorced from the run of the statement. A couple months down the line, someone is likely to notice that some author with a Wyoming zip code lives in LA. No one is likely to remember what action was taken that would have caused the change, but you then must undertake exhaustive comparisons looking for records that might be incorrect. In a large database, such corrections are impractical at best. The better you define the list of records for action by UPDATE, the better off you are.

Note

In case you have not noticed, UPDATE is a dangerous SQL statement. It has no explicit list of values that make up an entire row in a table, the way INSERT does. In addition, UPDATE changes existing rows in the table. Because the list of rows is hidden behind a WHERE clause, you want to think carefully about making mass updates to your database. The more you can do to uniquely identify the rows that will change, the better.

You need not use only equalities to select records using WHERE. The following is an equally valid statement:

```
UPDATE authors SET Contract = 1 WHERE Zip <> '40205'
```

Any mathematical or logical comparison operator works well in a WHERE clause. You can also undertake pattern matching with the LIKE operator. Take a look at the following statements:

```
UPDATE authors SET Contract = 1 WHERE Zip LIKE '402%'
UPDATE authors SET Contract = 1 WHERE Zip NOT LIKE '402%'
UPDATE authors SET Contract = 1 WHERE Zip LIKE '[456]0205'
UPDATE authors SET Contract = 1 WHERE Zip LIKE '[^456]0205'
UPDATE authors SET Contract = 1 WHERE Zip LIKE '4020_'
```

Each one of these statements uses a wildcard character to control the search. The first one finds the combination of 402 and any set of characters following the 402. It would match 40205, 40213, or 402AB. (It could match 402WXYZQ as well, but the zip column only holds five characters.) The last, obviously, is not a valid zip code. However, if you can depend on solid validation during data entry, you can rely on this LIKE comparison to locate zip codes with any combination of the last two characters.

Hint

If you need to use a wildcard character as a character to search for, enclose it in square brackets. For example, '4020[%]' in a LIKE statement searches for the string 4020%, a bogus zip code indeed.

The second example shows the use of the NOT keyword. This word negates what follows, so you match any pattern except that defined by the following string. You find all zip codes that do not begin with 402 and end in any two other characters. The third statement shows using a list of options. The square bracketed list of characters states to use one of these characters to match at this position. As a result, you would match 40205, 50205, and 60205. The fourth statement shows an abbreviation of NOT in the selection list. The caret character (^) translates as "use any character but the ones on this list to match at this position." The fourth statement matches any zip codes but 40205, 50205, and 60205. The last statement shows how to use a wildcard to match any single character. The underscore character (_) states "put any single valid character here." Thus, the matches must all begin with 4020, but the last character may be any valid character, allowing a match on 40201 or 4020&, for example.

You have another interesting option for use in WHERE clauses that is especially handy with UPDATE. You can use IN to specify a list of column values to use in the UPDATE, as shown here:

```
UPDATE authors SET Contract = 1 WHERE Zip IN ('40205', 40213', '40292')
```

IN takes a list of values separated by commas and enclosed in parentheses as its argument. It checks to see whether the named column has a value on that list. If the column has that value, then the UPDATE takes place.

LIKE offers one final trick for controlling a search. In the Pubs database, the discounts table has a forty-character field named discounttype. Suppose that you know the string 20% appears in a couple of the discount types, and you want to update the records containing this set of characters in the discounttype column. WHERE and LIKE allow you to make this change by using the following WHERE clause:

```
WHERE discounttype LIKE '%20!%%' ESCAPE '!'
```

4

What have we just done? First, ESCAPE tells the remainder of the SQL statement that an exclamation point (!) is going to identify the character immediately following to be treated as a literal, the equivalent of [%] in the string following LIKE, for example. As a result, the first % is treated as a wildcard character, matching any number of characters. The string 20 must follow any number of characters. The next %, identified by the exclamation mark, is treated as the character %. The next percent is treated as a wildcard matching any number of characters. As a result, you match any string of up to 40 characters (the width of the column) containing the three-character sequence 20%.

Hint

You can use any character not used in the string as a literal character with ESCAPE. Accordingly, you can save a lot of typing if you know that you are going to use several wildcard characters as literals in your search. Define an ESCAPE character, and simply place it before any wildcard character that must be treated as a literal character.

1-Minute Drill

● **What does a WHERE clause do in an UPDATE statement?**

● **What does LIKE do?**

● **What is an ESCAPE character?**

Adding a Having Clause

Having seen that you can use WHERE with UPDATE, you might wonder whether you can use HAVING. The answer is that yes, you can use HAVING, but you must remember what HAVING does. It works with grouped data. UPDATE does not provide you the opportunity

---

● **The WHERE clause identifies which records to update.**
● **LIKE allows you to search for patterns in a string.**
● **An ESCAPE character marks the character immediately following for treatment as a literal.**

to group data. However, you can use a FROM phrase with your UPDATE statement, which allows you to choose what to update from a set of records defined by another query. You might remember this query from Module 2:

```
SELECT title_id FROM sales GROUP BY title_id HAVING SUM(qty) > 30
```

We can use it to define the set of records for UPDATE to operate on in the following fashion:

```
UPDATE sales SET payterms = 'cash only' FROM (SELECT title_id FROM sales
GROUP BY title_id HAVING SUM(qty) > 30) AS MySelect WHERE sales.title_id =
MySelect.title_id
```

You must be thinking that this is a complex SQL statement of the sort you have not seen before. In some ways it is, but in most ways it is not. You have seen a basic UPDATE already. You have seen this SELECT already. What you have not seen is the particular method of linking them together. FROM says to get the group of records from the sales table according to the information following the FROM keyword. In this case, we defined a set of records to use by providing the SELECT statement. We named the recordset that this SELECT pulls from the database using AS so that we can refer to it later. We refer to it in the WHERE clause to allow us to link the results of the SELECT to the action of the UPDATE. In other words, we update payterms only where the title_id in the payterms table is on the list of title_id values pulled by the SELECT statement. We used the GROUP BY in the SELECT statement to allow us to use HAVING to define the set of records to operate on.

Hint

A query embedded inside another query has a technical name in SQL. It is called a *subquery*.

1-Minute Drill

● **How can you use HAVING to control an UPDATE?**

● **How do you link the actual update action to the result of the HAVING clause?**

Ask the Expert

Question: I have four tables that contain related information, and each one of them needs to be updated when my business sells a product. How do I make sure that I have updated all the proper values?

Answer: Having to update one table at a time may seem like a curse, but in fact, it's not. If you were able to update multiple tables in an UPDATE statement, the possibility for error would grow exponentially with the number of tables included.

The best way to make sure that you keep your four tables correctly up to date is to break the sales transactions into the four logical updates. Write each UPDATE statement out and then use this block of four statements each time you need to perform this transaction.

You might look at Module 12 to see how you can make these four statements into a stored procedure so that you can write the statements once and then reuse them whenever you need to.

● Embed the HAVING in a SELECT statement placed in the FROM phrase.
● Name the results of the SELECT statement that contains the HAVING clause using AS. Create a WHERE clause for the UPDATE that sets some column in the table to be changed equal to the value of the same column in the named results of the SELECT statement.

Question: **How do I make sure that I update only the correct rows?**

Answer: The best way to make sure that you are not making mistakes with an UPDATE statement is to identify the rows by values that are unique to each row. If a table has a primary key, for example, try to select the rows by this value. If you do not have a key, but you do have a row identifier, use the row identifier. If you are not able to select by a unique value per row, be as explicit as possible in identifying the rows for update.

Question: **Is it faster to update multiple columns in a single UPDATE or to use separate UPDATE statements for each column?**

Answer: First, if the answer to this question is critical, you might want to look carefully at the hardware that is running your database. A typical database server should have multiple processors and lots of memory. The multiple processors allow you to process multiple queries at the same time, and the memory keeps you from swapping to disk in support of query operations. If you are worried about the speed of updates, chances are your hardware needs to be upgraded to better support your database.

The only way you can verify which is faster is to test the queries on your combination of database software and hardware. Speed in SQL is dependent on the database vendor's query optimization strategies and the efficiency with which the database interacts with your hardware. In general, on a good database platform, you should not need to worry too much about the speed of updates. Typically you worry about the speed of SELECT statements, since they can introduce delays that produce noticeable pauses for the users.

Using Multiple Tables

FROM is a very helpful phrase in an UPDATE statement. It allows you to condition the update on information in other tables. You still may update only one table at a time, but you can use information stored in other tables to choose whether to update. For example, you may have noticed that titles has a year-to-date sales column (ytd_sales). Somehow that column has to be updated for each title. Here is the set of UPDATE statements that can do so:

```
UPDATE titles SET ytd_sales = 0
UPDATE titles SET ytd_sales = titles.ytd_sales + SUM(sales.qty) FROM titles, sales
WHERE titles.title_id = sales.title_id AND DATEPART(yyy, sales.ord_date) = 2000
```

The first UPDATE sets ytd_sales to 0. This clearing of the previous sum is important, because we need to add the qty column from each record pulled using FROM to ytd_sales. If we did not clear the value first, we would be adding the current sum to the previous sum already stored in ytd_sales. Subsequent runs of the UPDATE without clearing ytd_sales would cause our ytd-sales figures to skyrocket beyond belief. The second UPDATE sums the ytd_sales figure. Notice, however, that we need to add sales.qty to titles.ytd_sales. These values are in different tables. FROM allows us to solve the problem of how to pull the value from a table that will not be involved in the actual UPDATE.

In the FROM phrase, we include the two table names that must be involved in the complete operation. We use a WHERE clause to specify on what value the two tables are to be joined. We also included another WHERE condition to select a single year's sales to be involved in the summing operation. If you weren't watching carefully, a critical point may have slipped by. This FROM phrase acts like a JOIN in a SELECT statement. We joined the two tables together so that we could find values related to a single title_id to include in the operation. FROM acts like an abbreviated JOIN under these circumstances.

We used the DATEPART function to get the year value out of the ord_date column. DATEPART is a very useful function. It takes two arguments, the first being the part of the date you want, and the second, the column containing the datetime value from which a part of the date needs to be extracted. Table 4-1 shows the values that you can use for the first argument.

Part of Date to Return	Valid Abbreviations to Use As the First Argument
Year	yy, yyyy
Quarter	qq, q
Month	mm, m
Day of year	dy, y
Day	dd, d

Table 4-1   First Argument Values for DATEPART

Part of Date to Return	Valid Abbreviations to Use As the First Argument
Week	wk, ww
Weekday	Dw
Hour	Hh
Minute	mi, n
Second	ss, s
Millisecond	Ms

| Table 4-1 | First Argument Values for DATEPART *(continued)* |

The return value for DATAPART is an integer representing the part of the date you extracted. As a result, the comparison value need not be enclosed in single quotes. You can also do math with the return value if you need to.

You can also use a SELECT containing the full join syntax in FROM. Here is an example:

```
UPDATE authors SET Contract = 1 FROM (SELECT  authors.au_id,
titleauthor.title_id from authors inner join titleauthor on authors.au_id =
titleauthor.au_id) AS MySelect WHERE MySelect.au_id = authors.au_id AND
MySelect.title_id IN ('BU1111', 'PC9999')
```

This UPDATE uses a SELECT to locate the records for the authors associated with two title IDs, which we might assume were recently contracted and must have the contract column updated. The WHERE clause uses an IN phrase to select two titles. It uses an equality to link the authors table to the result of the SELECT clause.

Hint

When you use a SELECT in a FROM, you should not use a separate WHERE clause for the SELECT statement. All WHERE conditions should appear in the single WHERE clause associated with the FROM phrase.

Which version of the FROM syntax for using multiple tables should you use? The answer is straightforwardly the one that is (a) supported by your database and (b) the most comfortable for you to read. Some SQL programmers like to see all joins explicit in the SQL statements. Others find the more abbreviated syntax to be more readable. You want to be able to understand what your query does at a glance when you return to it after six months to make a slight change.

1-Minute Drill

● **What is the simplest syntax for using multiple tables with UPDATE?**

● **How can you use the JOIN syntax in an UPDATE statement?**

● **How many WHERE clauses can you use in an UPDATE statement?**

UpdatingData.vbp

Project 4-2: Update Data

Now it is time to learn how to include UPDATE statements in a program that modifies the database. We are going to extend the program we created to insert data to update data as well. We will add an Update button, and the code behind it will include embedded UPDATE statements. Users will be able to both insert and update data using the modified program. Note a couple of items. We are adding some limited navigation capability, and we are changing to a global set of database objects. We have not completed that conversion. And, if you try real hard, you can make the Update button choke on a single quote. We will be fixing these matters and adding some other enhancements in modules where there is less to talk about in terms of coding.

● **List the tables, separated by commas, following FROM.**
● **Use a SELECT following FROM to specify the rows to include in the UPDATE.**
● **Only one. If you have an embedded SELECT, its WHERE conditions should be included in the UPDATE statement's WHERE clause.**

Step-by-Step

1. Open the DataValidation.vpb project and save it as UpdatingData.vpb. Be sure to save the form as UpdatingData.frm.

2. Add two buttons to the form named cmdBack and cmdForward. Give them the captions shown in the next illustration.

3. For simplicity's sake, trim out the DAO code. We will pursue ADO examples so that we don't become too confusing.

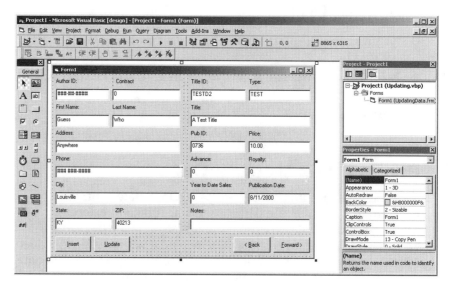

4. Add the following code to the General section of the form:

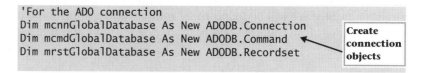

```
'For the ADO connection
Dim mcnnGlobalDatabase As New ADODB.Connection
Dim mcmdGlobalDatabase As New ADODB.Command
Dim mrstGlobalDatabase As New ADODB.Recordset
```

Create connection objects

5. Add the following code to the form Load event:

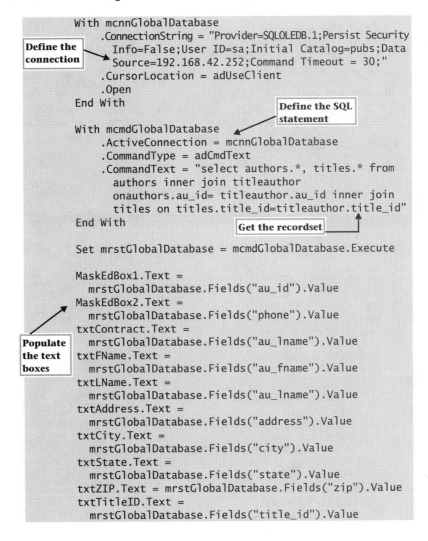

```
With mcnnGlobalDatabase
    .ConnectionString = "Provider=SQLOLEDB.1;Persist Security
        Info=False;User ID=sa;Initial Catalog=pubs;Data
        Source=192.168.42.252;Command Timeout = 30;"
    .CursorLocation = adUseClient
    .Open
End With

With mcmdGlobalDatabase
    .ActiveConnection = mcnnGlobalDatabase
    .CommandType = adCmdText
    .CommandText = "select authors.*, titles.* from
        authors inner join titleauthor
        onauthors.au_id= titleauthor.au_id inner join
        titles on titles.title_id=titleauthor.title_id"
End With

Set mrstGlobalDatabase = mcmdGlobalDatabase.Execute

MaskEdBox1.Text =
    mrstGlobalDatabase.Fields("au_id").Value
MaskEdBox2.Text =
    mrstGlobalDatabase.Fields("phone").Value
txtContract.Text =
    mrstGlobalDatabase.Fields("au_lname").Value
txtFName.Text =
    mrstGlobalDatabase.Fields("au_fname").Value
txtLName.Text =
    mrstGlobalDatabase.Fields("au_lname").Value
txtAddress.Text =
    mrstGlobalDatabase.Fields("address").Value
txtCity.Text =
    mrstGlobalDatabase.Fields("city").Value
txtState.Text =
    mrstGlobalDatabase.Fields("state").Value
txtZIP.Text = mrstGlobalDatabase.Fields("zip").Value
txtTitleID.Text =
    mrstGlobalDatabase.Fields("title_id").Value
```

Define the connection

Define the SQL statement

Get the recordset

Populate the text boxes

4

```
        txtType.Text =
          mrstGlobalDatabase.Fields("type").Value
        txtTitle.Text =
          mrstGlobalDatabase.Fields("title").Value
        txtPubID.Text =
          mrstGlobalDatabase.Fields("pub_id").Value
        txtPrice.Text =
          mrstGlobalDatabase.Fields("price").Value
        txtAdvance.Text =
          mrstGlobalDatabase.Fields("advance").Value
        txtRoyalty.Text =
          mrstGlobalDatabase.Fields("royalty").Value
        txtYTDSales.Text =
          mrstGlobalDatabase.Fields("ytd_sales").Value
        txtPubDate.Text =
          mrstGlobalDatabase.Fields("pubdate").Value
        txtNotes.Text =
          mrstGlobalDatabase.Fields("notes").Value
```

Repopulate the text boxes

6. Add the following code to the cmdBack_Click event:

```
mrstGlobalDatabase.MovePrevious

    MaskEdBox1.Text =
      mrstGlobalDatabase.Fields("au_id").Value
    MaskEdBox2.Text =
      mrstGlobalDatabase.Fields("phone").Value
    txtContract.Text =
      mrstGlobalDatabase.Fields("au_lname").Value
    txtFName.Text =
      mrstGlobalDatabase.Fields("au_fname").Value
    txtLName.Text =
      mrstGlobalDatabase.Fields("au_lname").Value
    txtAddress.Text =
      mrstGlobalDatabase.Fields("address").Value
    txtCity.Text = mrstGlobalDatabase.Fields("city").Value
    txtState.Text = mrstGlobalDatabase.Fields("state").Value
    txtZIP.Text = mrstGlobalDatabase.Fields("zip").Value
    txtTitleID.Text =
      mrstGlobalDatabase.Fields("title_id").Value
    txtType.Text = mrstGlobalDatabase.Fields("type").Value
    txtTitle.Text = mrstGlobalDatabase.Fields("title").Value
    txtPubID.Text = mrstGlobalDatabase.Fields("pub_id").Value
    txtPrice.Text = mrstGlobalDatabase.Fields("price").Value
```

Get the previous record

Repopulate the text boxes

```
    txtAdvance.Text =
      mrstGlobalDatabase.Fields("advance").Value
    txtRoyalty.Text =
      mrstGlobalDatabase.Fields("royalty").Value
    txtYTDSales.Text =
      mrstGlobalDatabase.Fields("ytd_sales").Value
    txtPubDate.Text =
      mrstGlobalDatabase.Fields("pubdate").Value
    txtNotes.Text = mrstGlobalDatabase.Fields("notes").Value
```

7. Add the following code to the cmdForward_Click event:

```
mrstGlobalDatabase.MoveNext        ← Move to the next record

    MaskEdBox1.Text =
      mrstGlobalDatabase.Fields("au_id").Value      Repopulate the
    MaskEdBox2.Text =                                text boxes
      mrstGlobalDatabase.Fields("phone").Value
    txtContract.Text =
      mrstGlobalDatabase.Fields("au_lname").Value
    txtFName.Text =
      mrstGlobalDatabase.Fields("au_fname").Value
    txtLName.Text =
      mrstGlobalDatabase.Fields("au_lname").Value
    txtAddress.Text =
      mrstGlobalDatabase.Fields("address").Value
    txtCity.Text = mrstGlobalDatabase.Fields("city").Value
    txtState.Text = mrstGlobalDatabase.Fields("state").Value
    txtZIP.Text = mrstGlobalDatabase.Fields("zip").Value
    txtTitleID.Text =
      mrstGlobalDatabase.Fields("title_id").Value
    txtType.Text = mrstGlobalDatabase.Fields("type").Value
    txtTitle.Text = mrstGlobalDatabase.Fields("title").Value
    txtPubID.Text = mrstGlobalDatabase.Fields("pub_id").Value
    txtPrice.Text = mrstGlobalDatabase.Fields("price").Value
    txtAdvance.Text =
      mrstGlobalDatabase.Fields("advance").Value
    txtRoyalty.Text =
      mrstGlobalDatabase.Fields("royalty").Value
    txtYTDSales.Text =
      mrstGlobalDatabase.Fields("ytd_sales").Value
    txtPubDate.Text =
      mrstGlobalDatabase.Fields("pubdate").Value
    txtNotes.Text = mrstGlobalDatabase.Fields("notes").Value
```

4

8. Add a button to the form named cmdUpdate.

9. Add the following code to cmdUpdate's Click event:

```
With mcmdGlobalDatabase
        .CommandType = adCmdText
        .CommandText = "update authors set au_id = '" &
         MaskEdBox1.Text
          & "', au_lname = '" & txtLName.Text & "',
            au_fname = '" &
          txtFName.Text & "', phone = '" &
            MaskEdBox2.Text & "',
          address = '" & txtAddress.Text & "', city = '" &
          txtCity.Text & "', state = '" & txtState.Text
            & "', zip =
          '" & txtZIP.Text & "' " & _
          "where au_id = '" & MaskEdBox1.Text & "'"
    End With

    Set mrstGlobalDatabase = mcmdGlobalDatabase.Execute

      With mcmdGlobalDatabase
        .CommandType = adCmdText
        .CommandText = "update titles set title_id = '" &
            txtTitleID.Text & "', title = '" &
              txtTitle.Text & "', type
            = '" & txtType.Text & "', pub_id = '" &
              txtPubID.Text & "',
            price = " & txtPrice.Text & ", advance = " &
            txtAdvance.Text & ", royalty = " &
              txtRoyalty.Text & ",
            ytd_sales = " & txtYTDSales.Text & ", notes = '" &
            txtNotes.Text & "', pubdate = '" & txtPubDate &
            "' " & _
            "where title_id = '" & txtTitleID.Text & "'"
      End With

    Set mrstGlobalDatabase = mcmdGlobalDatabase.Execute
```

Create the SQL statement

Execute the SQL statement

Execute the next SQL statement

Execute the SQL statement

☑ *Mastery Check*

1. An UPDATE statement can have the following parts:

   a. UPDATE, FROM, INSERT

   b. UPDATE, GROUP BY, INSERT

   c. UPDATE, SET, SELECT

   d. UPDATE, GROUP BY

2. A SET phrase can have the following parts:

   a. Table name, list of columns, list of joins

   b. Assignment operator, multiple values

   c. SET, INTO, FROM

   d. Column name, assignment operator, value

3. Explain what happens if you do not use WHERE or HAVING.

4. Explain how to use LIKE to search for a zip code that begins with 40 and then has any single character followed by 2 followed by another character.

5. What mathematical and logical operators can be used in a WHERE clause?

6. Can you do math in a WHERE clause?

7. What keyword allows you to use multiple tables in an UPDATE statement?

8. What does the DATEPART() function do?

9. What must you do to include a HAVING or a JOIN in an UPDATE statement?

10. How many tables can you update at once?

4

Module 5

Deleting Data

Goals

- Understand how to delete data from a table using two different methods
- Learn how to use a WHERE clause with DELETE to undertake selective deletions
- Have built a data entry application using an embedded DELETE statement to allow deletion of records

115

At some point, you will decide that you have obsolete data in your database. You need to get rid of it. Probably the most common occurrence of obsolete data occurs in temporary tables. These tables are storage places for data in transition. The data resides here while some SQL operation works on it to, for example, prepare a report of quarterly earnings. In the Pubs database, we have already seen that ytd-sales is a column that has to change values from day to day in order to report accurately the status of any title in the inventory. It is essentially a temporary data storage location that has to be cleared before the amount can roll up into it again. A temporary table is very similar, except it might hold an author's information and ytd_sales for every title in the author's set of books.

You will find many scenarios for deleting data. For example, in a nursing center, information on deceased residents need not be kept for longer than two years. Chances are you would copy the data to an archive database and delete the data from the active database in order to protect the efficiency of database operations. Why sift through hundreds of obsolete records when printing the current resident list, for example, when you don't have to?

SQL offers two options, DELETE and TRUNCATE TABLE, for deleting data. These are the two most dangerous commands in SQL. The results are catastrophic and permanent. So make certain that you intend to get rid of the data you have described in the statement before you execute the statement. There is no Undo button related to these two statements. Results are permanent and final.

Hint

Prior to undertaking a data deletion operation, you are wise to back up your database.

Deleting Data

Assume that you have an entire table that needs to be cleared of data. You have two options for undertaking the deletion. They look like this:

```
DELETE FROM authors
TRUNCATE TABLE authors
```

Both of these statements achieve the same purpose; they delete all the data in the table while leaving intact the column structure associated with the table. As a result, new data can easily be inserted after the deletion takes place.

What, you might ask, is the difference between these two operations? First, DELETE is supported by all SQL databases, while TRUNCATE TABLE might not be. In addition, DELETE is supported in all circumstances. TRUNCATE TABLE might not function in all situations. For example, Microsoft's SQL Server allows you to use TRUNCATE TABLE in most circumstances. However, when you are using the Data Transformation Services to copy a table from one database to another, you cannot use TRUNCATE TABLE to clear the table in the target database of preexisting data. You must instead use DELETE.

In addition, TRUNCATE TABLE undertakes only complete deletions of a table. You cannot use it to delete records selectively. DELETE, on the other hand, allows you to delete selected rows and leave others intact.

Adding a Where Clause

So far we have seen how to undertake complete deletions. Complete deletions are not your typical deletion task. You are more likely interested in undertaking selective deletions, where you delete some rows and leave others alone. DELETE is the SQL statement to use for this sort of operation, because DELETE supports the use of a WHERE clause.

Note

Having a WHERE clause available in a DELETE statement does not guarantee the safety of your data. SQL does not prompt you with dialog boxes to ask if you really want to delete the data. It just does what you tell it to do. Every database administrator has an awful tale about having forgotten to use a WHERE clause with DELETE. Double-check DELETE statements for the WHERE clause before executing them.

The WHERE clause for a delete obeys the same rules as any other WHERE clause. You can use an equality to control a deletion. For example, if you fire an author, you can delete information about that author with a DELETE statement like this one:

```
DELETE FROM authors WHERE au_lname = 'Gringlesby'
```

5

This statement deletes the author record for Burt Gringlesby. What happens after this row is gone depends on the database vendor and how the database administrator has set up the database.

Some SQL databases allow you to define sets of related records that will all be deleted if one of them is deleted. This kind of deletion operation is called a *cascading delete*. In this case, the deletion destroys the au_id for Burt Gringlesby. Au_id is the value that uniquely identifies an author. Once it is removed from the location where it first must be entered, any other references to that au_id should also be removed. They have no meaning after the defining information for Burt Gringlesby is destroyed. In databases that allow cascading deletes, key constraints control the deletion of other records. Once the first reference to a key value (which uniquely identifies some data element) is gone, the constraints force the deletion of the other records.

No matter how the database is designed or how the database administrator has configured the tables, you must regard DELETE as a potentially dangerous operation, one that you should be careful with. You need to actively inquire whether cascading deletes or triggers have been implemented, because you need to be able to predict what the delete should do. Never assume that cascading deletes or triggers will follow an intuitive path to deleting additional data. If they are well designed, you should be able to intuit what will happen. However, you are likely to discover that many database administrators do not think the way you do. What they see as intuitive operation may not be what you see as intuitive operation.

1-Minute Drill

- **Name two ways to completely delete the data in a table.**
- **Which statement would you use to selectively delete records from a table?**
- **How can you prevent the complete deletion of all records when using DELETE?**

- **DELETE and TRUNCATE TABLE**
- **DELETE**
- **Use a WHERE clause.**

Using a Query to Control Deletion

Like UPDATE, DELETE allows you to use a query to control deletion. Let's start by reviewing the query we used with UPDATE to control a data change operation. This is the query we used:

```
SELECT title_id FROM sales GROUP BY title_id HAVING SUM(qty) > 30
```

This query selects the title IDs that have a sum of the quantities for each individual sale greater than 30. It goes through the records in the sales table, groups them all by title_id, and then sums the qty field in all the individual records for a given title. When that sum is greater than 30, the query returns the title_id in the result set.

If we wanted to delete all titles from our titleauthor table that had sold more than 30 copies over their lifetime, we could do so using this statement:

```
DELETE FROM titleauthor WHERE title_id IN (SELECT title_id FROM sales GROUP
BY title_id HAVING SUM(qty) > 30)
```

This query looks up each title_id from titleauthor in the result set of the SELECT. If the title_id from titles is in the result set from the SELECT, the deletion takes place.

Note

The constraints in the Pubs database require that you delete all entries from titleauthor before you delete any entry sharing a title_id with titleauthor from titles.

The previous SQL syntax applies to all SQL databases. Microsoft's Transact SQL offers the following extension of this syntax, incorporating the JOIN keywords:

```
DELETE titleauthor FROM titleauthor INNER JOIN titles ON
titleauthor.title_id = titles.title_id WHERE titles.title LIKE '%novel%'
```

Note that we did not use the aggregate function and GROUP BY in this example. Microsoft's extension of the SQL 92 syntax for this sort of DELETE does not allow its use. You are focused on the JOIN syntax, and this form of the DELETE statement throws an error if you incorporate groups or aggregation. While Microsoft's extension allows you to use the familiar JOIN syntax, it does exclude other options. The more general SQL syntax therefore provides you more options.

1-Minute Drill

- **Why use a query with DELETE?**
- **When should you use the JOIN syntax allowed with DELETE?**
- **When can't you use the JOIN syntax?**

Using Transactions

DELETE is a dangerous operation. There is no better place, therefore, to introduce the concept of a *transaction*. Transactions provide you with an escape point that can save you from accidentally deleting records. This escape point is not a true undo, because once you tell the transaction to complete, you cannot turn back. However, transactions allow you to preview what will happen, and to make a decision based on that preview.

Transactions are groups of SQL statements that must either all succeed or all fail. The group can be as small as a single SQL statement. As a transaction processes, any error encountered causes failure of all the statements in the transaction. If there are no errors, all the statements succeed. You can also have the equivalent of a breakpoint in a transaction. At this point, you can check for errors and make a decision about how to complete the transaction.

At this point in our discussion, we are going to approach transactions from the point of view of working in the Query Analyzer. Assume that you want to undertake a delete operation, but you want to be able to back out of it at the last minute if something seems wrong. Here is what you do:

- **A query allows you great control over which records will be deleted.**
- **Use the JOIN syntax if you want to keep your delete operations consistent with all other statements that link tables.**
- **When you want to undertake aggregate operations.**

1. Begin your statements by entering BEGIN TRANSACTION as the first line of the statement group.

2. Make your second line the DELETE statement.

3. Run the set of transactions, and check the results. Most often you will see the number of rows affected in the results pane.

4. If you like what you see in the results, type COMMIT TRANSACTION on another line, highlight it, and click the Run button. The statements will complete to success, and you will delete the records.

5. If you don't like what you see in the results, type ROLLBACK TRANSACTION on another line, highlight it, and click the Run button. The statements will fail, and your database will be in the state it was before you attempted the DELETE. (Figure 5-1 shows how such a session would look in Query Analyzer. In this session, the user made each statement a comment. When you highlight just the SQL portion of the commented statement and click Run, the Query Analyzer interprets only the highlighted characters and runs the statement.)

5

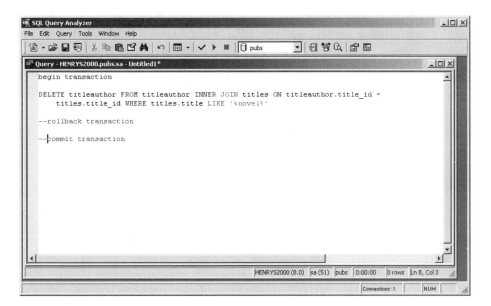

Figure 5-1   **A session using transactions in the Query Analyzer**

Hint

In the Query Analyzer, type both the COMMIT and ROLLBACK statements after your DELETE, and comment them out by placing two dashes (--) at the beginning of each line. These statements will not run when you attempt your delete. You can choose which to run, and cause it to run, by highlighting everything but the dashes on that line and clicking the Run button.

Transactions have many additional uses. Generally, the transaction statements bracket groups of SQL statements. When you write statements in groups, usually you save them as a stored procedure in the database (see Module 12). You can then run them by invoking the name of the stored procedure. We will explore the concept of transactions as we move along in additional modules. For now, see it as a way of protecting yourself from dangerous consequences when using DELETE in an interactive session with the database. You can also use transactions with UPDATE, of course, to provide the same protection.

1-Minute Drill

● **Define what a transaction is.**

● **How do you mark the beginning of a transaction?**

● **What statement cancels a transaction?**

● A transaction is a group of SQL statements that must all fail or succeed.
● Use a BEGIN TRANSACTION statement to mark the beginning of a transaction.
● ROLLBACK TRANSACTION

Ask the Expert

Question: What is the most common delete action I will take with a database?

Answer: Three kinds of events usually require deletes. One is the clearing of data from a temporary table. You undertake this action to make certain that no data lingers from a previous operation. You don't want leftover data showing up with yours to confuse the results.

Another action that requires a delete is a data entry error. If most of a row in a table gets entered correctly, then the best approach to correcting mistakes is to update the bad values in the row. However, sometimes the entire row is bad. Under those circumstances, a delete is required.

The last common scenario is purging obsolete data. Hospitals keep X-ray records for seven years, unless the film shows a diagnosis of disease. A routine operation would be to delete records that are over seven years old and do not yield a diagnosis. A DELETE with a WHERE clause handles this action well.

Question: How do I make sure that I delete only the correct rows?

Answer: The best way to make sure that you are not making mistakes with a DELETE statement is to identify the rows by values that are unique to each row, just as we suggested for UPDATE. If a table has a primary key, for example, try to select the rows by this value. If you do not have a key, but you do have a row identifier, use the row identifier. If you are not able to select by a unique value per row, be as explicit as possible in identifying the rows for update.

In addition, since DELETE is absolutely final in its results, use a transaction to give yourself a chance to preview what is happening.

5

Question: Is there a way to copy data you plan to delete to another location just for protection?

Answer: If you set up your DELETE to use a SELECT to condition which records will be deleted, you can always use SELECT INTO to create a table to hold a copy of the data that will be deleted. You can create this copy and examine it to make sure that what you expect to happen is what you want to happen. You should also use a transaction when you work interactively with the database, just to make sure that you get the same number of records affected as the SELECT INTO suggested there ought to be.

Your copy of the data can reside in the same database as the data to be deleted, or it could reside in another database.

Project 5-1: Data Deletion

DataDeletion.vbp

In this programming exercise, we are going to add a Delete button that will allow a user to delete any single record that links an author to a title. This change in our data entry project puts us dangerously close to the point where we need to use stored procedures and transactions to improve the integrity of both our program and our database. For now we will simply add a delete. Also, note that we still have not addressed the many issues that quickly adding functionality to this application has raised. We will do so in the next module, where we have fewer programming issues to address. In later modules, we will make the additional refinements to improve integrity.

Step-by-Step

1. Open the UpdatingData.vpb project and save it as DeletingData.vpb. Be sure to save the form as DeletingData.frm.

2. Add a button to the form named cmdDelete with the caption <u>D</u>elete.

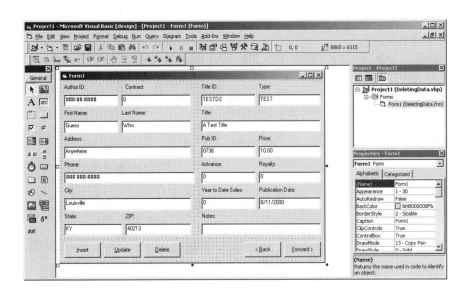

3. Add the following code to the cmdDelete_Click event:

```
With mcmdGlobalDatabase

    .CommandType = adCmdText

    .CommandText = "delete from titleauthor where au_id = '" &
        MaskEdBox1.Text & "' and title_id = '" & txtTitleID.Text & "'"

End With

Set mrstGlobalDatabase = mcmdGlobalDatabase.Execute
```

Now, you look at this code and you say "Why don't we delete from any of the other tables?" This is a good question. The answer is that (a) the author may have other books, so we may not be able to delete the author, (b) the title may have another author associated with it, so we may not be able to delete the title, and (c) the title has sales, and we may not wish to delete the sales history along with the link between the title and the author. What we have done is to delete the link between this author and this title. That is all our data entry application shows, and all it needs to rectify. We leave the other records to be handled in other ways by other applications. Ours needs only to deal with this one.

Keep in mind that we have left many unresolved issues in this application. By now, you must have noticed that we are overwriting our own recordset. Take an action such as update or delete, and you cannot continue to view the recordset. We've left these issues unresolved up to this point to acquaint you with some of the subtleties of database programming. You can't learn the best practices unless you experience the pitfalls. A programming exercise in the next module will address these issues and show you how to clean them up. For now, puzzle about your own solution, and see whether the one we work on in the next module matches your own thinking.

☑ *Mastery Check*

1. Which two statements can delete data?

   a. UPDATE and INSERT

   b. TRUNCATE TABLE and INSERT

   c. UPDATE and DELETE

   d. TRUNCATE TABLE and DELETE

2. A DELETE statement should have which one of the following elements:

   a. A WHERE clause

   b. A table name

   c. An INTO phrase

   d. A column name

☑ *Mastery Check*

3. Explain what happens if you do not use WHERE in a DELETE statement.

4. How can you make a quick copy of your data to protect against DELETE errors?

5. How do you start a transaction?

6. How do you roll back a transaction?

7. How do you complete a successful transaction?

8. What prompting does SQL provide to prevent you from making errors with the DELETE statement?

9. Can you use a join in a delete statement?

10. How many tables can you delete at once?

5

Module 6

Creating Tables

Goals

- Learn how to create a table in a database
- Understand how to use primary and foreign keys
- Understand data normalization
- Learn how to delete tables from a database

So far, we have worked through the basic data operations associated with any database. We have inserted, updated, and deleted data. Up to this point, however, we have assumed that some database administrator has created the database and the tables we have worked with. In this module, we are going to focus on how to build one part of that data-containing structure, a table.

We have used SELECT INTO to create a table in the previous modules. While this is a convenient method for you as a programmer to use for creating tables, it has several limitations. First, the table has to be based on a query. Not all tables, titleauthor in Pubs, for example, lend themselves to being created by a query. Good table designs for containing data often do not represent the results of a query. A good table design allows you to run queries efficiently. As we will see, what allows for efficient retrieval of data often does not look anything like the result of retrieving data.

Second, SELECT INTO does not allow you to address issues of unique identification. If you want a unique identifier in your table rows, you must place it there as a part of the query. The query you have in mind may not pull a unique identifier from the underlying tables. As a result, queries against the resulting table may not be able to distinguish among three authors named Smith.

Third, you cannot enforce data integrity when you use SELECT INTO. You cannot set constraints of the type we dealt with learning how to sequence insert and delete operations, for example. You cannot use a constraint to validate data inserted into the table. And you can take no action when a column's value matches a certain threshold value.

As you might guess, most of the time it is better to explicitly create tables so that you can take advantages of the features SQL provides to validate and protect your data. SELECT INTO is great for a quick temporary table that you create on the fly. If you are going to use the table for anything more than a temporary storage space, you should explicitly create the table with CREATE TABLE.

Using Create Table

Creating a table is easy. This is the minimal syntax necessary:

```
CREATE TABLE NewTable (NewValue INT)
```

Executing this statement against Pubs in the Query Analyzer creates a new table named *NewTable* with a column named *NewValue* that takes integer data. If you want to add additional columns, simply add the additional column names followed by their data type so that each pairing of name and data type between the parentheses is separated by a comma, as follows:

```
CREATE TABLE NewTable (NewValue INT, NextValue VARCHAR(6))
```

Since creating a table entails creating columns, and creating columns requires the use of data types, it's useful to review the data types available. Table 6-1 provides a way of reacquainting yourself with the data types we first described in Module 2.

6

Name	Storage
binary	Up to 8,000 bytes of binary data
bit	Integers 0 or 1
char	A fixed-length string of characters not encoded as Unicode
datetime	Date and time values from 1/1/1753 to 12/31/9999
decimal	Numbers containing decimal fractions from $-10^{38}-1$ to $10^{38}-1$
float	Floating-point decimals from $-1.79E+308$ to $1.79E+308$
image	A variable-length string of bits (binary data) with a maximum size of 2^{31}
int	Integers from $-2^{31}-1$ to $2^{31}-1$
money	Numbers representing monetary values from -2^{63} to $2^{63}-1$
nchar	A fixed-length string of characters encoded as Unicode
ntext	A variable-length string of characters not encoded as Unicode with a maximum size of $2^{31}-1$
nvarchar	A variable-length string of characters encoded as Unicode
numeric	Same as decimal
real	Floating-point decimals from $-3.40E+38$ to $3.40E+38$
smalldatetime	Date and time values from 1/1/1900 to 6/6/2079
smallint	integers from $-2^{15}-1$ to $2^{15}-1$
smallmoney	Numbers representing monetary values from $-214,748.3648$ to $214,748.3647$

Table 6-1   **SQL Data Types Used in Creating Columns**

Name	Storage
text	A variable-length string of characters not encoded as Unicode with a maximum size of 2^31–1
timestamp	A unique number in the database
tinyint	Integers from 0 to 255–failed copy
varbinary	A variable-length string of bits (binary data) with a maximum size of 8,000 bytes
varchar	A variable-length string of characters not encoded as Unicode
uniqueidentifier	A globally unique identifier (GUID), that is, a number unique in the world

Table 6-1   **SQL Data Types Used in Creating Columns** *(continued)*

Our concern with data types this time around, however, is not how to refer to them in a SELECT statement, but how to choose data types for columns appropriately. One thing that you have to consider is the ultimate size of your database and, to a certain extent, its speed. In general, you want to plan your tables by choosing table names and column names that are descriptive and self-documenting. People have to remember how to use your tables and columns, and table names and column names do not take up large amounts of space. (This statement should not suggest, however, that 256-character column names are a good idea.) The data type for a column, however, determines how much space is set aside even for a blank occurrence of that column. Even though disk space is no longer at a premium, many SQL databases require on database creation that you set the maximum file size for the database. Under these circumstances, you want to choose your data types wisely so that you do not bump up against that maximum size too quickly.

In choosing data types, therefore, apply the following suggestions:

● Choose varchar over char whenever possible. Char(256) sets aside 1 filled byte and 255 blank bytes for the value "A." Varchar(256), while it does incur some slight overhead to allow variable-length strings, only uses the number of bytes it requires for the string.

● If you absolutely know that you will never ever need to store a Unicode string, use the standard data types (like char) instead of the data types that begin with "n" (like nchar). Storing Unicode incurs some additional storage, because you are not using a character set that can be represented by a single byte. However, you need to be absolutely certain that you will not need to store Unicode, because you won't be able to if you try.

● Use a tiny data type or a small data type whenever it makes sense to do so. For example, you can use tinyint, smallint, or int. The int data type takes the most storage, because it has to be prepared to store very large integers. The smallint data type restricts the possible range of integers and takes less storage. The tinyint type takes the least storage but has a maximum value of 255.

● Avoid the binary and text data types whenever possible. If you need to store a collection of binary large objects (BLOBs), such as a collection of pictures, consider storing the path to the graphics file in the database and the BLOB in a folder set aside for holding the BLOB files. Your database will be smaller, storage for the BLOBs will actually be less, because you won't have the overhead the database wraps around the BLOB to keep track of it, and response time for queries will be faster. The same is true for large chunks of text.

6

In addition to planning data types, you need to consider default value and nullability when planning column layouts in tables. The default value is what is placed in the column when a row is created if no value for the column is provided. To provide a default value, you use the default keyword as follows:

```
CREATE TABLE NewTable (NewValue INT DEFAULT 0)
```

The column *NewValue* now takes a value of 0 if no other value is provided for it by an INSERT statement. A default value of 0 is somewhat redundant for any numeric data type, because the data type itself usually defaults the column to 0. However, there are many instances where 0 is not the appropriate default, such as when you want to specify a guaranteed interest rate for a life insurance contract. In addition, you need to specify whether the column can be null, that is, whether it can contain no data at all. You do so using the following syntax:

```
CREATE TABLE NewTable (NewText CHAR(6) NULL)
```

This table definition states that the column *NewText* can be null, which will be its value if an INSERT does not supply another value. You can also specify a default value for a nullable column, as follows:

```
CREATE TABLE NewTable (NewText CHAR(6) NULL DEFAULT 'ABCDEF')
```

In this definition, an INSERT that does not provide a value for this column creates a row that contains 'ABCDEF' in the column *NewText*. However, another INSERT statement could later set the value of this column to NULL if we so desired.

Note

If your database supports filenames or filegroups that represent the files that contain the data on the disk, you can usually specify which files to use in creating a table using the ON keyword. You will see examples of how SQL Server uses this keyword in examples in this chapter. You should check your database's documentation for the exact conventions to use, because they can differ.

Obviously, we have been simplifying the CREATE TABLE statements we have looked at to focus on certain features. Most tables have more than one or two columns, so let's take a brief look at a table definition for the Pubs database. Here is the basic definition for the Publishers table:

```
CREATE TABLE publishers
(
    pub_id   char(4) NOT NULL,
    pub_name      varchar(40)      NULL,
    city          varchar(20)      NULL,
    state      char(2) NULL,
    country       varchar(30)      NULL,
            DEFAULT('USA')
)
```

Note a couple of items here. First, note the use of indentation to make the statement more readable. Each column has its own line. Any additional lines necessary for a given column are indented well underneath that column name. In addition, note that you can use NOT NULL to indicate that a column absolutely cannot contain NULL as a value.

Planning Keys, Primary and Foreign

Tables usually contain *key values*. The key value uniquely identifies each row. In another module, we referred to columns as row identifiers. A key is a row identifier. However, a key need not be a single column. You can combine several columns to create a key, in which case the key is called a *multipart key*. Keys come in two general types, *primary* and *foreign*.

Because primary keys are the root of the key system in any SQL database, we will start with primary keys. Any given table ought to have a primary key, a single column or set of columns that uniquely identifies each row. You can have a table that functions perfectly well without a primary key, so long as you attempt no SELECT that requires the unique identification of data. Consider hospital patient records. People with all sorts of names are admitted to hospitals every day. If the Patients table has no primary key, we can select anything we want from the Patients table and always get a correct answer.

However, patients typically have multiple billing records. They incur pharmacy bills, room bills, nursing care bills, and physician bills, at the very least. Each bill will appear in a table that holds its bill type, and we have to be able to link John Smith the patient to John Smith's bills. Without a primary key in the Patients table, creating the join will be very difficult. In any given year, our hospital might admit twenty John Smiths, and some of them may have had the misfortune to have rented the same apartment on a six-month lease. We need to be able to tell which John Smith to link to all the bills incurred by that exact John Smith.

You have probably experienced several primary key schemes in use in retailing. Why do retailers ask for your phone number when they start to key in a purchase at the cash register? Your phone number is the primary key on your customer record. The social security number is similar in popularity, although with historical data even the social security number does not necessarily uniquely identify a person. Several years ago, a wife used her husband's social security number rather than applying for one of her own.

Note

SQL documentation often describes several kinds of keys. A *candidate key* is a column that could uniquely identify rows but may not be in use as a key at the moment. A *surrogate key* is a key that has no inherent meaning, like a serial number on a car. An *intelligent key* has some intrinsic meaning, such as longitude and latitude being used as a key to identify exact geographic locations in a table of places. A *super key* is a key that contains lots of columns.

Sometimes a multipart key makes sense. For example, if you collect a customer's address as well as name, but you do not wish to ask for further information, the combination of the name and address fields usually identifies each customer record uniquely. The exception, of course, is a junior who occupies the same residence as the parent and does not include "Jr." as a part of the name.

To create a primary key consisting of one column, use this syntax:

```
CREATE TABLE NewTable (NewText CHAR(6) NULL PRIMARY KEY)
```

Hint
Multipart keys are also called multivalue or composite keys.

A foreign key is an instance of a primary key that appears in another table. In Pubs, titleauthor is a table that contains foreign keys, namely au_id and title_id. The reason for referencing a primary key in another table is to provide an easy means of joining tables. As we have already seen, titleauthor allows us to select all the titles for a single author from the database. When you create a column that represents a foreign key, you indicate its source as a primary key using the REFERENCES keyword, as follows:

```
CREATE TABLE employees (job_id int REFERENCES jobs(job_id))
```

In this case, our new table Employees contains a column job_id that is the primary key for the preexisting jobs table.

Hint
Make sure that the primary key exists in the database before you attempt to create the foreign key.

Normalizing Data

The process of designing a set of tables is called *normalization*. In discussing relational database design, we often talk about normal forms. Think of these as stages you go through in table design. The goal of normalization is to avoid redundant storage of data, as when you store the customer's phone number in both the Customer table and the Order table. You have no real reason to store phone numbers in both tables, but it may have been convenient to do so as you added tables to your database over its evolution. One programmer added one table. Another programmer added another table. No one looked at the big picture, and the redundancy slipped in.

You definitely don't want to store the same data in two locations, because then you have to keep both locations updated if the data changes. In addition, you want to be certain that you locate the columns in tables properly to avoid awkward updates, or accidental failure to update. A brief look at normal forms will help to clarify what proper normalization avoids.

First normal form for data is the first goal of table design. To achieve first normal form, list all the data items you intend to store and create column names for them. Identify related columns, and group these related columns into tables. Establish a primary key for each table. Once you have undertaken this paper design task, you have achieved first normal form. Each data item appears as one and only one column, related columns appear together in tables, and each row in each table can be uniquely identified by a primary key.

So far, so good. You have, for example, gathered all the information about a single author into a table, you have created au_id to uniquely identify each author, and everything looks fine. To achieve second normal form, you do some further analysis. You examine each column and ask whether it depends fully or partially on the primary key. When your key is a single column, such as au_id, each additional column in the table depends on that column fully. Only when you have a multipart key can you have a partial dependency.

Suppose we create an authors table and use last name, zip code, and phone number as a multipart key. We add a column named postal zone to our authors table, so that we can estimate what the shipping costs are for sending complimentary books to that author. Postal zone is a function of the distance between our zip code and the author's zip code. Suppose that at some time after we establish the database, we move our offices to another city. We now have to go back through the database and calculate the postal zone for each author once again. We will be wasting processing and time if we have to do the calculation for each author. While the postal zone is related to each author, it really is related only to the zip code. We should only be doing the calculation once for each zip code. The rule for second normal form is that partially dependent columns should be moved to separate tables.

If we seem to be making a great deal of fuss about nothing, in some senses we are. The main goal of second normal form is really to make certain that each column relates to other columns through a meaningful relationship. Partial dependency in keys is one critical indicator that a column has been misplaced. Postal zone is partially dependent on our multipart key. However, if we define a single-column key, the partial dependency disappears, but the problem does not. Postal zone is still more a function of zip code than it is of the author. If the author moves, you have to recalculate the postal zone as well. However, if you store postal zone in a table with zip code as its primary key, the problem of having to change the postal zone as other factors in the data change dramatically reduces. If the author moves, the zip code changes and the postal zone changes along with the zip code. Storing postal zone in a separate table simplifies many data operations for us. A good way to understand second normal form is to see it as placing columns in tables according to their most elemental relationships.

Third normal form is the state of your columns when all transitive dependencies have been removed. A transitive dependency is a logical relationship. If A = B and B = C, then A = C. This rule describes transitivity in algebra. If I am heavier than you and you are heavier than your sister, then I am also heavier than your sister. This statement describes a logical transitivity. In our postal zone example, postal zone has a transitive relationship with author's name and zip code. If I know the author's name, then I know the zip code, because they are stored in the same table. If I know the zip code, then I know the postal zone.

In third normal form, you want all such transitive relationships removed from a single table. Columns that participate in a transitivity relationship should be moved to a separate table.

There are other normal forms that you can apply when designing tables. However, if you make sure you have achieved third normal form, your tables should be well optimized for use with SQL. Here are some practical suggestions for achieving the state of third normal form:

1. Seek out the basic relationships among columns. Put the authors stuff in the authors table and the title stuff in the titles table.

2. Establish single-column keys whenever possible.

3. Whenever you encounter one to many relationships, such as the fact that one author can write many titles, make sure the entities participating in the relationship are in separate tables.

4. Whenever you encounter one to one relationships, such as author–postal zone or zip code–postal zone, make sure that you group the most related columns together in a single table. In the postal zone case, you use zip code to calculate postal zone, not author. Postal zone and zip code should therefore be in a single table.

6

Ask the Expert

Question: Does the average SQL programmer get involved much with normalization?

Answer: Most programmers are not really allowed near the table structure of a database. The reason for this restriction is that someone has to be entrusted with guaranteeing the quality of the data. That person is usually the database administrator. If you are just programming against the database, you probably won't do much normalization. Your tables will probably be temporary tables, and you will design them to suit your needs, not the database administrator's needs.

On the other hand, in many jobs I've had as a programmer, I've also been the database administrator. Or, when I've needed a new set of tables, the DBA has said "Write me the script and I will run it." If that happens to you, you are thrust into the process of normalization, whether you are ready for it or not. It helps to know a bit about it.

Question: How do I figure out whether columns are related enough to go into a table for first normal form?

Answer: Recognizing relatedness for first normal form is largely a matter of logic and perception. In most cases, you will just see the relationship. In some cases, you need to puzzle it out logically. Really, what you have to do for first normal form is to make categories. Each table represents a category. The columns are the members of the category represented by the table. The troublesome cases are going to be the ones that might fit one category, or might fit another. Put these cases someplace just to make first normal form, and then deal with them later.

Question: Second normal form confuses me. I don't like to use multipart keys. How do I deal with this step?

Answer: Second normal form is problematic. I deal with it largely by not relying on multipart keys, and by looking at the issue from the point of view of one to one relationships and one to many relationships. If you've done first normal form correctly, you have probably grouped all the one to many relationships into separate tables. What you are really looking for in second normal form are one to one dependencies within a single table.

Question: But isn't the one to one dependency what you look for in reaching third normal form?

Answer: You're right. Most of the dependencies you work through in achieving second normal form and third normal form are related. There is not always a clear distinction between what you catch in second normal form and what you catch in third. The main point is to catch the problems, rather than worry about which one fits which normal form.

1-Minute Drill

● **Describe a primary key.**

● **Describe a foreign key.**

● **Which SQL statement do you use to create a multipart key?**

Adding Indexes

The most useful tool for improving the speed of queries against your database is to index your data. An *index* to a table is just like an index to a book. When you want to know what page in a book contains a certain word, you look in the index. When you want to know what row contains a certain value in a certain column, you look in the index.

More specifically, an index is a way of looking up values in a column quickly. Indexes employ fast search algorithms that allow you to spot a value in the list of values quickly, and then pair that value with a location or set of locations. As a result, you can get to a particular row or set of rows faster than the alternative, which is to scan each row in the table to see if it contains that value.

Imagine a phone directory in which the entries are randomly listed. Finding Henry Lee's phone number would take a great deal of time, because you would have to check each entry to see if the name was Henry Lee, and then you could use the number associated with the name. Indexing the phone directory by last name makes finding a number faster. You can skip over all the irrelevant first letters of last names and turn directly to the "L" listings. You can then skip to the "Le" listings rapidly as well, and save the detailed scanning for a small subset of the records in the phone directory.

An index on a table works the same way. Looking up Lee in the index is faster than scanning the table, largely because of the search algorithms that can be used to move you directly to the value "Lee" quickly. Once you are there, you can retrieve the associated row identifiers, and retrieve

6

● **A primary key uniquely identifies rows in a table.**
● **A foreign key is a primary key referenced from another table.**
● **ALTER TABLE**

only those rows that relate to "Lee." If you have included other constraints on your query, you have to scan only a restricted subset of the rows in the table to see whether those constraints apply.

Creating an index on a key value is easy. Most databases automatically index the primary key in a table. Since the primary key uniquely identifies rows, it's a good bet that it will be used in joins. Joins need to be fast, and indexing the primary keys is a safe optimization strategy that permits speeding up joins without much user or administrator intervention. You can explicitly create an index in many SQL databases when you create a constraint (the topic of the next section). You can also explicitly create and index using CREATE INDEX.

Indexing a database is both a simple topic for a book like this and an advanced topic that could occupy a book of its own. For this reason, we are going to explore the basics of creating an index. If you need to create them often and need to engage in serious database optimization using indexes, then you want to turn to an advanced SQL primer.

Indexes can be of three types. A unique index allows no two rows to have the same index value. Thus, each row is uniquely identified in the index. No duplicate values are allowed in the index, so no index entry can refer to multiple rows. A clustered index is an index in which the values are sorted, and the sort structure of the index dictates the storage order of the rows. Indexing on last name, for example, typically causes rows to be sorted in alphabetical order by last name in the index and dictates that rows will be stored in the same order. As a result, when you add a new row to the table, it is stored in the sort order dictated by the clustered index. A nonclustered index indexes the rows in the table but does not change their storage order. Nonclustered indexes also need not be unique, while clustered indexes must be unique. Because clustered indexes affect storage order, you may have only one clustered index per table. You should choose this column wisely. It should be the column you are most likely to join on, or most likely to use for data lookup in a WHERE clause. If you face a choice between the two options, choose the one you are most likely to join on.

To create an index when you create a key, use the following syntax:

```
CREATE TABLE NewTable (NewText CHAR(6) NULL) PRIMARY KEY CLUSTERED
```

You can use any of the three index-defining keywords, CLUSTERED, UNIQUE, or NONCLUSTERED, in this statement. To use CREATE INDEX, use the syntax illustrated in this example:

```
CREATE UNIQUE CLUSTERED INDEX employeeID_ind ON employees (employeeID)
```

Note that the keywords describing the index precede the INDEX keyword. Following INDEX, you specify the name of the index. It is a good idea to give the index a name, because the default naming can be both nonmeaningful and confusing. After ON, you specify the table (column) on which to create the index.

Hint

CREATE INDEX with no keywords describing the index type creates a simple nonclustered index.

You have one other option for creating indexes. You can include keywords defining them in a CONSTRAINT statement. More about that in the next section.

Adding Constraints

Constraints can be primary keys, foreign key references, or data validation rules. They can also specify what happens when a key changes. We've already seen that you can create a primary key or a foreign key by using the following statements:

```
CREATE TABLE NewTable (NewText CHAR(6) NULL) PRIMARY KEY
```

```
CREATE TABLE employees (job_id  REFERENCES jobs(job_id))
```

You can also create similar keys using the CONSTRAINT keyword. Let's look at the following complete definition of the Publishers table in Pubs:

```
CREATE TABLE publishers
(
    pub_id  char(4) NOT NULL
            CONSTRAINT UPKCL_pubind PRIMARY KEY CLUSTERED
            CHECK (pub_id IN ('1389', '0736', '0877', '1622', '1756')
              OR pub_id LIKE '99[0-9][0-9]'),
    pub_name       varchar(40)     NULL,
    city           varchar(20)     NULL,
    state          char(2) NULL,
    country        varchar(30)     NULL
            DEFAULT('USA')
)
```

Note the use of the CONSTRAINT keyword to create the primary key with a clustered index. Note that it follows the definition of the pub_id column, to which the constraint applies. You can place constraints on any column by listing them one after the other, no punctuation between them, right after the column name. Why create a key in this fashion? You get to supply a constraint name meaningful to you immediately after the CONSTRAINT keyword. In the other method, your database supplies a random name. When you look at the constraint name, you are not likely to know what column or table it applies to.

Note

The term *referential integrity* refers to the use of constraints. Data that has referential integrity is data for which all the constraints are true at the end of a database action. If one of the constraints turns up false, the data has lost logical consistency and may have lost the ability to refer to the world. For example, in the table of places example we have mentioned, longitude and latitude represent a multipart key. Were one of those keys to have the value null, we could no longer locate the place on a map.

Note that following the key constraint is a check constraint. In this case, whatever you are to check follows the keyword CHECK in parentheses. You use OR or AND to specify multiple conditions, and each condition is enclosed in parentheses. In this case, we use IN to verify whether the pub_id appears on a list of possible values. We use LIKE to verify its match against a pattern.

You can create constraints that are foreign keys as well. This SQL fragment shows the syntax:

Hint

Module 8 covers the use of IN and LIKE in detail.

```
CONSTRAINT FK_backorder FOREIGN KEY (stor_id, ord_num, title_id)
   REFERENCES sales (stor_id, ord_num, title_id)
```

Note in this case that the foreign key is a multipart key, and it references a primary key in the sales table that is multipart. Note that multipart keys are simply a comma-separated list of fields enclosed in parentheses. The following table definition shows how to create a multipart primary key using the CONSTRAINT keyword:

```
CREATE TABLE NewTable (
        [stor_id] [char] (4),
    [ord_num] [varchar] (20),
    [ord_date] [datetime] NOT NULL ,
    [qty] [smallint] NOT NULL ,
    [payterms] [varchar] (12) ,
    [title_id] [tid] NOT NULL
        CONSTRAINT [UPKCL_new] PRIMARY KEY  CLUSTERED
            (
        [stor_id],
        [ord_num],
        [title_id]
    )  ON [PRIMARY]
) ON [PRIMARY]
```

6

Note that the constraint definition must follow the creation of all the columns involved. For this reason, CREATE TABLE can become confusing when you must include a multipart key, or several different constraints on different columns. Therefore, the most common method for creating multipart keys or long lists of constraints is ALTER TABLE.

In addition to keys and check constraints, you can create an index with a constraint that enforces uniqueness on nonkey columns in the database. Here is an example of such a constraint that applies within Pubs:

```
CONSTRAINT U_store UNIQUE NONCLUSTERED (stor_name, city)
```

This SQL fragment actually creates a unique index on the columns stor_name and city, requiring that the pairings must be unique in the table. Under this constraint, you may not have two stores named Franklin's in Louisville. Each store must have a unique name.

On foreign key constraints, you may specify what happens if you attempt a DELETE or UPDATE on the foreign key. You use the ON DELETE or ON UPDATE phrases, as in the following fragment, the definition of the employees table in Pubs with the addition of an ON DELETE action:

```
CREATE TABLE employee
(
    emp_id  empid
        CONSTRAINT PK_emp_id PRIMARY KEY NONCLUSTERED
        CONSTRAINT CK_emp_id CHECK (emp_id LIKE
            '[A-Z][A-Z][A-Z][1-9][0-9][0-9][0-9][0-9][FM]' or
            emp_id LIKE '[A-Z]-[A-Z] [1-9][0-9][0-9][0-9]
                [0-9][FM]'),
    fname   varchar(20)     NOT NULL,
    minit   char(1) NULL,
    lname   varchar(30)     NOT NULL,
    job_id  smallint        NOT NULL
        DEFAULT 1
        REFERENCES jobs(job_id) ON DELETE NO ACTION,
    job_lvl tinyint
        DEFAULT 10,
    pub_id  char(4) NOT NULL
        DEFAULT ('9952')
        REFERENCES publishers(pub_id),
    hire_date       datetime        NOT NULL
        DEFAULT (getdate())
)
```

In specifying an ON DELETE or ON UPDATE, you specify either NO ACTION or CASCADE. NO ACTION means not to cascade the action into the table where the primary key resides. The update or delete fails because it violates a constraint, and the DELETE or UPDATE rolls back, leaving the database in the state it was in before you attempted the action. If you specify CASCADE, however, the action extends into the table where the primary key resides. If the action violates no other constraints, the delete or update will also occur on the row containing the primary key value in the table where the primary key resides.

Note

ON DELETE and ON UPDATE are the two options on keys that allow you to enforce referential integrity. They prevent you from deleting a primary key while a foreign key still references it. They also allow you to delete all references to a key if there are no references left to it elsewhere in the database, indicating that the key value is no longer valid.

Altering Tables

As you might guess, ALTER TABLE is a statement that changes an existing table. Its basic syntax is as follows:

```
ALTER TABLE MyTable ADD MyColumn VARCHAR (20) NULL
```

This form of the statement adds a column. As you can see, the name of the table follows the ALTER TABLE keywords, and then the action to be taken follows. This example adds two constraints to a table; it was taken from a script that SQL Server generated for building the table:

```
ALTER TABLE [dbo].[sales] ADD
    FOREIGN KEY
    (
        [stor_id]
    ) REFERENCES [dbo].[stores] (
        [stor_id]
    ),
    FOREIGN KEY
    (
        [title_id]
    ) REFERENCES [dbo].[titles] (
        [title_id]
    )
```

You can also drop a column or a constraint using syntax like the following:

```
ALTER TABLE MyTable DROP COLUMN MyColumn
```

6

You can also perform many actions at once on a single table, as in this example:

```
ALTER TABLE MyTable ADD

/* Add several items. First a primary key identity column. */
column_1 INT IDENTITY
CONSTRAINT column_1_pk PRIMARY KEY,

/* Next a column referencing another column in the same table. */
column_2 INT NULL
CONSTRAINT column_2_fk
REFERENCES MyTable(column_0),

/* Next a column with a check constraint to enforce that   */
/* nonull follows a valid phone number format.   */
column_3 VARCHAR(16) NULL
CONSTRAINT column_3_chk
CHECK
(column_3 IS NULL OR
column_3 LIKE "[0-9][0-9][0-9]-[0-9][0-9][0-9][0-9]" OR
column_3 LIKE
"([0-9][0-9][0-9]) [0-9][0-9][0-9]-[0-9][0-9][0-9][0-9]"

/* Finally, a nonnull column with a default.   */
column_4 DECIMAL(3,3)
CONSTRAINT column_4_default
DEFAULT .081
```

Note that you use one ADD keyword, and each item to add follows in a comma-separated list. For your own sanity, use separate ALTER TABLE statements for each intended action. ALTER TABLE statements can become confusing when they are complex, and complex ALTER TABLEs can lead to accidental and unintended consequences. Keep them as simple and straightforward as possible.

Deleting Tables

You can also delete tables with the DROP statement. The syntax is straightforward:

```
DROP TABLE [dbo].[sales]
```

Keep in mind that DROP needs a keyword to identify what you want to delete, in this case a table. Following this keyword is the table name. DROP is final and does not prompt you to have your sanity checked before you carry through the deletion. Make sure you have the names right. If there is data in the table, it will be deleted along with the table.

> **Hint**
>
> Drop can be used with the keyword COLUMN or CONSTRAINT in an ALTER TABLE statement.

1-Minute Drill

● **Explain how to delete a table.**

● **How would you delete a column from a table?**

● **How can you get exact examples of how to perform complex SQL tasks for your database?**

BugFix1.vbp

Project 6-1: Fix the Recordset Handling Bugs

In this programming exercise, we are going to fix the recordset handling bugs that you must have noticed in the code by now. Our reason for leaving these bugs is to help you struggle through some of the issues associated with database programming with SQL. In particular, using SQL statements through a database connection can cause destructive consequences to the recordset you want to hold in memory to present to the user. If you execute an INSERT, UPDATE, or DELETE as the code now stands, you lose the recordset that populates the text boxes as you navigate.

There are a couple of solutions to this problem. One is to attach your presentation recordset to a data control, and let the data control handle the data changing operations. This may seem an attractive alternative, but it incurs high overhead and speed penalties. The data control has to break down the SELECT that defines the recordset into the UPDATEs, INSERTs, or DELETEs that are required for the changes.

● **Use DROP TABLE *tablename*.**
● **Use ALTER TABLE with DROP COLUMN.**
● **Use the database's "generate scripts" option to create scripts that drop and create the objects in the database.**

A better solution is to use two recordset objects. In most cases, you can get away with one command object, but a better practice is to use two so that you don't have to keep resetting the command to present the recordset. One command and recordset pair handles the presentation. The other pair handles data changing operations. Now you always have your presentation recordset. After a change, call the Recordset.Refresh method to make sure that the changes are available for presentation. Or reexecute the command.

You might notice that I am recommending only one connection object. The reason for the recommendation is that connections are high-cost items on SQL databases. The fewer the connections, the faster the database transactions. For this reason, since we have no inherent need to open a new connection, we avoid it.

Please note that we have not fixed all the bugs we have introduced. In the next module, in addition to building a database, we will fix some of the navigation problems that remain.

Step-by-Step

1. Open the DeletingData.vpb project and save it as BugFix1.vpb. Be sure to save the form as BugFix1.frm.

2. Add a module-level command object and a module-level recordset object. Name them as you wish. We are using module-level objects because they need to be available to all procedures on the form.

3. Substitute your new command and connection objects for each of the SQL actions that change data.

4. After each set of SQL statements associated with a change have completed, be sure to refresh the presentation recordset using one of the two methods described.

☑ *Mastery Check*

1. A multipart key is also called:

   a. A composite key

   b. A multivalue key

   c. A referential integrity constraint

   d. All of the above

2. ALTER TABLE can have the following parts:

   a. A DROP clause

   b. An ADD clause

   c. Columns to add

   d. All of the above

3. Explain what happens when you use ON UPDATE CASCADE.

4. How would you add a column named Here with data type char(6) to a table named Places?

5. What is the best data type for an integer column?

6. You need to store the computer name in a column, and you know that NetBIOS names have been extended to 255 characters for Windows 2000. What is the best data type, char, nchar, varchar, or nvarchar?

7. Do you think it is better to use float, decimal, or money for monetary values?

8. How do you delete a table?

9. How do you delete a column?

10. Can a DROP take place within an ALTER TABLE?

6

Module 7

Creating Databases

Goals

- Learn how to create a database
- Understand how to use primary and foreign keys in the context of a database
- Understand more about data normalization

M odule 6 taught you a lot about creating tables. At this point, you should feel comfortable creating a table in an existing database. You should feel comfortable normalizing that table to fit into an existing set of tables.

This module adds one new statement to your repertoire, CREATE DATABASE. Teaching you to use that command takes very little time. However, planning a database from scratch is different from adding tables to an existing database. The process of normalization requires different thinking. As a result, we are going to return to the topic of planning tables, and we are going to plan a database to track and manage evaluation portfolios for a school district. We will also cover planning security for your database, even though most programmers are not allowed to manage security directly. You need to know at least how it works.

Using Create Database

To create a database, you need to know the following from the start:

- The name you want to use for the database

- The minimum database size you want to use

- The maximum database size you expect to use

- The minimum transaction log size you want to use

- The maximum transaction log size you expect to use

- The file growth factor you want to use

- The file location where you want the database to reside

- The file location where you want the transaction log to reside

Let's go over each of these items to make sure we understand them. The name should be pretty obvious. We have been talking about Pubs for six modules now, and it should be pretty clear that each database has a name and that is how we refer to it when we want to interact with it. The minimum size is the amount of file storage space to allocate for the blank database after we create it. This is the file size that we start out with. There is no good rule about file start size, but 10MB is a very common number.

The size of the transaction log is a different matter. We have mentioned transactions briefly along the way. Most SQL databases treat each data-altering operation as a transaction by default. If you attempt an INSERT and it really goes wrong, the database rolls itself back to the state before you started. These implicit transactions do not allow you any control. They just function, statement by statement, as you work with the database. Each transaction is logged for backup purposes, and the name of the log is the transaction log. It is stored in a separate file from the data, so that if you lose one, you don't lose the other. If you do lose your data, you restore from your last good tape backup and then replay all recent transactions until the point of failure. If you are doing your backups correctly, you can restore to within minutes of the point of failure.

Hint

You should store your transaction log on a physically different drive if at all possible. Losing a single drive, therefore, will not take out both the data and the transaction log.

7

Obviously, you want a good chunk of space for the transaction log, because if it fills to capacity and can no longer expand, you will receive an out of space error and you will not be able to continue executing database modifications. This figure we are talking about now is the starting figure. Again, there are no good rules, but 5MB is a common starting size for a transaction log.

The maximum sizes for the database and the transaction log can be frustrating matters. How you handle these sizes depends on the database you use. Some SQL databases require that you change these sizes manually with an ALTER DATABASE statement if you run out of space. Other databases allow the files to grow until they physically run out of space on the designated storage medium. The best advice is, if your database supports unlimited sizes, use unlimited sizes; if your database does not support unlimited sizes, use the largest number practical for the operating system and storage devices involved. Murphy has an axiom about the amount of data growing to fill the storage space planned in less than half the time anticipated.

The growth factor can be expressed in different ways, depending on the database. You can express a number of megabytes, or a percentage. Usually, if you must use a number of megabytes, using the initial size of the database as the growth factor makes sense. You allocate enough new storage space to hold another starting database. You introduce a linear growth pattern as well, so that you can predict when you may run out of space easily. You need to know only the time factor in which you fill each allocated amount, and then you can plot growth against time and predict when you need to add storage space.

If you select a percentage, you introduce an exponential growth pattern. Each new amount of space allocated will be larger than the previous amount allocated. As a result, growth accelerates with time, and predicting the out of storage space point is more difficult.

We are going to create a database called Portfolio under SQL Server 2000. We will use the following statement:

```
CREATE DATABASE Portfolio
```

This is the minimal CREATE DATABASE statement. It puts the database on the SQL server using default options. The database goes on PRIMARY, a keyword that indicates to use the default file settings. Each database includes some form of a blank database to use as a template for creating new databases. SQL Server has a database named Model that serves this purpose.

A more common statement might be the following:

```
CREATE DATABASE Portfolio
ON
( NAME = Portfolio_dat,
   FILENAME = 'c:\mssq17\data\portfoliodat.mdf',
   SIZE = 10,
   MAXSIZE = 50
   FILEGROWTH = 5 )
LOG ON
( NAME = 'Portfolio_log',
   FILENAME = 'c:\mssq17\data\portfoliolog.ldf',
   SIZE = 5MB,
   MAXSIZE = 25MB,
   FILEGROWTH = 5MB )
```

In this statement, we give the logical names for the database file and log file, the names we can use in SQL statements to refer to them if we wish. We also give an exact filename and location. (Here is where you can place the log file on a separate device.) We have also given start sizes, maximum sizes, and growth factors.

Hint

SQL Server creates the logical names as databasename_dat and databasename_log by default. It provides roughly the same start sizes by default. Maximum and growth factors in the more terse statement we used are governed by the settings in force when the primary file group was set up. The only thing we really gain by using a more verbose CREATE DATABASE statement is the ability to specifically locate the files where we want them.

Creating databases is a topic that is very implementation specific. We have given you the critical information that you need to create a database on our teaching server using SQL Server 2000 or the Microsoft Data Engine. Other databases may require different statements in different sequences, and they may have special requirements because of the way that they allocate storage space to databases. To become proficient with your database, you need to dig into its documentation and find out its requirements.

Planning Tables

So we have a database named Portfolios. Currently, it has nothing in it. We have to figure out what should go in it. Probably your first question is "Just what is a portfolio?" A portfolio is a collection of work that is presented for evaluation purposes. This practice has become increasingly popular as schools have begun to realize that traditional testing does not allow the evaluation of critical skills like writing very effectively. For example, a timed writing test allows you to evaluate what a student can do in a given period of time on a given topic. It makes predictions about what a student might do in a similar situation, but it cannot make predictions about how well a student might do when writing a research paper in a period of two weeks. A portfolio evaluation schema allows the evaluator to study a variety of pieces in order to gain a broader sense of a student's capabilities.

The practice of using portfolios for evaluation grew out of the need to evaluate writing, art, and other areas where typical testing technologies fail. Its success in these areas has encouraged other disciplines, such as mathematics, to try portfolio evaluation. If you are interested in evaluating problem-solving skills in mathematics, whether the student chooses the right answer from among four or five offered on a standard test tells you little. You don't see any of the student's notations. You do not see how the student framed the problem while preparing the answer. At best, you only know whether the student guessed the right answer. Standard tests do not tell you anything more about how the student arrived at the answer.

We have, therefore, a basic definition of the thing this database is to track. A portfolio is a collection of work. Each item of work is an unknown quantity. It may be a piece of writing. It may be a written proof in geometry. It may be a piece of art. Because we are managing portfolios electronically, we can validly assume that whatever this database manages will be in electronic form, storable as a computer file. As a result, we can begin to understand how the database will relate to the pieces of work. Work will be stored on disk in a folder as computer files. The database will keep track of the work, organizing it into a portfolio.

Other relevant entities must play a role in this database. The most obvious entity is a student. A student owns a portfolio, and the portfolio describes a student's performance in a subject matter. Because portfolios can represent different subjects, subject matter or discipline is a relevant entity. Teachers are also important entities. Teachers are the evaluators of the portfolio, but students also have a belonging relationship to teachers. Classes are also relevant, because students are grouped into classes, and classes belong to or are assigned to teachers.

Somehow we need to arrange these entities and relationships into a set of tables. You can draw an entity–relationship diagram, but that is usually a tool that tells you about the tables you have created rather than a planning tool for tables. In the process of planning a database, normalization begins by finding the primary entities and describing them in as much detail as necessary. That is how we shall begin. We will create tables that describe our primary entities, and then look for ways to link the entities in appropriate ways.

Normalizing Tables

The most primary element we have is the portfolio. Let's enumerate its essential attributes. We have to have some way to identify the portfolio uniquely, because there will be lots of portfolios to manage. This requirement implies that we need a unique portfolio ID. Another primary attribute of a portfolio is its owner, whom we shall also have to identify uniquely. The owner is a student, so we will need a unique ID for each student to avoid name confusion. Let's call this attribute the student ID. We will also need to identify the subject matter, and each subject should have a unique identifier. Let's call this attribute the subject matter ID. Portfolios also have to have contents. The contents attribute leads us to our first dilemma. We have a one to many relationship. One portfolio contains multiple pieces of work. If we review the normalization suggestions in the last module, this requirement implies that contents should be represented by a separate table.

So far, therefore, we have discovered that we need two tables to represent a portfolio accurately in our database. One we will call Portfolio, and it will have the fields Portfolio_ID, Student_ID, and Subject_Matter_ID. The second table will be named Portfolio_Contents. It must contain the Portfolio_ID so that we can tell which portfolio these are contents for. It must also contain the path to the content matter. We will assume that the path will uniquely identify each content object. Portfolio_Contents, therefore, contains Portfolio_ID and Content_Path.

We are also going to add another column to this table. It will be called Deleted. In any portfolio tracking system, one of the things you want to prevent is students losing work. Once a content item is checked into the portfolio, we need to have a means of marking the item for deletion if it is not supposed to be in the portfolio any longer. We don't want to delete in actuality, because we want to recover the item in case the student changes

7

her mind. Marking it deleted means that it can persist but not appear in the student's or teacher's view of the portfolio. However, it can easily be recovered in case the student wants the item back in the portfolio.

This discussion has caused us to mention that items have to be checked in. Clearly, a content item has to have a pathway into the portfolio. We will call this pathway "checking in" and leave until later exactly what we mean by that. Once an item is checked in, it can be used. The student may want to edit the item's contents, or an evaluator may want a static view of the item while grades are being assigned. We also need to have an In_Use field for each content item, so that we can prevent two users from attempting to use the content item in conflicting ways at the same time. This statement implies that there must be a "check out" procedure, and again we will wait until later to define what that might actually be.

Tables 7-1 through 7-3 define the nature of the database that we have puzzled out so far.

The next entity most closely associated with the portfolio is the student, who both owns and creates the portfolio. We need, obviously, a table of students named Student. This table must contain a unique ID for each student, a column named Student_ID. As we have indicated in the previous tables, Student_ID will serve as a foreign key, but it is the primary key in the Student table. In addition, we need at least First_Name and Last_Name fields. We need to be able to address students by their name if our data access program for this database is to be user friendly. In addition, we need a Password column. We want to be certain that only the student can access his or her records in the database. (We will come back to the question of who should have access when we talk about teachers as entities in the database.)

The question of how to identify students to the database uniquely is an interesting one. When we look up a student, we pretty much have to do it

Column Name	Data Type	Key
Portfolio_ID	int, identity	Primary
Student_ID	int	Foreign, referencing Students table
Subject_Matter_ID	int	Foreign, referencing Subject_Matter table

Table 7-1   Preliminary Draft of the Table Portfolio

Column Name	Data Type	Key
Portfolio_ID	smallint, identity	Foreign, referencing Portfolio table
Content_Path	varchar(256)	None
Deleted	bit	None
In_Use	bit	None

Table 7-2 Preliminary Draft of the Portfolio_Contents Table

by first name, last name, and password. However, when we look up student information, like what portfolios they are building, we don't want to have to repeat a composite key in the Portfolio table just to look up a student's portfolios. To do so would be inefficient, as well as forcing us to maintain three pieces of data in multiple tables. As a result, for lookups, we will use Student_ID. But we must make certain that passwords are not repeated in the database. Some names are common, and schools will have multiple students with the same name at any given time, and they will be working on portfolios. We therefore need to make certain that passwords are unique in the Student table. A uniqueness constraint will guarantee that this column will contain unique values. Therefore two combinations, either first name, last name, and password or student ID and password, allow us uniquely to identify any given student for access to a portfolio. Table 7-4 summarizes our thinking about the Student table.

We have three additional entities we have to be concerned about. Students are grouped into classes. Classes are taught by teachers. And administrators want control over everything. We should expect to have a Class table, a Teacher table, and an Administrator table. Teachers will need to be able to view the portfolio for any student in their classes. As a result, we need to be able to identify the students belonging to a given teacher easily. Administrators need to be able to review the entire

Column Name	Data Type	Key
Subject_Matter_ID	int, identity	Primary
Subject_Matter_Name	varchar(50)	None

Table 7-3 Preliminary Draft of the Subject_Matter Table

Column Name	Data Type	Key
Student_ID	int, identity	Primary
First_Name	varchar(50)	None
Last_Name	varchar(50)	None
Password	varchar(50)	Unique

Table 7-4 Preliminary Draft of the Student Table

database, and they bear a supervisory relationship to teachers. Curiously, if we want this database to serve an entire school district, we need to include schools as entities. Certain administrators, like building principals, should be able to view information for their buildings only. Other administrators, superintendents for example, should be able to view information for the entire district.

How to organize these groupings may seem like a puzzle. We can begin to unravel the problem if we ask which entity organizes all the rest. The answer, actually, is the school. Students, classes, and teachers belong to a school. Some administrators belong to a school, and some don't. If we agree on what a school represents, we can easily plan the relationships among the other entities.

A school is a very simple entity. It must have an ID, School_ID, to uniquely identify it, and for easy sharing as foreign keys with other tables. It must also have a name, School_Name. Our draft of the School table therefore looks like that in Table 7-5.

The administrators table, shown in draft form in Table 7-6, needs to be a table that contains First_Name, Last_Name, Administrator_ID, and Password. However, it needs to contain a School_ID field. This field will be a foreign key referencing the School table; however, it will be a nullable field. Some administrators do not belong to a school.

Column Name	Data Type	Key
School_ID	int, identity	Primary
School_Name	varchar(50)	None

Table 7-5 Preliminary Draft of the School Table

Column Name	Data Type	Key
Administrator_ID	int, identity	Primary
School_ID	int	Foreign referencing School table, nullable
First_Name	varchar(50)	None
Last_Name	varchar(50)	None
Password	varchar(50)	Unique

Table 7-6 Preliminary Draft of the Administrator Table

Hint

SQL Server allows nullable foreign keys. Be sure to check your database documentation to make sure that this implementation is a part of your database.

The Teacher table, shown in Table 7-7, must have the same definition as the administrator table, right down to the nullable foreign key.

The Class table has to link together only three items. Why will be apparent in a moment. The Class table needs Class_ID, Class_Name, and Grade_Level columns. It cannot contain students, because any number of students may be in a single class. It cannot contain teachers, because more than one teacher may teach a class. This entity is a little like a portfolio. It is small, is easy to define, and has a slew of one to many relationships to deal with. Table 7-8 shows our draft of what the Class table should be.

Column Name	Data Type	Key
Teacher_ID	int, identity	Primary
School_ID	int	Foreign referencing School table, nullable
First_Name	varchar(50)	None
Last_Name	varchar(50)	None
Password	varchar(50)	Unique

Table 7-7 Preliminary Draft of the Teacher Table

Column Name	Data Type	Key
Class_ID	int, identity	Primary
Class_Name	varchar(50)	None
Grade_Level	varchar(50)	None

Table 7-8   Preliminary Draft of the Class Table

Note

We are making the assumption that all one-on-one and small group tutoring arrangements will be defined as classes.

The Class table starts us down the path of creating bridging tables. We need ways to create bridges between classes and multiple teachers, as well as classes and multiple students. To link to teachers, we need a table that bridges between Class_ID and Teacher_ID. Table 7-9 suggests how to accomplish the bridge.

The Class_Student table has the same structure, as shown in Table 7-10. Its purpose is to link students to a class. What do we gain by building the database this way, you might ask? Several things. If we want a list of teachers for a class, we do a three-way inner join among Class, Teacher, and Class_Teacher, and we have the list. The same approach works for finding a list of students in a class. However, we can easily remove a student from a class without deleting either the class or the student. The same is true of removing a teacher from a class.

One factor has so far escaped our attention. What do we do when a teacher retires? What happens when a student leaves the district? What do

Column Name	Data Type	Key
Class_ID	int	Foreign, referencing Class table
Teacher_ID	int	Foreign, referencing Teacher table

Table 7-9   Preliminary Draft of the Class_Teacher Table

Column Name	Data Type	Key
Class_ID	int	Foreign, referencing Class table
Student_ID	int	Foreign, referencing Student table

Table 7-10 | Preliminary Draft of the Class_Student Table

we do if a student wants to throw out a portfolio and start over? We can't just delete a teacher or a student. Teachers have been known to return to teach on a part-time basis, and students have been known to return after short-term moves out of the district. Students have also been known to change their minds about throwing work away. As a result, we need to be able to mark any of these entities as inactive. Just as we can mark a content item as deleted for a portfolio, and then recover it, we need to be able to do so with these entities. As a result, the final drafts of our tables that appear in Project 7-1 include appropriate Active columns for just this purpose.

Note

You might expect to need a Student_Portfolio table. The Portfolio table serves this purpose, because we link the Portfolio_ID to the Student_ID in this table.

1-Minute Drill

- **What purpose do bridge tables serve?**
- **Can a foreign key be nullable?**
- **In SQL Server, which statement creates a database?**

- **Bridge tables serve to represent one to many relationships.**
- **A foreign key can be nullable, but whether it is depends on database implementation of the feature.**
- **CREATE DATABASE**

7

Portfolio.sql

Project 7-1: Create the Portfolio Database

In this programming exercise, we are going to create the tables and constraints that we just discussed. Execute the required CREATE DATABASE, then use CREATE TABLE and ALTER TABLE to build the tables and constraints necessary. Tables 7-11 through 7-20 represent final drafts of the database tables and constraints we intend to build.

Step-by-Step

1. Use a CREATE TABLE statement to create each table. Include primary keys in the CREATE TABLE statements.

2. Create each foreign key with an ALTER TABLE statement.

Column Name	Data Type	Key
Portfolio_ID	int, identity	Primary
Student_ID	int	Foreign, referencing Students table
Subject_Matter_ID	int	Foreign, referencing Subject_Matter table
Active	bit	None

Table 7-11 Final Draft of the Table Portfolio

Column Name	Data Type	Key
Portfolio_ID	smallint, identity	Foreign, referencing Portfolio table
Content_Path	varchar(256)	None
Deleted	bit	None
In_Use	bit	None

Table 7-12 Final Draft of the Portfolio_Contents Table

Column Name	Data Type	Key
Subject_Matter_ID	int, identity	Primary
Subject_Matter_Name	varchar(50)	None
Active	bit	None

Table 7-13 Final Draft of the Subject_Matter Table

Column Name	Data Type	Key
Student_ID	int, identity	Primary
First_Name	varchar(50)	None
Last_Name	varchar(50)	None
Password	varchar(50)	Unique
Class_ID	int	Foreign, referencing Class table
Active	bit	None

Table 7-14 Final Draft of the Student Table

7

Column Name	Data Type	Key
School_ID	int, identity	Primary
School_Name	varchar(50)	None
Active	bit	None

Table 7-15 Final Draft of the School Table

Column Name	Data Type	Key
Administrator_ID	int, identity	Primary
School_ID	int	Foreign referencing School table, nullable
First_Name	varchar(50)	None
Last_Name	varchar(50)	None
Password	varchar(50)	Unique
Active	bit	None

Table 7-16 Final Draft of the Administrator Table

Column Name	Data Type	Key
Teacher_ID	int, identity	Primary
School_ID	int	Foreign referencing School table, nullable
First_Name	varchar(50)	None
Last_Name	varchar(50)	None
Password	varchar(50)	Unique
Active	bit	None

Table 7-17 Final Draft of the Teacher Table

Column Name	Data Type	Key
Class_ID	int, identity	Primary
Class_Name	varchar(50)	None
Grade_Level	varchar(50)	None

Table 7-18 Final Draft of the Class Table

Column Name	Data Type	Key
Class_ID	int	Foreign, referencing Class table
Teacher_ID	int	Foreign, referencing Teacher table

Table 7-19	**Final Draft of the Class_Teacher Table**

Column Name	Data Type	Key
Class_ID	int	Foreign, referencing Class table
Student_ID	int	Foreign, referencing Student table

Table 7-20	**Final Draft of the Class_Student Table**

7

Ask the Expert

Question: Why didn't you invoke any normalization rules as you discussed designing the tables and constraints in this database?

Answer: Normalization rules are really just aids to thinking. What I really wanted to expose in this module was how a working programmer thinks about building data tables. This thinking style represents an internalization of normalization rules and procedures. You can apply the rules if you want. I find them most usefully applied after you have designed the tables to verify that the design is correct. They don't help me to think productively about the design, but they do help me to verify it.

Question: Why allow 50 characters for each name?

Answer: Allowing 50 characters for each name is probably overkill. On the other hand, I have run into some long, hyphenated names for which 50 characters might be insufficient. The choice is to be more efficient with space, or to risk offending users. Each programmer develops an intuitive sense of where that line should be with experience.

Question: Why not use smallint for key values?

Answer: Most school districts will fit into the smallint range of data values, but many school districts won't. If you use smallint to save space, this choice has to be verified for each implementation. You probably need to use int for large school districts, especially those that serve tens of thousands of students, if not more. Using int for every database implementation enables you to avoid having to verify whether the school district will fit the data type. In addition, you avoid problems associated with the school district growing in size.

Question: You mentioned procedures that remain unspecified. When will we fill those in?

Answer: The programming exercises in the coming modules will show you how to build those procedures. For now, the important point is that they are actions that will be taken by a program. They will be combinations of intentions demonstrated by users and SQL statements embedded in the program.

Planning Security

So far we have created a database that no one can use, except us, because we know how to log into the database server and the database. To allow a program to access the Portfolio database, we need to grant security to users, or at least one user. To do that, we need to understand database security schemas.

All SQL databases implement their own security schemes. The database has a set of tables that contain a list of usernames, passwords, and access rights to individual databases. Some SQL databases also accept the operating system's security schema. SQL Server, because it runs on Windows NT, for example, can use Windows NT logins to grant access to databases and tables.

Which method is better? Microsoft would like you to believe that using Windows NT security with SQL Server is always better. You need to maintain only one list of users in the domain Security Account Manager database, and you assign database privileges to those users. This is certainly one point of view. It works well when you have a large group of users all of whom must have different access privileges on the database. Why indeed would you want to keep two copies of the user base, one in the operating system and one in the database? Under such circumstances, implementing database-level security is a waste of effort.

However, in the case of our Portfolio database, we have lots of users who will access the database, but we will be providing some kind of program that handles the access for them. Under this circumstance, creating an operating system login for the program can be dangerous. You must secure this login from malicious use, and doing so can be difficult. In the case of Windows NT, very bright and very careful system administrators have found themselves vulnerable to security breaches because of unexpected events relating to operating system security. For example, over the history of Microsoft's Internet Information Server, a Windows NT user account was used to grant anonymous FTP access. Turning off the FTP service or disallowing anonymous access did not disable this account. Any user could log into it using the username anonymous and no password. And this account had full access to many directories. (A subsequent service pack has closed this security breach.)

Our point is that, when programmatic access is concerned, opening an account on the database need not imply opening an account on the operating system. Using a database account, you can allow your program to obtain appropriate access. Only the program "knows" the username and password, because they are hard coded. No one can accidentally log into the account, because it is not generally available to anyone but the developer, and the password is never distributed.

In the case of Portfolio, we recommend creating a SQL Server account named Portfolio_User to allow programmatic access to the database. A common practice is to use the username as the password when connecting to the database. You can create a user account in any number of ways using a special stored procedure. To create a database login and grant access to the user to a specific database, use the following script as a template:

```
USE master
sp_addlogin @loginame = 'Portfolio_User', @password = 'Portfolio_User',
    defdb = 'Portfolio'
GO
USE Portfolio
sp_grantdbaccess 'Portfolio_User'
GO
```

This script defines a login name and a password, and sets the default database for that user to Portfolio. Setting the default database allows you to guarantee that the user cannot make accidental changes to some other database. The user is defined in the master database, as are all SQL Server users. Other databases use a similar construct for defining users. The second stored procedure grants the user access to the database Portfolio. Note the use of USE to change the database operated on in the midst of the script.

Hint

GO breaks SQL scripts into units that execute separately. The reason for using GO to force sp_addlogin to execute before sp_grantdbaccess is to guarantee that the user exists before you attempt to grant the user access.

If, on the other hand, you wish to use operating system security, you will use the following as a script template:

```
USE master
GO
sp_grantlogin 'DOMAIN\Portfolio_User'
GO
sp_defaultdb @loginame = 'DOMAIN\ Portfolio_User', defdb = 'Portfolio'
GO
USE Portfolio
GO
sp_grantdbaccess 'DOMAIN\Portfolio_User ', 'Portfolio_User'
GO
```

In this script, sp_grantlogin imports the username from the operating system domain (substitute the actual domain name for DOMAIN) into the database for use in managing security. The procedure sp_defaultdb pairs a default database with the imported login. The procedure sp_grantdbaccess grants the imported login access to the database named in the preceding USE and associates a short name (Portfolio_User) for use in any graphical view of the database security. You can also use this alias in stored procedures that manage security.

1-Minute Drill

● **What does sp_grantaccess do?**

● **When is the use of operating system security the best approach?**

● **Why use GO in scripts?**

BugFix2.vbp

Project 7-2: Fix Bugs

In this programming exercise, we are going to fix the miscellaneous bugs that you must have noticed in the code by now. Our reason for leaving these bugs is to help you struggle through some of the issues associated with database programming with SQL. In particular, using NULLs and navigation buttons leads to problems. By now, you have probably noticed that the program throws an error when you attempt to assign a NULL to a text box and when the recordset hits the Beginning of File or End of File marker. Follow the steps in this project to handle these problems.

You will notice that data validation kicks in aggressively on fields that are left blank. As you scroll past a record with blank fields, an announcement that you must enter a numeric value, for example, pops up. If you want, you can handle this error by adding "and Not

7

● **Nothing. The proper name of the stored procedure is sp_grantdbaccess, and it grants a particular username access to a database.**

● **Relying on operating system security for granting database access is most efficient when you have large numbers of database users who must have different access permissions.**

● **GO breaks scripts into units that execute separately. When the database encounters GO, it executes whatever came before, up to any preceding GO. You can use GO to guarantee that the results of previous statements will be available to the next statement.**

IsNull()" to the validation code for any field that may take a null value, like this:

```
Private Sub txtAdvance_Change()
    If Not IsNumeric(txtAdvance.Text) and Not IsNull(txtAdvance.Text) Then
        MsgBox "You must enter a numeric value in this field"
        txtAdvance.SetFocus
    End If
End Sub
```

Step-by-Step

1. Open the BugFix1.vpb project and save it as BugFix2.vpb. Be sure to save the form as BugFix2.frm.

2. Change each text box assignment statement to end with '& "".' This addition converts any null value to an empty string, and you can assign an empty string to a text box. Here is an example of what these lines should look like:

```
txtYTDSales.Text = mrstGlobalDatabase.Fields("ytd_sales").Value & ""
```

3. Add the following logic, which traps the error and turns on appropriate navigation buttons, to the Forward button:

```
    mrstGlobalDatabase.MoveNext

    If mrstGlobalDatabase.EOF Then
        cmdForward.Enabled = False
        cmdBack.Enabled = True
    Else
        cmdForward.Enabled = True
        MaskEdBox1.Text = mrstGlobalDatabase.Fields("au_id").Value & ""
        MaskEdBox2.Text = mrstGlobalDatabase.Fields("phone").Value & ""
        txtContract.Text = mrstGlobalDatabase.Fields("au_lname").Value & ""
        txtFName.Text = mrstGlobalDatabase.Fields("au_fname").Value & ""
        txtLName.Text = mrstGlobalDatabase.Fields("au_lname").Value & ""
        txtAddress.Text = mrstGlobalDatabase.Fields("address").Value & ""
        txtCity.Text = mrstGlobalDatabase.Fields("city").Value & ""
        txtState.Text = mrstGlobalDatabase.Fields("state").Value & ""
        txtZIP.Text = mrstGlobalDatabase.Fields("zip").Value & ""
        txtTitleID.Text = mrstGlobalDatabase.Fields("title_id").Value & ""
        txtType.Text = mrstGlobalDatabase.Fields("type").Value & ""
        txtTitle.Text = mrstGlobalDatabase.Fields("title").Value & ""
        txtPubID.Text = mrstGlobalDatabase.Fields("pub_id").Value & ""
        txtPrice.Text = mrstGlobalDatabase.Fields("price").Value & ""
        txtAdvance.Text = mrstGlobalDatabase.Fields("advance").Value & ""
        txtRoyalty.Text = mrstGlobalDatabase.Fields("royalty").Value & ""
        txtYTDSales.Text = mrstGlobalDatabase.Fields("ytd_sales").Value
            & ""
        txtPubDate.Text = mrstGlobalDatabase.Fields("pubdate").Value & ""
        txtNotes.Text = mrstGlobalDatabase.Fields("notes").Value & ""
    End If
```

4. Add the following logic, which traps the error and turns on appropriate navigation buttons, to the Back button:

```
mrstGlobalDatabase.MovePrevious

If mrstGlobalDatabase.BOF Then
    cmdForward.Enabled = True
    cmdBack.Enabled = False
Else
    cmdBack.Enabled = True
    MaskEdBox1.Text = mrstGlobalDatabase.Fields("au_id").Value & ""
    MaskEdBox2.Text = mrstGlobalDatabase.Fields("phone").Value & ""
    txtContract.Text = mrstGlobalDatabase.Fields("au_lname").Value & ""
    txtFName.Text = mrstGlobalDatabase.Fields("au_fname").Value & ""
    txtLName.Text = mrstGlobalDatabase.Fields("au_lname").Value & ""
    txtAddress.Text = mrstGlobalDatabase.Fields("address").Value & ""
    txtCity.Text = mrstGlobalDatabase.Fields("city").Value & ""
    txtState.Text = mrstGlobalDatabase.Fields("state").Value & ""
    txtZIP.Text = mrstGlobalDatabase.Fields("zip").Value & ""
    txtTitleID.Text = mrstGlobalDatabase.Fields("title_id").Value & ""
    txtType.Text = mrstGlobalDatabase.Fields("type").Value & ""
    txtTitle.Text = mrstGlobalDatabase.Fields("title").Value & ""
    txtPubID.Text = mrstGlobalDatabase.Fields("pub_id").Value & ""
    txtPrice.Text = mrstGlobalDatabase.Fields("price").Value & ""
    txtAdvance.Text = mrstGlobalDatabase.Fields("advance").Value & ""
    txtRoyalty.Text = mrstGlobalDatabase.Fields("royalty").Value & ""
    txtYTDSales.Text = mrstGlobalDatabase.Fields("ytd_sales").Value
        & ""
    txtPubDate.Text = mrstGlobalDatabase.Fields("pubdate").Value & ""
    txtNotes.Text = mrstGlobalDatabase.Fields("notes").Value & ""
End If
```

7

☑ Mastery Check

1. When you are ready to create a database, you must:

a. Check the documentation to confirm which statements to use

b. Use CREATE DATABASE

c. Use a special stored procedure

d. None of the above

☑ *Mastery Check*

2. To import an operating system user, use the following procedure:

   a. sp_grantlogin

   b. GO

   c. sp_grantdbaccess

   d. None of the above

3. What is a key clue that you must use bridge tables?

4. How do you locate the primary entities in any given database?

5. Why didn't you need to include a Student_Portfolio table?

6. Why use the bit data type for the columns named Active?

7. What is an entity–relationship diagram?

8. Why use the data type varchar for names?

9. Why include a Delete field in Portfolio_Contents?

10. What procedure adds a database login?

Part II

Building Skills

Module 8

Using Operators

Goals

- Understand relational and Boolean operators
- Learn how to check for the existence of a value
- Learn how to locate an item in a set

In SQL as in any programming language, you need ways to express relationships among data items. The category of items that expresses such relationships is the operators. Each item in the category operates on the data items in a query to express something about their relationship. The operators are what we build SQL clauses from.

Any SELECT that has a WHERE clause uses operators in the WHERE clause to express a selection condition. We want data returned where a column is equal to some value, or greater than some value, or simply not some value. Operators allow us to express these conditions. In this module, we will focus on enriching your understanding of the SQL operators so that you can be more expressive in selecting data.

Using Relational and Boolean Operators

Relational operators express what we commonly call mathematical relationships. If you have survived public education, you are certainly familiar with the operators shown in Table 8-1.

These operators have a familiar meaning in mathematics. They have the same meaning in SQL expressions: $1 + 1 = 2$, for example, and $2 > 1$, and $2 <> 1$. When you are working with numbers, you will find that the conventional meanings of these symbols apply, as do the normal actions of the arithmetic operators ($+$, $-$, $\times$, and $/$).

However, these operators can apply to other values besides numbers. Their exact meaning depends on the coding scheme, ASCII or EBCDIC, your database uses for characters. In the coding scheme, each character has

Operator	Meaning
=	Equal to
>	Greater than
<	Less than
>=	Greater than or equal to
<=	Less than or equal to
<>	Not equal to

Table 8-1   **SQL Relational Operators**

a numeric value in the code. In ASCII, "D" is 68, for example. A line feed is 9. When you use relational operators with characters, you are actually comparing their code values. For ASCII, the statement is true. The code value of "D" is larger than the code value for line feed.

```
D > line feed
```

> **Hint**
>
> When you start comparing characters using relational operators, you are wise to use the ASCII function provided by SQL, or the equivalent function for the coding scheme used by your database. This function returns the ASCII value associated with the character. When you see this function in use, you know you are comparing code values, and you are less likely to be confused by the results returned from the relational comparison.

Use of relational operators is very straightforward. The following two SQL statements use them:

```
SELECT * FROM authors WHERE contract = 1
SELECT * FROM authors WHERE contract <> 1
```

8

Table 8-2 shows the Boolean operators. These operators belong to a set of logical operations originally defined by George Boole. They are meant to encapsulate truth relationships in logic.

Operator	Meaning
AND	Takes two expressions that can be evaluated as true or false. Returns true if both are true and false if one or both are not true.
OR	Takes two expressions that can be evaluated as true or false. Returns true if either is true and false if both are not true.
NOT	Takes a single expression that can be evaluated as true or false. Returns false if the expression is true and true if the expression is false.

Table 8-2 Boolean Operators in SQL

Boolean operators are a bit tricky. The first question that comes to mind is what kinds of expressions can be evaluated as true or false. In general, these are expressions built with the relational operators. The following expression is false, for example:

```
1 = 2
```

And the following expression is true:

```
1 < 2
```

The simplest expression that can be evaluated as true or false is a column name for a column that takes only the values true and false.

Hint

Often we say that True = 1 and False = 0 in working with logic. You need to be careful of this assumption in programming. Some languages define False as some other value, such as –1, in order to distinguish between False and 0 in certain contexts. Be sure you know how your implementation defines True and False before you rely on any assumption about what the values will be.

Using Boolean operators, we can build WHERE clauses that can contain more than one condition. For example, in a hypothetical database, you could use this expression:

```
SELECT * FROM addresses WHERE city = 'Louisville' AND state = 'KY'
```

Here we are saying that we want all addresses returned from a city named Louisville (there is one in Kentucky and one in Colorado) and for any address in the state of KY. Both of the conditions must be true for the SELECT to pull the record. As a result, the SELECT will pull addresses for Louisville, KY, but not for Louisville, CO.

We can allow the SELECT to get Louisville, CO, from the database by switching to OR, as in the following:

```
SELECT * FROM addresses WHERE city = 'Louisville' OR state = 'KY'
```

Now only one of the conditions must be true for the SELECT to pull data. We will get records from both Louisville, KY, and Louisville, CO, as well as for any other city in Kentucky.

If we want to find all addresses for cities named Louisville outside the state of Kentucky, we can use AND combined with NOT, as in the following:

```
SELECT * FROM addresses WHERE city = 'Louisville' AND NOT state = 'KY'
```

NOT converts the value of *state* = *'KY'* to its opposite, making the result false where the expression is true and true where the expression is false. We select no cities from the state of Kentucky, therefore, but any city named Louisville in any other state.

Finding What Exists

Sometimes you want to know whether a set of rows exists in your database. The EXISTS keyword allows you to undertake this task. We can use EXISTS to find, for example, only those authors who have titles in the Pubs database. (This assumes, of course, that we enter authors into the database when they start a contract, but enter a title only when it is actually published.) The following example clarifies:

```
SELECT * FROM authors WHERE EXISTS (SELECT * FROM titles INNER JOIN
titleauthor ON titles.title_ID = titleauthor.title_ID WHERE
titleauthor.au_ID = authors.au_ID)
```

EXISTS requires the use of a subquery, which is simply a query within a query. Subqueries are entered in parentheses following the EXISTS keyword. To link the main query to the subquery, some value in the main query must appear in the WHERE clause of the subquery. If you do not make certain to do so, the EXISTS will always return True. Without a conditional relationship between the two queries, the subquery will always return rows. The main query and the subquery will be completely independent of one another. Suppose we phrase the query like this:

```
SELECT * FROM authors WHERE EXISTS (SELECT * FROM titles INNER JOIN
titleauthor ON titles.title_ID = titleauthor.title_ID)
```

We will find that all authors will return in the resultset, regardless of whether they have titles in the titles table. The subquery will always return all the rows in the titles/titleauthor join. Adding the clause

```
WHERE titleauthor.au_ID = authors.au_ID
```

forces the check of each row in the authors table against a resultset based on the au_ID field. If we have never entered a title for the author, then we should have no records in the titleauthor table for that author. If the subquery does not return rows, that author does not appear in the overall resultset.

1-Minute Drill

● **Give the results of the following query:**

```
SELECT * FROM authors WHERE EXISTS (SELECT * FROM titles INNER JOIN
titleauthor ON titles.title_ID = titleauthor.title_ID WHERE
NOT titleauthor.au_ID = authors.au_ID)
```

● **Give the truth value of the following: NOT 1 = 2 AND NOT 1 < 2**

● **Give the truth value of the following: 1 + 2 + 3 = 6**

Finding Something in a Set

EXISTS introduces the idea of being able to find subsets of a set. The EXISTS subquery uses a set of rows as the basis for selecting rows into a resultset. Other operators allow you to work with sets of rows to select other rows in similar fashion. With each of these options, you need to remember that you are finding a set of rows and then operating on that set of rows in some fashion to choose another set of rows. These tools can be very powerful in narrowing queries appropriately.

● **All authors would be returned. The subquery will always return results for any given author in the main query, because it will return a list of authors who are not the current author in the main query. As a result, for any given author in the main query, there will always be rows in the subquery.**
● **False**
● **True**

Finding Items In Between

BETWEEN allows you to generate a set of column values that will be used to return rows into a recordset. Its basic syntax is as follows:

```
SELECT title, ytd_sales FROM titles WHERE ytd_sales BETWEEN 1000 and 7000
```

BETWEEN allows you to get rows where a column value is within a given range. Note that in this case AND is not a Boolean operator. It is used to link the lower and upper limits of the column value. BETWEEN can be combined with NOT, as in the following statement:

```
SELECT title, ytd_sales FROM titles WHERE ytd_sales NOT BETWEEN 0 AND 5000
```

This query filters out the low-selling titles, showing us only those that have achieved 5,001 sales and above.

Note

Often you can do the same work as you can with BETWEEN using relational operators. You should use the expression that makes the most sense for the query. If we are serious about expressing that we want high sellers on our list of titles, using ytd_sales > 5000 probably more correctly expresses our intention than the use of the BETWEEN phrase.

8

Finding In, Any, All, or Some

The IN keyword allows you to use a subquery to control generation of a resultset in another way. IN seeks a column value in a list of values. The overall syntax of this expression is as follows:

```
SELECT au_lname, au_fname FROM authors WHERE au_id IN (SELECT au_id FROM titleauthor
    WHERE royaltyper = 10)
```

This query selects author first name and last name from the authors table. The WHERE clause states that the author ID must be on the list generated by the subquery. In this case, the list is the list of authors whose royalty percentage is 10%.

HINT

IN does not require the use of subqueries. You can use a list of comma-separated values within the parentheses instead.

Two operators allow you to force particular kinds of comparisons to the result of the subquery. ALL requires that the current row in the main query match all the results of the subquery in the way specified. Assume that we want to estimate the costs for the annual authors party. We plan a gathering of authors in each city where we have a publishing facility, and we need to find which authors are not located in those cities. In the following query, we seek to find the authors in Pubs who are not located in a city where we have a publishing facility. We also collect the city so that we know where the outlying authors are located.

```
SELECT au_lname, city FROM authors WHERE city <> ALL (SELECT city FROM publishers)
```

In the main query, we are pulling from a single table, the authors table. In the subquery, we also pull from a single table, the publishers table. The WHERE clause requires that we check the column city in the main query against the column city in the subquery. The two columns must not be equal. What is more, authors.city must not equal ALL of the values returned from the subquery. If there are five cities returned by the subquery, each will be compared to authors.city, and the author's name will be pulled only if authors.city does not equal any of the five values returned from publishers.

To plan this party well, we also need to find the list of authors in cities where we have facilities. The following query uses the ANY operator to accomplish this task.

```
SELECT au_lname, city FROM authors WHERE city = ANY (SELECT city FROM publishers)
```

ANY allows us to match any one of the values returned by the subquery. As a result, we will find the authors who live in a city where we have an office. While the subquery might return five cities, we need only to match one of them to pull that author's name and city information.

Note

The ANY and SOME operators are equivalent in function. They mean the same thing. Use the phrasing that is more intuitive for you.

Ask the Expert

Question: Don't ANY and SOME get confusing?

Answer: Yes, they do get confusing. I recommend using them sparingly, because they do lead to confusion. Someone who is not on their toes while working with a database can easily be lulled into thinking that ANY and SOME mean different things. They are two different words, after all, and in English they mean different things. You need to frame your queries as precisely as possible using the operators that make the most intuitive sense.

Question: Can't ALL, IN, and EXISTS accomplish the same task?

Answer: Yes, they can. The answer to the question which is best depends on the semantics of the question you are asking in the query. If you need all the items on a list that you can retrieve with a query, ALL makes more sense than EXISTS or IN. If you need one item from a list of many, IN makes more sense. EXISTS is the trickiest to think about, because it can easily return rows in the subquery when you do not intend to return rows. You must be very careful with your WHERE clauses when you use EXISTS.

Question: Are there any rules about whether relational operators are better than Boolean operators for certain tasks?

Answer: Good rules of thumb are these. If you are working with numbers, stick to relational operators. If you are working with true and false values, use Boolean operators. If you are comparing characters, use ASCII or the equivalent function to make obvious that you are comparing character codes. And don't waste time thinking about how you could express the query in one set of operators or another. Let the situation that gives rise to the query suggest the most appropriate set of operators.

8

Using Like and Is Null

Often when you frame queries, you need to match patterns in columns in order to return the correct data. You know, for example, that you want to select all phone numbers with a 502 area code. It would be nice to search the phone_number column for phone numbers that begin with 502. The LIKE keyword allows you to undertake this action.

We first looked at LIKE in Module 4, when we examined how to use UPDATE. Let's review what we saw in that context. A basic LIKE statement looks like this:

```
SELECT * FROM authors WHERE phone LIKE '502%'
```

LIKE triggers pattern matching on the column phone, and the string '502%' indicates that the first three characters of the field must be 502. The '%' character is a wildcard that stands for any number of characters.

Other wildcards can be used with LIKE. Here is the basic list of examples:

```
UPDATE authors SET Contract = 1 WHERE Zip LIKE '[456]0205'
UPDATE authors SET Contract = 1 WHERE Zip LIKE '[^456]0205'
UPDATE authors SET Contract = 1 WHERE Zip LIKE '4020_'
```

A square bracketed list of characters states to use one of these characters to match at this position. The caret character (^) translates as "use any character but the ones on this list to match at this position." The underscore character (_) states "put any single valid character here."

Hint

If you need to use a wildcard character as a character to search for, enclose it in square brackets. For example, '4020[%]' in a like statement searches for the string 4020%, a bogus zip code indeed.

When you work with LIKE, you must be excruciatingly careful. LIKE matches exactly the pattern you type, not what you intended to type. A stray blank space in the string will be matched. It could prevent data from returning, or it could match the wrong data. You also need to know the exact format in which data has been stored. Are phone numbers stored as sequences of 10 characters? Have the area codes been placed in parentheses and a dash been placed between the prefix and the suffix of the phone number? Do dashes alone separate all three elements? Or have periods been used to separate the elements? All of these are common phone number formats in the United States. If you must store phone numbers from other countries, you need to know what items are being stored (country codes, for example) and what format is being used.

Hint

The wildcards used in LIKE are common to other SQL elements. You can use them in check constraints, for example, to force correct data entry.

In the last module, we showed you one way to deal with inappropriate null characters appearing in a recordset. The problem was that text boxes could not accept the value NULL in an assignment statement. As a result, we appended an empty string to the values returned to keep the NULLs from interfering with presenting the data.

SQL provides a way for you to check for inappropriate NULL characters when the data gets pulled from the database. You use the ISNULL function, which checks for the NULL character and returns a specified character if the value of the column is NULL. Here is the syntax:

```
SELECT ISNULL(price, $0.00) FROM titles
```

In this example, we are retrieving price information from the titles table in Pubs. If we encounter a NULL, it makes no sense to pass the NULL on for presentation. A more appropriate value is $0.00. ISNULL checks price. If it is not NULL, the value of price is returned. If it is NULL, the value $0.00 is returned.

Notice that ISNULL is different from the following expression:

```
SELECT price FROM titles WHERE price IS NULL
```

This statement simply checks to see if price is NULL, and returns all NULL prices to the rowset. This is a rather boring query, because the result is a set of rows that contain nothing.

ISNULL is also different from this expression:

```
SELECT price FROM titles WHERE price IS NOT NULL
```

This expression checks for all prices that are not NULL, and returns them to the rowset.

ISNULL is the only SQL function that can be used to return any value you want. As a result, you can deliberately use an expression that evaluates to NULL in a query to trigger a certain response, or deliberately allow a column to be set to NULL so that you can trigger a certain response in

8

queries. Of course, using such schemes requires advance planning about what a NULL means when you encounter it, and what the appropriate responses should be. Such plans need to be documented so that subsequent programmers can take advantage of deliberate NULLs.

1-Minute Drill

- **What is unique about ISNULL?**
- **What is the difference between SOME and ANY?**
- **How is IN different from EXISTS?**

InsertCritical.vbp

Project 8-1: Build an Administrative Tool

In this programming exercise, we are going to begin building the administrative tool that populates the portfolio database with data and handles administrative functions like deleting outdated records. To begin populating the database, we must have a program that will enter the primitive data elements, those that others depend on. In our database, we must have schools, classes, and subjects defined so that they can be used in other entries in other tables. Once we have these items defined, teachers, administrators, or students can enter the rest as they register themselves to use portfolios. By having these users enter and maintain their own information, we reduce the burden of managing even a district-wide portfolio database to a relatively minor task for a central administrator. In fact, we can define an administrator per building if we wish, so that no single central database administrator needs to manage this database. To create this administrative tool, follow these steps.

- It is the only SQL function to return any value you want to return.
- There is no difference.
- EXISTS checks for a set of rows returned. IN looks for certain values in the list of rows returned.

Step-by-Step

1. Create a standard VB project with a form, and enter the buttons on the form shown here.

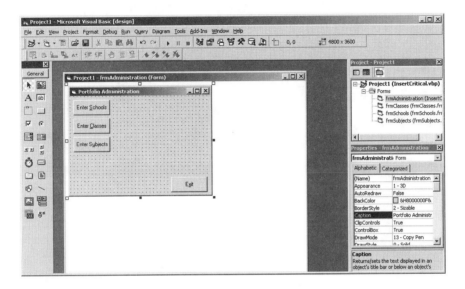

2. Name the buttons cmdExit, cmdSchools, cmdClasses, and cmdSubjects.

3. Set the Cancel property for cmdExit to True.

4. Set the caption property for the form to "Portfolio Administration."

5. Add the ADO Data Control to your project using Project | Components from the menu.

6. Create three more forms that look like the one here. Each one will be attached to one of the three left-hand buttons. Name the form after a button and set its Caption property appropriately.

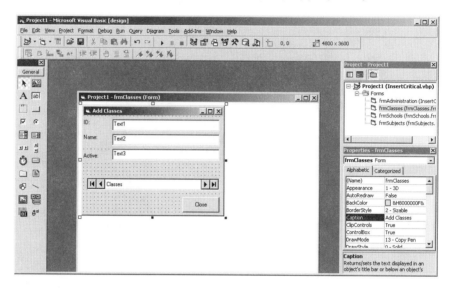

7. Set the Cancel property of the Close buttons to true.

8. Set the caption properties of the ADO Data Controls to match the caption on the form.

9. Use the custom properties of the ADO Data Control to build a connection string and a select command for the Class, School, and Subject_Matter tables for the appropriate form.

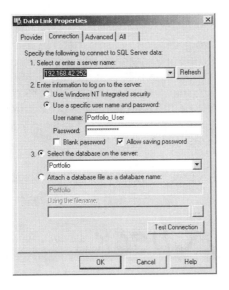

10. Add text boxes to the forms, one for each column in the table, and bind the text boxes to the data control using the Data Source and Data Field properties.

11. Add the data validation that you deem appropriate to the Change event for each text box.

12. Link the data forms to the command buttons in the main form by placing the show command in the click event for the button.

13. Add Me.Unload to the click events for the Close and Exit buttons.

14. Place the End command in the QueryUnload event for the main form.

15. Save the project, compile it, and run it to add the data to these tables.

8

Note

When the layout of your data entry form matches the layout of a table, then using the data control to manage the recordset is efficient. You can easily allow users to enter data into a single table, edit that data, and update the tables with minimal code. When your recordset involves multiple tables, don't use the data control. You are more likely to get efficient and accurate results managing the queries yourself, as we have in previous applications.

☑ Mastery Check

1. When you want to select one item from a list returned by a subquery, you must:

a. Use EXISTS

b. Use ISNULL

c. Use IN

d. Use ADO

2. To pattern-match in strings, you use:

a. The % wildcard

b. IN

c. FIND

d. None of the above

3. Assume that you have set up a table of book chapters. For each chapter record, you store book_ID, chapter_number, chapter_title, and page_count. If the author has not yet assigned a chapter title, you want to display "Title not yet assigned" in any query results. How could you do this?

☑ Mastery Check

4. If you want to match the values A, B, and C in one position in a string, how would you do it?

5. What is the crucial trick in using EXISTS?

6. Does IN require a subquery?

7. What does *WHERE city = ANY (SELECT city FROM publishers)* match?

8. What does *WHERE city = ALL (SELECT city FROM publishers)* match?

9. What is the truth value of *NOT 1 = 2?*

10. What is the truth value of *NOT 3 = 4 AND NOT 1 = 1?*

8

Module 9

Using Functions

Goals

- Understand how to use aggregate functions
- Learn how to manipulate dates and times
- Understand how to use string functions
- Understand how to use the essential system functions

Programming languages provide functions, and SQL is no different from any of the others. Functions are useful routines that perform common actions. They are predefined so that you do not have to write them yourself. If you want to average a column, you could write the routine to read all its values into a recordset, add them together, and divide by the number of rows. You will need to perform this action so frequently, however, that you would either rewrite the same lines of code over and over again or store them as a stored procedure so that you could reuse them over and over again without rewriting them. Functions are basically stored procedures that someone else wrote for you to reuse.

This module serves as your handy guide to the critical SQL functions. There are others, of course, besides the ones we cover here. They are of greater use to database administrators than they are to programmers. Our focus is on the functions that programmers often need to use to get at critical data. Our format here will be to define the purpose of the function, show its basic syntax, explain the arguments, and give an example. You can then follow the example in using the function on your own.

Aggregating Data

As we have seen in previous modules, aggregating is the process of summarizing data in some way. Your purpose in performing aggregation is to allow whoever is reading the results to understand trends quickly. SQL provides several means of quickly summarizing what is in the columns of your tables. If you combine aggregation and arithmetic operations, you can easily summarize the results of multiple columns.

AVG

Purpose

Returns the average of the values in a group defined either by AVG or GROUP BY.

Syntax

```
AVG(sql_expression)
```

Arguments

Sql_expression is typically a column name, but it can be a more complex expression. ALL or DISTINCT can be used to modify the expression. The return value matches the data type of the *sql_expression*.

Example

```
SELECT AVG(DISTINCT price) FROM titles
```

COUNT

Purpose

Returns the count of the number of items in a group defined by COUNT or GROUP By.

Syntax

```
COUNT(sql_expression)
```

Arguments

Sql_expression is typically a column name, although more complex expressions are possible. ALL and DISTINCT may be used to qualify *sql_expression*. The return type is an integer representing the count.

Example

```
SELECT COUNT(city)FROM authors
```

MAX

Purpose

Returns the maximum value associated with an expression.

Syntax

```
MAX(sql_expression)
```

9

Arguments

Sql_expression is typically a column name, although arithmetic expressions can be used. ALL and DISTINCT may be used to qualify *sql_expression*, although DISTINCT has no real meaning in the context of this function. There is only one maximum value for any given expression. ALL forces the function to apply to all values of the expression; it is the default mode of operation for the function. The return type matches that of *sql_expression*.

Example

```
SELECT MAX (ytd_sales) FROM titles
```

MIN

Purpose

Returns the minimum value associated with an expression.

Syntax

```
MIN(sql_expression)
```

Arguments

Sql_expression is typically a column name, although arithmetic expressions can be used. ALL and DISTINCT may be used to qualify *sql_expression*, although DISTINCT has no real meaning in the context of this function. There is only one minimum value for any given expression. ALL forces the function to apply to all values of the expression; it is the default mode of operation for the function. The return type matches that of *sql_expression*.

Example

```
SELECT min(ytd_sales) FROM titles
```

SUM

Purpose

Returns the sum of the items designated in the expression.

Syntax

```
SUM(sql_expression)
```

Arguments

Sql_expression is typically a column name. However, other types of expressions can be used. *Sql_expression* must represent numeric data, and NULLs are discarded. ALL and DISTINCT may be used to modify *sql_expression,* and ALL is the default. DISTINCT forces the sum of only the unique values; duplicate values are discarded. The return data type matches that of *sql_expression.*

Example

```
SELECT SUM(advance) FROM titles
```

STDEV

Purpose

Returns the standard deviation for a sample of the values associated with an expression.

Syntax

```
STDEV(sql_expression)
```

Arguments

Sql_expression is typically a column name, and it must represent a numeric data type. Aggregate functions may not be used in the expression. NULL values are discarded.

Example

```
SELECT STDEV(ytd_sales) FROM titles
```

9

STDEVP

Purpose

Returns the standard deviation for a population of the values associated with an expression.

Syntax

```
STDEVP(sql_expression)
```

Arguments

Sql_expression is typically a column name, and it must represent a numeric data type. Aggregate functions may not be used in the expression. NULL values are discarded.

Example

```
SELECT STDEVP(ytd_sales) FROM titles
```

VAR

Purpose

Returns the variance for a sample for the data elements represented by an expression.

Syntax

```
VAR(sql_expression)
```

Arguments

Sql_expression is typically a column name, and it must represent a numeric data type. Aggregate functions may not be used in the expression. NULL values are discarded.

Example

```
SELECT VAR(ytd_sales) FROM titles
```

VARP
Purpose
Returns the variance for a population for the data elements represented by an expression.

Syntax

```
VARP(sql_expression)
```

Arguments
Sql_expression is typically a column name, and it must represent a numeric data type. Aggregate functions may not be used in the expression. NULL values are discarded.

Example

```
SELECT VARP(ytd_sales) FROM titles
```

 ## 1-Minute Drill

- **Get the standard deviation for a sample of royalties.**
- **Get the maximum royalty paid.**
- **Get the average royalty paid.**

- SELECT STDEV(royalty) FROM titles
- SELECT MAX(royalty) FROM titles
- SELECT AVG(royalty) FROM titles

PortfolioBugFix1.vbp

Project 9-1: Fix the Bug

In this programming exercise, we are going to fix the bug that you must have noticed in the Portfolio database administration program. If you haven't found the bug, then we know that you haven't tried to enter data yet. The problem is what happens when you try to enter an ID value for a school, class, or subject. You should get an error, because we set these values up to be generated by the database itself as identity values, thus ensuring uniqueness of the ID values.

Why did we leave this little problem to lurk in the program? Why not tell you up front? First, this is one of the most common errors that creep into database client programs. You need to experience it first-hand. Second, programmers rarely learn by being told. They learn by doing, and doing means experiencing the common bugs that plague any database program. So we set the agenda to help you learn from building these samples. Here is how to fix the bug.

Hint

If you want to enter data on a form that uses the ADO data control, you must set its EOFAction property to 2—adDoAddNew. If you want to scroll backward, you must process the control's Error event and include the adodc1.Recordset.CancelUpdate method followed by the adodc1.Recordset.MovePrevious method in your error-handling code.

Step-by-Step

1. Open the BugFix1.vpb project and save it as PortfolioBugFix1.vpb.

2. Open each data entry form and set the Locked property on the ID text box to True.

3. Save the project and try it out.

Handling Dates and Times

For reports or for summarizing data, you often need to work with dates, times, and ranges thereof. SQL provides functions that allow you to add and subtract dates, get parts of datetime strings, and get current date and time stamps.

DATEADD

Purpose

To perform math with date values.

Syntax

```
DATEPART(Part_of_date_code, Number, sql_date)
```

Arguments

Part_of_date_code is a set of characters, not enclosed in single quotes, that represent the portion of the date on which you wish to do math. Valid values are the following:

year	yy, yyyy
quarter	qq, q
month	mm, m
dayofyear	dy, y
day	dd, d
week	wk, ww
hour	Hh
minute	mi, n
second	ss, s
millisecond	Ms

Number is the value that you want to add to the date part. Remember that the only math function allowed is addition, so to subtract, *Number* must be a negative value. *Sql_date* is a valid date expression on which to do the math.

Example

```
DATEADD(d, 21, Posting_Date)
```

DATEDIFF

Purpose

Returns the number of date units between the two dates specified. This function answers questions like "How many days are left to the end of the quarter?"

9

Syntax

```
DATEDIFF(Part_of_date_code, sql_startingdate,
sql_endingdate)
```

Arguments

Part_of_date_code is a set of characters, not enclosed in single quotes, that represent the portion of the date you wish to count. Valid characters are those described for DATEADD. *Sql_startingdate* and *sql_endingdate* are valid date expressions that mark the beginning and ending of the period in question.

Example

```
DATEDIFF(d, Posting_Date, getdate())
```

This example answers the question "How many days have elapsed since the posting date and today?"

DATENAME

Purpose

Returns the specified part of the date as a character string.

Syntax

```
DATENAME(Part_of_date_code, sql_date)
```

Arguments

Part_of_date_code is one of the date part codes described for DATEADD. *Sql_date* is a valid SQL date expression.

Example

```
DATENAME(m, getdate())
```

DATEPART

Purpose

Returns the specified part of the date as an integer.

Syntax

```
DATEPART(Part_of_date_code, sql_date)
```

Arguments

Part_of_date_code is one of the date part codes described for DATEADD. *Sql_date* is a valid SQL date expression.

Example

```
DATEPART(m, getdate())
```

DAY

Purpose

Returns the day associated with a date expression as an integer.

Syntax

```
DAY(sql_date)
```

Arguments

Sql_date is a valid SQL date expression.

Example

```
DAY('12/27/1954')
```

GETDATE

Purpose

Returns the current date and time for the system on which the function runs. In most cases, this is the date and time at the server, not at the client. For distant servers, remember that you may need to take into account shifts in time zones.

Syntax

```
GETDATE()
```

9

Arguments

None

Example

```
GETDATE()
```

MONTH

Purpose

Returns the month associated with a date expression as an integer.

Syntax

```
MONTH(sql_date)
```

Arguments

Sql_date is a valid SQL date expression.

Example

```
MONTH('12/27/1954')
```

YEAR

Purpose

Returns the year associated with a date expression as an integer.

Syntax

```
YEAR(sql_date)
```

Arguments

Sql_date is a valid SQL date expression.

Example

```
YEAR('12/27/1954')
```

1-Minute Drill

- **Get the current system date and time.**
- **Get the date that is twelve months previous to now.**
- **Get the current year.**

TextFunction.sql

Project 9-2: Test Functions

In this programming exercise, we are going to try out some of these functions. Not all functions will be relevant to the work of all programmers. For this reason, you ought to try the ones that seem relevant to your work. You can usually force a function to run by typing SELECT in the Query Analyzer and then entering the sample code provided in this reference. The output demonstrates the resultset returned by the function.

Step-by-Step

1. Type the word SELECT on a new line in the query anaylyzer.

2. Press Enter to move to a new line.

3. Enter the function code.

4. Click the Run button.

5. To check the results of a new function, highlight the function code and type the new function code in its place.

9

- **GETDATE()**
- **DATEADD(m, -12, GETDATE())**
- **YEAR(GETDATE())**

Using Math Functions

We've mentioned being able to collect aggregation statistics with functions. In addition, you can perform several mathematical functions beyond arithmetic with SQL's mathematical functions. These are most useful if you are storing information about angles, working with powers, or collecting information about the numeric values themselves.

ABS

Purpose

Returns the positive value of an expression, known as the absolute value.

Syntax

```
ABS(sql_number)
```

Arguments

Sql_number is a valid numeric expression.

Example

```
ABS(5+12)
```

ACOS

Purpose

Returns the radian value of the angle whose cosine is represented by the argument.

Syntax

```
ACOS(sql_float_expression)
```

Arguments

Sql_float_expression is any valid expression that evaluates to a floating-point number.

Example

```
ACOS(-1.00)
```

ASIN

Purpose

Returns the radian value of the angle whose sine is represented by the argument.

Syntax

```
ASIN(sql_float_expression)
```

Arguments

Sql_float_expression is any valid expression that evaluates to a floating-point number.

Example

```
ASIN(-1.00)
```

ATAN

Purpose

Returns the radian value of the angle whose tangent is represented by the argument.

Syntax

```
ATAN(sql_float_expression)
```

Arguments

Sql_float_expression is any valid expression that evaluates to a floating-point number.

Example

```
ASIN(-46.00)
```

9

ATN2

Purpose

Returns the radian value of the angle whose tangent is between the two values represented by the arguments.

Syntax

```
ATN2(sql_float_expression_low, sql_float_expression_high)
```

Arguments

Sql_float_expression_low and *sql_float_expression_high* are valid expressions that evaluate to floating-point numbers.

Example

```
ATN2(35.1, 128.01)
```

CEILING

Purpose

Returns an integer that represents the smallest value greater than the value of the numeric expression represented by the argument.

Syntax

```
CEILING(sql_numeric_expression)
```

Arguments

Sql_numeric_expression is any valid SQL expression that evaluates to a number.

Example

```
CEILING(10.95)
```

COS

Purpose

Returns the cosine of the angle represented by the argument. The argument must be expressed in radians.

Syntax

```
COS(sql_float_expression)
```

Arguments

Sql_float_expression is any valid SQL expression that can evaluate to a floating-point number.

Example

```
COS(14.2)
```

COT

Purpose

Returns the cotangent of the angle represented by the argument. The argument must be expressed in radians.

Syntax

```
COT(sql_float_expression)
```

Arguments

Sql_float_expression is any valid SQL expression that can evaluate to a floating-point number.

Example

```
COT(14.2)
```

DEGREES

Purpose

Returns the measurement in degrees for the angle measured in radians represented by the argument.

Syntax

```
DEGREES(sql_numeric_expression)
```

Arguments

Sql_numeric_expression is any valid SQL expression that evaluates to a number.

Example

```
DEGREES(14.2)
```

EXP

Purpose

Returns the natural logarithm base *e* raised to the power of the argument.

Syntax

```
EXP(sql_float_expression)
```

Arguments

Sql_float_expression is any valid SQL expression that evaluates to a floating-point number.

Example

```
EXP(2.5)
```

FLOOR

Purpose

Returns an integer that represents the largest value less than or equal to the value of the numeric expression represented by the argument.

Syntax

```
FLOOR(sql_numeric_expression)
```

Arguments

Sql_numeric_expression is any valid SQL expression that evaluates to a number.

Example

```
FLOOR(10.95)
```

LOG

Purpose

Returns the natural logarithm of the argument.

Syntax

```
LOG(sql_floating_point_expression)
```

Arguments

Sql_floating_point_expression is any valid SQL expression that evaluates to a floating-point number.

Example

```
LOG(6.21)
```

LOG10

Purpose

Returns the base-10 logarithm of the argument.

Syntax

```
LOG(sql_floating_point_expression)
```

Arguments

Sql_floating_point_expression is any valid SQL expression that evaluates to a floating-point number.

Example

```
LOG(6.21)
```

9

PI

Purpose
Returns the value of PI.

Syntax

```
PI()
```

Arguments
None

Example

```
PI()
```

POWER

Purpose
Returns the first argument raised to the power represented by the second
argument.

Syntax

```
POWER(sql_numeric_expression, power)
```

Arguments
Sql_numeric_expression is any valid SQL expression that evaluates to
a number, except a value of the bit data type. *Power* is a number
representing the power to which *sql_numeric_expression* will be raised,
except a number of the bit data type.

Example

```
POWER(2, 3)
```

RADIANS

Purpose
Returns the measurement of an angle in radians associated with the
measurement of an angle in degrees provided as the argument.

Syntax

```
RADIANS(sql_numeric_expression)
```

Arguments

Sql_numeric_expression is any valid SQL expression that evaluates to a number. This expression may not be of the bit data type.

Example

```
RADIANS(45)
```

RAND

Purpose

Returns a random floating-point number with a value between 0 and 1.

Syntax

```
RAND(sql_integer_seed)
```

Arguments

Sql_integer_seed is a value of one of the integer data types that serves to seed, or provide an initial value for calculation for, the random number generator algorithm.

Example

```
RAND(5)
```

9

ROUND

Purpose

Returns a numeric value that represents the rounded or truncated value based on the first argument.

Syntax

```
ROUND(sql_number_to_round, sql_precision, [sql_truncate])
```

Arguments

Sql_number_to_round is any numeric expression not of the bit data type.
Sql_precision is an integer representing the number of places to round to.
If *sql_precision* is positive, *sql_number_to_round* is rounded to the number of
decimal places identified by *sql_precision*. For example, ROUND(745.045, 2)
returns 745.05. If *sql_precision* is negative, *sql_number_to_round* is rounded
to the number of places to the left of the decimal point. For example,
ROUND(745.045, -2) returns the number 700.

Sql_truncate indicates whether to round or truncate the number. If
omitted or 0, the function rounds. If a nonzero value is used, the function
truncates the number. For example, ROUND(745.055, 0, 1) returns 745.

Example

```
ROUND(780.045, 2)
```

SIGN

Purpose

Returns 1 if the number is positive, 0 if the number has no sign, or −1 if
the number is negative.

Syntax

```
SIGN(sql_numeric_expression)
```

Arguments

Sql_numeric_expression is any valid SQL expression that evaluates to a
number, except an expression of the bit data type.

Example

```
SIGN(200)
```

SIN

Purpose

Returns the sine of an angle represented by the argument as a floating-
point number expressed in radians.

Syntax

```
SIN(sql_floating_point_expression)
```

Arguments

Sql_floating_point_expression is any valid SQL expression that evaluates to a floating-point number.

Example

```
SIN(35.234)
```

SQUARE

Purpose

Returns the argument multiplied by itself.

Syntax

```
SQUARE(sql_floating_point_expression)
```

Arguments

Sql_floating_point_expression is any valid SQL expression that evaluates to a floating-point number.

Example

```
SQUARE(2.3)
```

SQRT

Purpose

Returns the square root of the argument.

Syntax

```
SQRT(sql_floating_point_expression)
```

Arguments

Sql_floating_point_expression is any valid SQL expression that evaluates to a floating-point number.

Example

```
SQRT(25.25)
```

TAN

Purpose

Returns the tangent of the argument expression.

Syntax

```
TAN(sql_floating_point_expression)
```

Arguments

Sql_floating_point_expression is any valid SQL expression that evaluates to a floating-point number or a real number.

Example

```
TAN(PI())
```

 ## 1-Minute Drill

- Obtain the square root of the value in the column **data_variance**.

- Determine whether the value in **quarterly_income** represents a deficit or a profit.

- Make sure that the value in **revenue_returned** always rounds down to the nearest dollar.

- SQRT(data_variance)
- SIGN(quarterly_income)
- ROUND(revenue_returned, 2, 1)

Using String Functions

Data is often stored as strings of characters, and often you need to get information about the strings themselves. SQL's string functions allow you to get parts of strings, remove blank spaces, or get information about strings.

ASCII

Purpose

Returns the ASCII code value associated with the first character, also called the left-most character, in a string expression.

Syntax

```
ASCII(string_expression)
```

Arguments

String_expression is any valid SQL expression that evaluates to a character string, or any expression of the char or varchar data type.

Example

```
ASCII('Le Monde')
```

CHAR

Purpose

Returns the character associated with the ASCII code provided by the argument.

Syntax

```
CHAR(sql_integer)
```

Arguments

Sql_integer is an integer value that represents a value on the ASCII code page.

Example

```
CHAR(68)
```

CHARINDEX

Purpose

Returns the starting position of the designated string to search for in the string to be searched.

Syntax

```
CHARINDEX(string_to_find, string_to_search[,
starting_position])
```

Arguments

String_to_find and *string_to_search* are valid SQL expressions that evaluate to a string data type. *Starting_position* is an integer indicating the character position in *string_to_search* at which to begin searching. If *starting_position* is omitted, the search begins at position 1 of *string_to_search*.

Example

```
CHARINDEX('find me', 'look here to find me')
```

DIFFERENCE

Purpose

Calculates the SOUNDEX values of two strings and returns the difference. Use this function to evaluate whether two strings are close enough to be considered spelling variants of one another. Use the DIFFERENCE function to determine how closely related two forms are. A difference of 4 indicates highly related spellings, and so you can assume that the two strings are spelling variants.

Syntax

```
DIFFERENCE(string_expression1, string_expression2)
```

Arguments

String_expression1 and *string_expression2* are valid SQL expressions that evaluate to a string data type.

Example

```
DIFFERENCE('Jane', 'Jayne')
```

LEFT

Purpose

Returns the number of characters specified by the second argument from the left side of the string specified by the first argument.

Syntax

```
LEFT(sql_string_expression, sql_integer_expression)
```

Arguments

Sql_string_expression is any valid SQL expression that evaluates to a string.
Sql_integer_expression is any valid SQL expression that evaluates to an integer.

Example

```
LEFT('My string', 3)
```

9

LEN

Purpose

Returns the number of characters in the string designated by the argument.

Syntax

```
LEN(sql_string_expression)
```

Arguments

Sql_string_expression is any valid SQL expression that evaluates to a string.

Example

```
LEN('My string')
```

LOWER

Purpose

Returns the string designated by the argument with all uppercase characters converted to lowercase characters.

Syntax

```
LOWER(sql_string_expression)
```

Arguments

Sql_string_expression is any valid SQL expression that evaluates to a string.

Example

```
LOWER('My string')
```

LTRIM

Purpose

Returns the string designated by the argument with leading blanks removed.

Syntax

```
LTRIM(sql_string_expression)
```

Arguments

Sql_string_expression is any valid SQL expression that evaluates to a string.

Example

```
LTRIM('  My string')
```

NCHAR

Purpose
Returns the Unicode character with the code indicated by the argument.

Syntax

```
NCHAR(sql_integer_expression)
```

Arguments
Sql_integer_expression is any valid SQL expression that evaluates to an integer.

Example

```
NCHAR(68)
```

PATINDEX

Purpose
Returns the starting position of the first occurrence of the pattern indicated in the first argument in the string designated by the second argument.

Syntax

```
PATINDEX('%sql_pattern%', sql_string_expression)
```

9

Arguments
Sql_pattern is any sequence of characters, including the wildcards described for use with LIKE. Normally, you use the % wildcard to start and end *sql_pattern*. Leave the first one off to search only for initial characters in the string. Leave the last one off to search only for final characters in the string. Leaving out one of the % wildcards means that the pattern must either begin or end the string. Leaving out both % characters means that the pattern must match the entire string exactly. *Sql_string_expression* is any valid SQL expression that evaluates to a string.

Example

```
PATINDEX('%My%', 'My string')
```

QUOTENAME

Purpose

Takes a Unicode string and adds quote characters at the beginning and end to make it a valid SQL quote-delimited identifier, such as a column name.

Syntax

```
QUOTENAME ( 'sql_character_string' [ ,
'sql_quote_character' ] )
```

Arguments

Sql_character_string is a Unicode string. *Sql_quote_character* is any valid quote character, such as " or '. If omitted, square brackets, the standard designator for a column name, are used.

Example

QUOTENAME('Column_1')

REPLACE

Purpose

Searches the string designated by the first argument for the pattern designated by the second argument and replaces that pattern with the characters designated by the third argument.

Syntax

```
REPLACE(sql_string_to_search, sql_string_to_find,
  sql_string_to_replace_with)
```

Arguments

All three arguments *Sql_string_expression* are valid SQL expressions that evaluate to strings or to binary data. This function works both on strings and on binary data.

Example

```
REPLACE('My string', 'My', 'Our')
```

REPLICATE

Purpose

Returns a string with the string designated by the first argument repeated the number of times indicated by the second argument.

Syntax

```
REPLICATE(sql_string_expression, sql_integer_expression)
```

Arguments

Sql_string_expression is any valid SQL expression that evaluates to a string. *Sql_integer_expression* is any valid SQL expression that evaluates to an integer.

Example

```
REPLICATE('one', 3)
```

REVERSE

Purpose

Returns the string designated by the argument with the characters in reverse order.

Syntax

```
REVERSE(sql_string_expression)
```

Arguments

Sql_string_expression is any valid SQL expression that evaluates to a string.

Example

```
REVERSE('My string')
```

9

RIGHT

Purpose

Returns the number of characters specified by the second argument from the right side of the string specified by the first argument.

Syntax

```
RIGHT(sql_string_expression, sql_integer_expression)
```

Arguments

Sql_string_expression is any valid SQL expression that evaluates to a string. *Sql_integer_expression* is any valid SQL expression that evaluates to an integer.

Example

```
RIGHT('My string', 3)
```

RTRIM

Purpose

Returns the string designated by the argument with trailing blanks removed.

Syntax

```
RTRIM(sql_string_expression)
```

Arguments

Sql_string_expression is any valid SQL expression that evaluates to a string.

Example

```
RTRIM('  My string')
```

SOUNDEX

Purpose

SOUNDEX is useful for evaluating whether two items sound alike, as when you search for the name Smith and want to locate all variant spellings, such as Smythe. It returns a four-digit soundex code, which evaluates the similarity of two strings. Use this function to return the soundex code for any given string. Use the DIFFERENCE function to determine how closely related two forms are. A difference of 4 indicates highly related spellings, and so you can assume that the two strings are spelling variants.

Syntax

```
SOUNDEX(string_expression)
```

Arguments

String_expression is any valid SQL expression that evaluates to a string data type.

Example

```
SOUNDEX('Jane')
```

SPACE

Purpose

Returns a string with the space character repeated the number of times indicated by the argument.

Syntax

```
SPACE(sql_integer_expression)
```

Arguments

Sql_integer_expression is any valid SQL expression that evaluates to an integer.

9

Example

```
SPACE(3)
```

STR

Purpose

Returns a floating-point number as a string that represents that number.

Syntax

```
STR(sql_float_expression[, sql_length[, sql_decimal]])
```

Arguments

Sql_float_expression is any valid SQL expression that evaluates to a floating-point number. *Sql_length* is the total number of characters that can be in the resulting string. The default value is 10. *Sql_decimal* is the number of places allowed to the right of the decimal point.

Example

```
STR(111.12, 6, 2)
```

STUFF

Purpose

Modifies a string by deleting a specified number of characters at the starting point designated and inserting a specified set of characters at the designated starting point.

Syntax

```
STUFF(sql_string_expression_to_modify, sql_integer_start,
  sql_integer_length, sql_string_expression_to_insert)
```

Arguments

Sql_string_expression_to_modify is the string you wish to modify. *Sql_integer_start* is an integer indicating the position from the left of the starting character. *Sql_integer_length* is the number of characters to delete. *Sql_string_expression_to_insert* is the string of characters to insert.

Example

```
STUFF('To be or not to be', 7, 2, 'well, maybe')
```

SUBSTR

Purpose

Returns the part of a string, text, binary, or image expression designated by the starting position and the length arguments.

Syntax

```
SUBSTRING(sql_expression, sql_integer_start,
sql_integer_length)
```

Arguments

Sql_expression is a string, text, binary, or image expression. *Sql_integer_start* is an integer that indicates the starting character or byte. *Sql_integer_length* indicates the number of characters or bytes after the starting position to return.

Example

```
SUBSTRING('To be or not to be', 7, 2)
```

9

UNICODE

Purpose

Returns the Unicode code value associated with the first character, also called the left-most character, in a string expression.

Syntax

```
UNICODE(string_expression)
```

Arguments

String_expression is any valid SQL expression that evaluates to a character string, or any expression of the nchar or nvarchar data type.

Example

```
UNICODE('Le Monde')
```

UPPER

Purpose

Returns the string designated by the argument with all lowercase characters converted to uppercase characters.

Syntax

```
UPPER(sql_string_expression)
```

Arguments

Sql_string_expression is any valid SQL expression that evaluates to a string.

Example

```
UPPER('My string')
```

1-Minute Drill

- **Remove the trailing padding from a column's value.**

- **How can you make sure that LIKE will match any set of upper- and lowercase characters?**

- **You want the code value for the first character in a column of the nchar data type. What function do you use?**

- **RTRIM(column_name)**
- **Use UPPER to place the value of the column to search in all uppercase characters and have LIKE search for uppercase characters only.**
- **UNICODE**

Using Critical System Functions

System functions typically give information about the state of the database system. For programmers, several of the system functions are useful in forcing changes of data type, locating NULLs, locating dates, or identifying numbers. Here is the list of the system functions most useful to you.

CASE

Purpose

Examines a list of conditions and returns a value based on which of the conditions is true. This function is like the IIF statement in Basic.

Syntax

To check for values of a given expression:

```
CASE sql_expression
  WHEN sql_expression_value THEN return_value
  ELSE return_value
```

To check for values of multiple expressions:

```
CASE
  WHEN sql_Boolean_expression THEN return_value
  ELSE return_value
```

9

You may repeat the WHEN clause multiple times in either form of the CASE function. CASE returns when it finds the first match, so order your WHEN expressions carefully.

Arguments

Sql_expression is any valid SQL expression. *Sql_Boolean_expression* is any valid SQL expression that evaluates to a Boolean value of true or false. *Return_value* may be any valid SQL expression.

Example

```
CASE column1
  WHEN 'Linclon' THEN 'Issued Emancipation Proclamation'
  WHEN 'King' THEN 'Fought for civil rights'
  WHEN 'Kennedy' THEN 'Managed the world's first nuclear conflict'
  ELSE 'You have not chosen a political leader on the list'

CASE
  WHEN column1 > 0 THEN column1 * 10
  WHEN column2 > 0 THEN column2 * 10
  ELSE 0
```

CAST

Purpose

Converts the argument to the data type indicated.

Syntax

```
CAST(sql_expression AS sql_data_type)
```

Arguments

Sql_expression is any valid SQL expression. *Sql_data_type* is any valid SQL data type.

Example

```
CAST(date_column AS varchar(10))
```

CONVERT

Purpose

Converts the expression to the data type indicated in the format indicated.

Syntax

```
CONVERT(sql_data_type, sql_expression, sql_format_code)
```

Arguments

Sql_data_type is any valid SQL data type. *Sql_expression* is any valid SQL expression. *Sql_format_code* is one of the format codes defined by your database. Format codes are provided for formatting dates. Common ones are the following:

1	mm/dd/yy
101	mm/dd/yyyy
2	mm.dd.yy
102	mm.dd.yyyy
3	dd/mm/yy
103	dd/mm/yyyy
4	dd.mm.yy
104	dd.mm.yyyy

The default date codes of 0 or 100 provide the following formats:

- mon dd yy hh:mmAM

- mon dd yyyy hh:mmAM

Example

```
CONVERT(datetime, column1, 101)
```

9

ISDATE

Purpose

Returns true if the expression can be evaluated as a valid date for your database.

Syntax

```
ISDATE(sql_expression)
```

Arguments

Sql_expression is any valid SQL expression.

Example

```
ISDATE(column1)
```

ISNULL

Purpose

Returns true if the expression can be evaluated as NULL.

Syntax

```
ISNULL(sql_expression)
```

Arguments

Sql_expression is any valid SQL expression.

Example

```
ISNULL(column1)
```

ISNUMERIC

Purpose

Returns true if the expression can be evaluated as a number.

Syntax

```
ISNUMERIC(sql_expression)
```

Arguments

Sql_expression is any valid SQL expression.

Example

```
ISNUMERIC(column1)
```

1-Minute Drill

- **How do you verify that a varchar column's value can be converted to a number for calculations?**
- **How do you verify whether a nullable column is NULL before attempting an assignment to a text box?**
- **How do you convert a string representation of a date to a datetime value to store in a datetime column?**

Ask the Expert

Question: Scanning down the list of functions, I don't see many that I can imagine using. Do I really need to memorize all these functions?

Answer: I don't think you need to memorize the functions at all. You want to scan the list to build familiarity. You definitely want to know about the system functions, because you will use them the most often. Next in importance are the string functions. You will be led to the others by the nature of your data.

Question: Do all databases support all these functions?

Answer: All SQL databases should support the functions defined in the SQL standard. Expect to see some special functions that belong only to your database, however, in the documentation. You might also expect implementations to vary slightly on different platforms.

9

- ISNUMERIC
- ISNULL
- Use CAST or CONVERT.

Question: I am porting a database from Microsoft Access to a SQL database. Is there any way to convert the SQL function code automatically?

Answer: In a word, no. Microsoft Access provides perhaps the least standard implementation of SQL available. Basic functions can be incorporated into SQL code, and there is no automatic translation to standard SQL functions. All the IIF statements need to become CASE functions in SQL. Many functions will translate to their SQL counterparts with some simple adjustment of the arguments (changing their order, for example). Porting nested IIF statements, however, is just torture. Use lots of white space to lay out the CASE functions necessary to make clear which condition triggers what return value.

Project 9-3: Enter Your Own Database Connections

PortfolioConnection.vbp You may have noticed that our portfolio database administration program has a significant limitation. It connects only to the database on our server in our development lab. This is a significant problem, because any implementation of our database in the field will not be able to connect using the connection string we are currently using. As a result, we need to provide a way for users to enter their own database connections. That is what we will be about in this exercise.

Step-by-Step

1. Open the PortfolioBugFix1.vpb project and save it as PortfolioConnection.vpb.

2. Add a form named frmDatabase. Make it look like the one shown here.

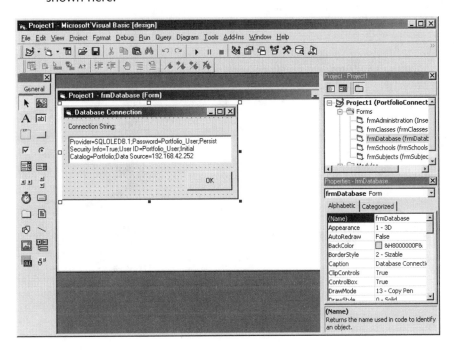

3. Name the button cmdOK and the text box txtConnection.

9

4. Copy the connection string you used for your ADO data controls into the Text property of the text box and set its Multiline setting to True.

5. Add a Database button to frmAdministration. Enter the code to cause this button to show frmDatabase.

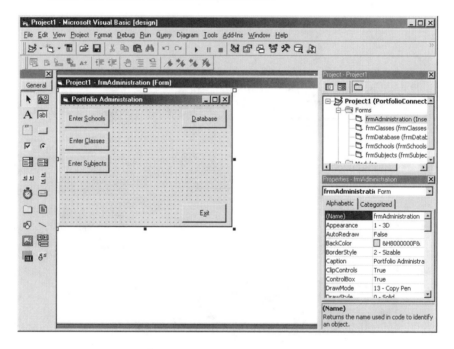

6. Use Project | References to add a reference to Registry Access Functions.

7. Place the following code into the OK button on frmDatabase:

```
Private Sub cmdOK_Click()
  SaveSetting "Portfolio Administration", "Form Load",
    "ConnectionString", txtConnection.Text
  gstrConnectionString = txtConnection.Text
  Unload Me
End Sub
```

8. Add a module to the project named modGlobal.

9. Add the following line to the module:

```
Public gstrConnectionString As String
```

10. Add the following line to the Load event for frmAdministration:

```
Private Sub Form_Load()
  gstrConnectionString = GetSetting("Portfolio Administration", "Form
Load", "ConnectionString", "Empty")
  If gstrConnectionString = "Empty" Then
    gstrConnectionString = "Provider=SQLOLEDB.1;
      Password=Portfolio_User;Persist Security Info=True;User
      ID=Portfolio_User;Initial Catalog=Portfolio;Data
      Source=192.168.42.252"
  End If
End Sub
```

☑ *Mastery Check*

1. When you want to count the number of records that match a specific criterion, which function do you use?

    a. AVG

    b. MAX

    c. COUNT

    d. ISNUMERIC

2. To pattern match in strings, you use:

    a. LIKE

    b. PATINDEX

    c. FIND

    d. Either a or b

3. To get the length of a string, which function do you use?

4. To make certain that you are viewing an angle's measurement in degrees, which function do you use?

9

✓ Mastery Check

5. In SQL, what is the default measurement system for angles?

6. Which function returns the sine of an angle?

7. Which functions return the upper and lower bounds of a measurement?

8. What function do you use to get a square root of a number?

9. How do you make certain that the value returned from column1 has no padding?

10. How do you get the date at the database server?

Module 10

Building Subqueries

Goals

- Learn how to select a single item using a subquery
- Learn how to set a condition on a subquery
- Learn how to use subqueries as a substitute for joins
- Learn how to use subqueries in INSERT and UPDATE statements

Sometimes a single query is simply not enough. You need to ask your database to provide an answer about the students in the student table, but you want to pull one item of information from another table as well. Perhaps you need their teacher, or you need to verify whether that student has active portfolios in the system. Subqueries are ideally suited to such a task.

A subquery is a query within a query. Within one SELECT statement, you include another SELECT statement to allow retrieval of an item or two from another table. You may react by saying "But we can get those items with a JOIN." Yes, you can retrieve some types of information in related tables with a JOIN. However, sometimes joins become very complex to manage, or the item of information you want has no shared field on which to join. In these cases, subqueries can be much more efficient.

Suppose, for example, you want to build a report from the Pubs database that lists each title in the database, its price, and some sales comparison data. You want to show the average price for all titles. The following query will not do the job:

```
SELECT title, price, AVG(price) FROM titles
```

Your database will complain that title and price are not included in either an aggregate function or a GROUP BY phrase. If you switch to using the following query, you will not get the average you want:

```
SELECT title, price, AVG(price) as AveragePrice FROM titles
    GROUP BY title, price
```

The GROUP BY phrase causes the average price to be calculated for the group title. As a result, both price and average price are identical, as shown in Figure 10-1.

To circumvent such problems, you must use a subquery. Here is what the SQL statement looks like:

```
SELECT title, price, (SELECT AVG(price) FROM titles) as AveragePrice
    FROM titles
```

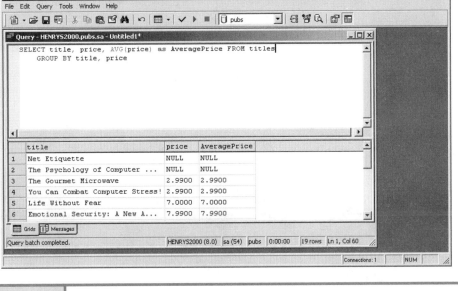

Figure 10-1 The effects of using GROUP BY when averaging

When you run this query, you see the correct average, as shown in Figure 10-2. In this case, the subquery removes the need to include a GROUP BY phrase on the main query that forces aggregates to be calculated for the group only.

Subqueries therefore have their place in your work. The only rule to remember is that subqueries go in parentheses. You are always wise to name their results using AS when those results must appear in a recordset. You will find that subqueries can accomplish a great deal of work, and they can appear in several different locations in a statement. In the remainder of this module, we will explore the different options and the type of work that you can accomplish with subqueries.

10

Note

Subqueries are often said to be nested within the main query.

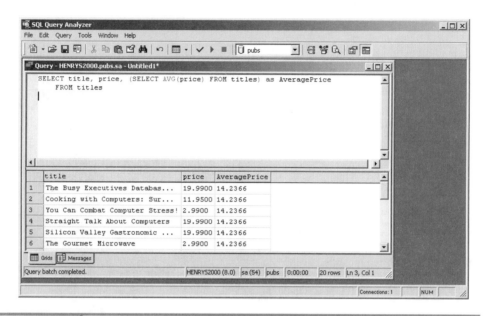

Figure 10-2 Using a subquery provides the correct results for the average

Selecting an Item

The preceding example shows how and why to use a subquery to obtain a single item. Typically, you use a subquery within a SELECT statement to obtain a value that the rules for the remainder of the select cannot return. In this case, we wanted the average of all book prices in the Pubs database. Using a single select would require us to group the data so that we could use the aggregate function AVG, yielding averages by groups, not for the entire table. Using a subquery breaks the stranglehold of the required grouping, allowing us to obtain the results we want.

Subqueries that retrieve an item for inclusion in a superordinate query obey certain rules. Such subqueries are enclosed in parentheses so that the SQL parser will treat them as separate entities. Whatever is within the parentheses obeys the rules that apply to any given single query. If you group, that query obeys the grouping. Typically, you use AS to name the results of the selection so that you can manipulate those results in your program. However, such subqueries must return a single value; otherwise, you will receive an error.

When you are retrieving a single item to include in a superordinate query, your SELECT statement must return one and only one value. In cases where your SELECT might return more than one value, you must use the DISTINCT or TOP keyword to limit the returned results to a single value. The query itself is inserted into the list of items selected by the superordinate query, just as if it were a column name.

If you wish to correlate the contents of the subquery to some value in the main query, you must include a WHERE clause in the subquery. A condition in the WHERE clause must equate a column value in the subquery to a column value in the main query. The following example returns a list of students and the count of the portfolios they are using from the Portfolio database:

```
SELECT First_Name, Last_Name, (SELECT COUNT(Portfolio_ID)
    FROM Portfolio where Portfolio.Student_ID = Student.Student_ID)
    AS PortfolioCount FROM Student
```

Note

Subqueries that reference a column in a table referred to in the main query are called correlated subqueries.

Setting a Condition

You can also use subqueries in a WHERE or HAVING clause to set conditions. In this case, you have three options. You can use a subquery that returns one and only one value, in which case the clause will check to see whether a column in the main query or a constant value has a relationship with the value returned. You can use any relational operator to check whether the value returned from the subquery relates to the column value in the main query, as in the following:

```
SELECT First_Name, Last_Name FROM Student WHERE (SELECT COUNT(Portfolio_ID)
    FROM Portfolio where Portfolio.Student_ID = Student.Student_ID) > 0
```

This query returns a list of student names where the count of portfolios is greater than zero. The subquery returns the count of portfolios for each individual student. As a result, the subquery correlates with the main query, so that each record in the recordset returned relates to one and only one student.

10

You can also use the IN keyword to determine the condition. Suppose you want to get a list of students who have active portfolios. You don't particularly care how many they have; you just want to be certain that any student returned by the main query has a portfolio in the system. You can use a subquery to return a list of all the student IDs in the portfolio table. You can use this recordset to set up the appropriate condition in the following manner:

```
SELECT First_Name, Last_Name FROM Student WHERE Student.Student_ID IN
    (SELECT Student_ID FROM Portfolio)
```

This query returns the list of student names where each student's ID appears in the list of student IDs returned from the Portfolio table. As a result, if a student is on our list, we know that the student has at least one entry in the Portfolio table.

To give you a sense of how this query would look if we used HAVING, let's add a GROUP BY to the query so that we can use HAVING. The query would look like this:

```
SELECT First_Name, Last_Name FROM Student GROUP BY Last_Name, First_Name,
    Student_ID Having Student.Student_ID IN (SELECT Student_ID
    FROM Portfolio)
```

In this case, we have to put every column used in the query into the GROUP BY phrase, since we have no aggregate functions. Obviously, such a query is artificial and contrived. We've presented it here to allow you to compare a WHERE form closely with a HAVING form. You would use HAVING when you have used aggregate functions in the main query and are forced, as a result, to use a GROUP BY with the other column names. Our main point is that subqueries work with HAVING as well as with WHERE.

You can also use subqueries with EXISTS to set conditions. When you work with EXISTS, you are asking if the subquery returns a recordset at all. You don't seek a count of records; you want simply to know if any records exist. Our first example in this section can therefore be rephrased in the following way, since the count itself is actually irrelevant:

```
SELECT First_Name, Last_Name FROM Student WHERE EXISTS (SELECT
    Portfolio_ID FROM Portfolio where Portfolio.Student_ID =
    Student.Student_ID)
```

The net result is the same as the first query, where we sought a count of the portfolio IDs and checked to see whether the count was greater than zero. Here, we simply asked if any portfolio IDs came back. If they did, we place the student's name on the list returned by the main query.

Note

You can use the ANY keyword with a subquery to check whether a constant or a column has a relation with every value returned by the subquery. You can use the ALL keyword with a subquery to check whether a constant or a column has a relation with any single value returned by the subquery.

1-Minute Drill

● **How would you include the count of student IDs in a query that returns a count of all portfolios?**

● **What does IN tell you about a subquery?**

● **What does EXISTS tell you about a subquery?**

Substituting for Joins

Subqueries can substitute for complex joins. Earlier we noted that, while you can obtain some of the same information a subquery yields using joins, subqueries can yield that information free from the grouping

10

● **SELECT COUNT(Portfolio_ID) AS PortfolioCount, (SELECT COUNT(Student_ID) FROM Student) as StudentCount FROM Portfolios**
● **Whether the value of a column or a constant appears in the list returned by the subquery**
● **Whether the subquery returned any records at all**

restraints that a SELECT using joins might impose. When we say that a subquery can substitute for a join, we mean that using a condition with EXISTS or IN can replace complex join logic.

Let's review our last query:

```
SELECT First_Name, Last_Name FROM Student WHERE EXISTS (SELECT
    Portfolio_ID FROM Portfolio where Portfolio.Student_ID =
    Student.Student_ID)
```

Here we used EXISTS to check whether a student has an active portfolio. We could also express this query using a JOIN. Here is the query:

```
SELECT First_Name, Last_Name FROM Student INNER JOIN Portfolio ON
Portfolio.Student_ID = Student.Student_ID
```

This is in fact a simple query. But notice, for comparison's sake, how the action of the query is hidden in the JOIN logic. You have to know that an inner join will select only the records from both tables where a student ID appears in the Student table and where the same student ID appears in the Portfolio table. Because the student ID must appear in both tables to be selected, we get a natural filter that prevents students without active portfolios from appearing on our list. We need to emphasize that you have to know this information and extract it from memory and apply it appropriately when the occasion arises. In other words, this form of the query will be more difficult to maintain than the query that uses a subquery because the logic is obscured.

Now imagine a complex join and the means by which it might obscure the logic behind the query. Imagine a combination of inner and outer joins that filter the records for display. A quick rule of thumb begins to emerge. Wherever possible, express your logic explicitly and clearly. If you have the choice between the implicit logic of joins and the explicit logic of subqueries, use the explicit logic. Six months later when you have to revisit your queries to undertake maintenance, you will thank yourself over and over.

Hint

Sometimes you will detect performance differences between the use of joins and the use of subqueries, especially on large databases that sustain lots of transactions per second. Subqueries make less effective use of indexes than joins. Where performance is the issue, obviously you should choose the fastest option.

Deleting, Updating, and Inserting

Subqueries can be used with other SQL statements. The fact that they can appear in a WHERE clause should tip you off to some possible uses. For example, in a DELETE statement, you can use a subquery in a WHERE clause to determine what to delete. The following query deletes students who have no active portfolios:

```
DELETE FROM Student WHERE NOT EXISTS (SELECT Portfolio_ID FROM Portfolio
    where Portfolio.Student_ID = Student.Student_ID)
```

An UPDATE statement can also use a subquery in the WHERE clause. The following example updates the Student table to capitalize all the students' names for those who have failed to start a portfolio:

```
UPDATE Student SET First_Name = UPPER(First_Name), Last_Name =
    UPPER(Last_Name) WHERE NOT EXISTS (SELECT Portfolio_ID FROM Portfolio
    where Portfolio.Student_ID = Student.Student_ID)
```

10

Note

You can also use a subquery in an UPDATE to obtain a value to update a column. The subquery is a SELECT that appears to the right side of an equal sign in the list of columns to SET.

INSERT statements work a little differently. You can use a subquery in a WHERE clause to express a condition if you want to. The more typical use of a subquery is to provide a list of values to insert. The following query illustrates:

```
INSERT INTO TempTable (First_Name, Last_Name, PortfolioCount) SELECT
    First_Name, Last_Name, (SELECT COUNT(Portfolio_ID) FROM Portfolio where
    Portfolio.Student_ID = Student.Student_ID) AS PortfolioCount FROM
    Student
```

This query assumes, of course, that you have built a temporary table named TempTable to insert values into. This temporary table receives values from a select statement, and the select statement uses a subquery to generate one of the values to insert. In this case, we could possibly have obtained the portfolio count for an individual student using a JOIN and a GROUP BY. The logic in this case would be almost equivalent and about as explicit. Compare this query:

```
INSERT INTO TempTable (First_Name, Last_Name, PortfolioCount) SELECT
    First_Name, Last_Name, COUNT(Portfolio_ID) FROM Student INNER JOIN
    Portfolio ON Portfolio.Student_ID = Student.Student_ID GROUP BY
    First_Name, Last_Name
```

In such cases, you should use the version of the query that, to you, most naturally expresses the logic behind the query.

1-Minute Drill

- **When is a subquery preferred over a join?**
- **Where is a subquery used in a DELETE statement?**
- **Where is a subquery used in an UPDATE statement?**

- **When the subquery more explicitly expresses the logic of the query**
- **In the WHERE clause**
- **In the WHERE clause or in the list of values to SET**

Ask the Expert

Question: Now we seem to have too many options. Why have the choice between a subquery and a join in the first place?

Answer: Actually, you were probably not intended to have a choice. Joins link tables for extracting data from multiple tables. Subqueries return a recordset for use in another query. They do have separate purposes. However, those separate purposes allow you to overlap their functionality. Perhaps the best way to keep their use straight is to choose which to use according to purpose. If you need to get a recordset to use in another query, use a subquery. If you intend to extract data from multiple tables, use a join. If you start from this perspective, a choice between the alternatives arises only when query logic becomes confusing. Then you want the simplest alternative.

Question: Can a GROUP BY in a subquery change the grouping in a main query?

Answer: The likelihood that a grouping in a subquery will affect the main query is minimal. Such an effect is only likely when a value returned by the subquery is used for grouping in the main query. If, for example, you return a value of 1, 2, 3, or 4 from the subquery and the main query assumes that you will be grouping into five groups based on this value, something will go wrong in the main query. Aggregates will not be calculated properly at the very least. Such a problem could occur quite independently of grouping in the subquery. However, if the values returned are calculated as a result of grouping in the subquery, grouping in the subquery could affect grouping in the main query.

Quite honestly, you want to avoid linking groups in this way. The bugs that could arise will be difficult to track, and you need to remember that SQL does not provide extensive debugging facilities. You cannot step into a SQL statement from your code debugger. Instead, you must use a tool like the query analyzer to diagnose the problem. Your debugging procedure is to separate the queries so that you can determine what each is returning. Start with your subquery, and determine that it returns what you expect. Then move to the main query without the subquery in place.

10

Make sure that it is returning what you expect it to. Then link the two together, and try to predict what will happen given the earlier trials of the separate queries. When the unexpected happens, you must try to imagine the circumstances that could create what happens. This process is neither fun nor easy.

Project 10-1: Delete Records

DeleteMarked.vbp

In this programming exercise, we continue building the administrative tool that populates the portfolio database and handles administrative functions. In this exercise, we are going to build the buttons that allow deletion of records from the database. If you recall, we said when we designed the database that users (that is, students or teachers) can mark something in the Portfolio_Contents table for deletion, but they cannot actually delete the item. Users can also mark a portfolio as inactive in the Portfolio table, but they cannot actually delete it. We will add an administrative cleanup button that performs the actual deletion of portfolio contents, and a button that can delete inactive portfolios whose contents have been deleted. Follow these steps to create these buttons.

Note

If you have not added any data to your database, you might want to add some schools, classes, and subjects at this time. The delete functions will be vacuous until we build the client portion of the Portfolio application. However, soon we will provide administrators with a way to enter teachers and students, and we will need some schools, classes, and subjects to undertake those additions.

Step-by-Step

1. Open Project 9-2 and save it as DeleteMarked.vbp.

2. Add two buttons named cmdDeleteContents and cmdDeletePortfolios.

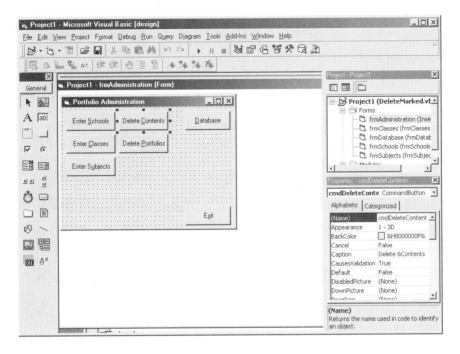

3. For each button, we need to add a warning dialog box. Add the following code to the cmdDeleteContents button:

```
Private Sub cmdDeleteContents_Click()
    Dim msgboxReturn As Integer
    Dim cnnConnection As ADODB.Connection
    Dim cmdSQLStatement As ADODB.Command
    Dim rstRecordset As ADODB.Recordset

    msgboxReturn = MsgBox("Are you sure you want to delete
all portfolio contents marked for deletion?", vbYesNo)

    If msgboxReturn = vbYes Then
        Set cnnConnection = CreateObject("ADODB.Connection")
        Set cmdSQLStatement = CreateObject("ADODB.Command")
        Set rstRecordset = CreateObject("ADODB.Recordset")

    With cnnConnection
        .ConnectionString = gstrConnectionString
        .Open
```

Create connection objects

Issue warning

If the user clicks Yes

Instantiate connection objects

Create connection

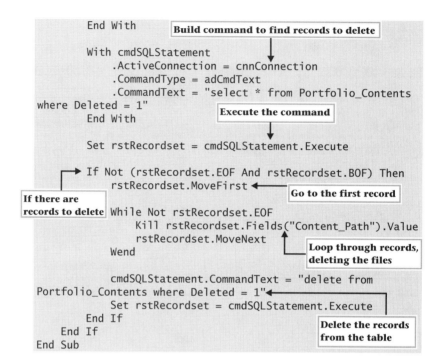

```
            End With                    Build command to find records to delete

        With cmdSQLStatement
            .ActiveConnection = cnnConnection
            .CommandType = adCmdText
            .CommandText = "select * from Portfolio_Contents
where Deleted = 1"
            End With                    Execute the command

        Set rstRecordset = cmdSQLStatement.Execute

        If Not (rstRecordset.EOF And rstRecordset.BOF) Then
            rstRecordset.MoveFirst      Go to the first record

            While Not rstRecordset.EOF
                Kill rstRecordset.Fields("Content_Path").Value
                rstRecordset.MoveNext
            Wend                        Loop through records,
                                        deleting the files

            cmdSQLStatement.CommandText = "delete from
Portfolio_Contents where Deleted = 1"
            Set rstRecordset = cmdSQLStatement.Execute
            End If                      Delete the records
        End If                          from the table
End Sub
```

If there are records to delete (annotation)

4. Add the following code to the cmdDeletePortfolios button:

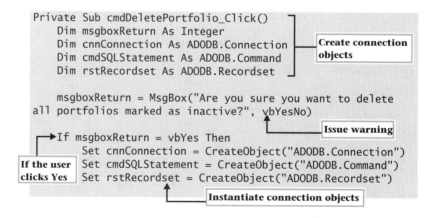

```
Private Sub cmdDeletePortfolio_Click()
    Dim msgboxReturn As Integer
    Dim cnnConnection As ADODB.Connection      Create connection
    Dim cmdSQLStatement As ADODB.Command       objects
    Dim rstRecordset As ADODB.Recordset

    msgboxReturn = MsgBox("Are you sure you want to delete
all portfolios marked as inactive?", vbYesNo)
                                               Issue warning

    If msgboxReturn = vbYes Then
        Set cnnConnection = CreateObject("ADODB.Connection")
        Set cmdSQLStatement = CreateObject("ADODB.Command")
        Set rstRecordset = CreateObject("ADODB.Recordset")
                                    Instantiate connection objects
```

If the user clicks Yes (annotation)

```
        With cnnConnection
            .ConnectionString = gstrConnectionString
            .Open                    ← Create connection
        End With

        With cmdSQLStatement
            .ActiveConnection = cnnConnection ←
            .CommandType = adCmdText
            .CommandText = "delete from Portfolio where
Active = 0"
        End With                         Create SQL statement

        Set rstRecordset = cmdSQLStatement.Execute
                              ↑
    End If             Execute SQL statement
End Sub
```

5. Save the project and run it to verify that it works.

☑ *Mastery Check*

1. Give the purpose of a subquery.

2. What are the two most common locations for a subquery?

3. Can you use a subquery in a HAVING clause?

4. Where do you place the subquery in a DELETE statement?

5. Where do you place a subquery in an INSERT statement?

6. How do you use a subquery to check to see whether a recordset has been returned?

7. How do you tell if the subquery has returned a specific value?

8. What does the ANY keyword achieve in relation to a subquery?

9. How do you debug queries containing subqueries?

10. How do you prevent a grouping in a subquery from affecting the grouping in the main query?

10

Module 11

Building Views

Goals

- Learn how to plan a database view
- Learn how to create the query for a view
- Learn how to test the query for the view
- Learn how to use the view you have created
- Practice more embedded SQL by adding to the Portfolio database project

So far we have considered the database table as the primary unit of information storage. Tables have columns and rows that define the storage locations for individual data items. If you want to examine the data stored in the tables, you query the tables. If you want to see data in more than one table, you use joins within your queries.

Relying on tables alone is perfectly appropriate methodology. However, when you have users who must browse a table, you may see a reason to worry just the slightest bit. Every database administrator who has been on the job for any time at all has at least one tale of having to resort to backup tapes because somebody—often the DBA—made a mistake when browsing a table. Your protection against such mistakes is providing users who have update and delete privileges with a special login with limited rights to use when accessing data tables directly. The most significant limitation of this approach is that most users are too lazy to log out and log back in under the right ID when they wish to access tables directly.

Enter a construct called a *view* to the rescue. A view is like a table, except it has no physical existence within the database. A view is created on demand when a user accesses it. As a result, a user accessing a view sees a table structure with the data up-to-date as of the time the view was accessed. Views are like temporary tables that you do not have to create, populate, and drop when users are finished with them. In fact, the physical structure that underlies a view is a temporary table. Because a view has an underlying table structure, you can set security on the view. If you want to guarantee read-only browsing access to data, you can define the view as read-only. No matter who uses it, the view remains read-only in nature. You need not worry about the use of special logins.

Note

Because they have no permanent physical existence as tables in the database, views are often called *virtual tables*. (Views have physical existence as database objects that you can see listed in management tools like Enterprise Manager. However, they are different from tables in kind.)

Rationalizing the Use of Views

The speed fiends among your development group may grouse a bit about views. They have their limitations. First, they have to be created on demand when they are accessed. If your database has high usage demands, you could find views to be performance bottlenecks. The process of creating the view must be merged into the query execution plan for the query that accesses the view. As a result, when you compare running identical queries, one against a table and the other against a view of a table, the execution plan for the query that accesses the view has slightly more work to do. Second, any time a view accesses a view, sometimes a necessary evil, you can expect the performance delay to increase. Even though the query optimizer is very good at building the optimal execution plan, the plan has to accommodate the fact that View #1 must present results before View #2 can present results. The dependence on the execution of the first view's query so that the second view can return data introduces a sequential set of events into the execution plan. Sometimes the query optimizer can work around such dependencies very well. Sometimes it can't. In some instances, the delays are serious problems.

Dependencies among views create interesting problems for the query optimizer to solve. The dependencies themselves are not inherently a problem. However, when the dependencies introduce significant recursion into the execution plan, delays will happen. You need to realize that any database's query optimizer is a black box to you as a programmer. You are not well equipped to predict what it will do. Because of this fact, you can only plan your views and queries carefully, and test their performance carefully. In my experience, changing the way you implement view dependencies can dramatically improve query performance. In one project, shifting from using a single view to using five views, each of which evaluated one element that appeared as a column in the final query, dramatically improved performance.

11

Note

The process of instantiating a view to make it ready for use is called *materialization*.

With such potential problems, views may seem dangerous. However, views are actually very useful. You just need to be aware of their pitfalls and know how to manage them properly. First, consider these advantages:

- You can present data from multiple tables, because the underlying query can contain joins.

- You can easily provide read-only access to data.

- You can look up values from tables using a view and then use IN to verify whether those values are relevant to another query.

- You can look up values using a view and use a join to the view within a query to include those values in a query.

As a practical example of when to use views, consider the new Health Care Finance Administration (HCFA) requirements for nursing homes. If a home falls into trouble, it can be fined. If it falls into trouble over more than one survey of its conditions, it can be fined immediately, without having an opportunity to correct the deficient condition. The interval for determining "No Opportunity to Correct" runs from the last standard survey forward, unless a serious deficiency occurred on the last standard survey. (Other types of surveys can take place between the standard surveys.) In a database of surveys, views allow you to conveniently locate the interval boundary points. In the first view, you simply select MAX(SurveyDate) where the survey type is "standard." In a second view, you can identify the preceding standard survey by selecting MAX(SurveyDate) where the survey type is "standard" and the survey date is older than the one identified in the first view. (Use a subquery to pull that date from the first view.) You can now easily locate the boundary points for determining whether a nursing home meets the "No Opportunity to Correct" criteria.

In using views, you need to follow a few practical precautions. You need to remember that views introduce an intervening layer between a table and the database user. This intervening layer provides protection for your tables; however, it can also rob you of performance. You should therefore observe these cautions:

● Keep the query that defines a view as simple as possible. If the query takes a long time to run, your view will take a long time to materialize before it can be used.

● Avoid views that use views that use views. Unfortunately, views that reference views are often very handy.

● Test and optimize views. Avoid the big surprises that can occur when you rush a slow-going view into production without testing.

● Combine views with bit fields in a table that can describe the results of a view where performance suffers. In creating a query that lists nursing homes that meet the "No Opportunity to Correct" criteria for a client, I used one query with four views. Because of the complexity of the views, the query took five minutes to return the data. I added a bit field to the facilities table for NOTC, converted the query that pulls data from the views to update this field, and scheduled the query to run overnight. The query for building the No Opportunity to Correct report became SELECT * FROM facilities WHERE NOTC = 1, and it ran very fast indeed.

Create the Query

As we have said, a view requires a query. The first step in creating a view is therefore to write a query. You can use a query tool like Query Analyzer to build the query, but your database may provide a specialized tool for creating the query behind a view. (SQL Server 2000 provides the tools shown in Figure 11-1.) In this tool, you can enter your query by hand, or, if you have experience with Microsoft's graphical query builder from your Access days, you can define the query graphically. You can run the query and see the results in a grid in the tool's lower pane. You can rapidly develop and test a single view using this tool.

11

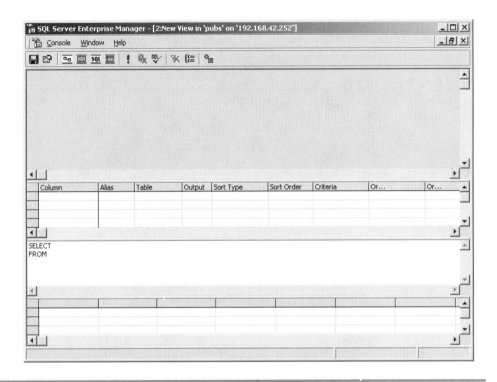

Figure 11-1 The View Builder in SQL Server 2000

There are a couple of cautions that attend using a graphical view builder, however. Pay attention to the following:

● SQL syntax may not be the same within the tool. Because your query is ultimately destined to be part of a CREATE VIEW statement, you may be surprised that you cannot use certain SQL elements. A semicolon to terminate your SQL statement, common in many implementations, may not be accepted in the tool.

● The SQL you write may not be the SQL you see. Many view-building tools optimize your SQL for you so that it runs more efficiently. Expect to see what you expressed as a WHERE condition being conflated into JOIN syntax as a part of the ON phrase, for example.

1-Minute Drill

- **What is perhaps the most common use of views?**
- **Why might syntax be different in a view-building tool?**
- **How do you control access to a view?**

Create the View

To create the view, use a CREATE VIEW statement. It has the following syntax:

```
CREATE VIEW tablename [(column1, column2, . . .)] AS query
    [WITH CHECK OPTION]
```

The CREATE VIEW statement looks a lot like INSERT INTO. You name the view that will result following the VIEW keyword. You can include a list of column names to use in the resulting table. If you do not include the names, the column names from the underlying table(s) will be used. The query is the SELECT query you have already created and tested.

The remaining syntax element applies only to views that you wish to be updatable. For a view to be updatable, you must grant update permission to it using the security scheme for your database. The view must also be based on one and only one table, because SQL does not allow updates across multiple tables. (Some databases allow the update of a view based on more than one table, as long as the columns updated come from only one table.) Assuming that your view is updatable, WITH CHECK OPTION forces any update to match the WHERE conditions in the query that defines the view.

Hint
You can drop a view using DROP VIEW *viewName*.

11

- **To protect data in tables from accidental alteration by database users**
- **The tool inserts whatever you write into a CREATE VIEW statement, and it may not check what you write for correct syntax before making the insertion. The tool also might optimize your SQL statements for faster execution.**
- **By granting permissions using your database's security scheme**

Suppose that we define a view in the following way:

```
CREATE VIEW StudentPortfolio AS SELECT * FROM portfolio WHERE StudentID
    IS NOT NULL
```

The view StudentPortfolio contains a list of records where StudentID has a value. If we make the view updatable, we can execute the following update:

```
UPDATE StudentPortfolio SET StudentID = NULL
```

This update will run and remove all records from the view. None of the records will meet the WHERE condition that defines the view. While this behavior might be desirable if we were processing the Done check box on a To Do list, it may not be the behavior we desire for our view. We may prefer to allow updates, but no updates that would remove a record from the view. Suppose we define the view in the following way:

```
CREATE VIEW StudentPortfolio AS SELECT * FROM portfolio WHERE StudentID
    IS NOT NULL WITH CHECK OPTION
```

When we try an update, SQL checks the update against the WHERE conditions in CREATE VIEW and issues an error if the WHERE conditions are violated. By using WITH CHECK OPTION, we have made certain that we cannot remove a record from the view by updating the view. You also cannot add a row that wouldn't be in the view, and you cannot update a record in the view in such a way as to make it no longer meet the criteria of a view.

> ## Hint
>
> You can execute INSERT statements against an updatable view.

CreateView.sql

Project 11-1: Create a View

A useful view in the Portfolio database would be a set of records that lists each student's name, each portfolio, and each portfolio's contents. We could easily get a list of a portfolio's contents using a query like the following:

```
SELECT * FROM TheView WHERE StudentID  = X AND PortfolioID = Y
```

Create the view that would allow this access.

Step-by-Step

1. Run the following CREATE VIEW statement in the Query Analyzer:

```
CREATE VIEW dbo.vwStudentPortfolioContents
AS
SELECT dbo.Student.Student_ID, dbo.Student.First_Name,
    dbo.Student.Last_Name, dbo.Subject_Matter.Subject_Matter_Name,
    dbo.Portfolio_Contents.Content_Path, dbo.Student.Active AS
    ActiveStudent, dbo.Portfolio.Active AS ActivePortfolio

FROM dbo.Student INNER JOIN dbo.Portfolio ON dbo.Student.Student_ID =
    dbo.Portfolio.Student_ID INNER JOIN dbo.Portfolio_Contents ON
    dbo.Portfolio.Portfolio_ID = dbo.Portfolio_Contents.Portfolio_ID
INNER
    JOIN dbo.Subject_Matter ON dbo.Portfolio.Subject_Matter_ID =
    dbo.Subject_Matter.Subject_Matter_ID

WHERE (dbo.Student.Active = 1) AND (dbo.Portfolio.Active = 1)
```

?—Ask the Expert

Question: If the main reason for using views is to prevent damage to data, why even allow updatable views?

Answer: That's a very good question to which there is no logical answer. It's just a feature of SQL. The standard wisdom is to let DBAs have direct access to tables, and to force those who need to consume data to use views so that an accidental ad hoc query does not go awry. Those who are creating data entry applications typically work directly with tables.

However, you may have a table with a set of records you want screened from view by someone who will insert data. Imagine a table that contains employee names and sensitive information about security clearances. You can define an updatable view that allows data entry for nonsensitive fields so that any clerk can enter this information. Only those with appropriate security clearances would be able to access the full table. Note that, if you

11

have a view that only shows the first two columns of a table with four columns, an update will fail if the two columns not in the view do not have defaults values defined, allow nulls, or support a system-supplied value of some kind. You will receive an error if none of these stipulations applies. You might also note that data entry applications for such settings should not allow the user to view any sensitive portion of a table. An updatable view affords protection against someone getting access to a query tool and exploring the database on their own. Such a view is just one more measure of protection. You typically cannot grant access to a table column by column (although some databases allow column-level permissions).

Question: **Are there any restrictions on the syntax elements used in views?**

Answer: Yes, there are some restrictions, and these will vary with the database you are using. CASE is typically disallowed. You may find that the number of joins is limited. Unions are commonly disallowed. Usually you discover these limitations at the exact moment their support would be most useful to you.

Project 11-2: Add Forms

`InsertNonCritical.vbp`

Let's continue our development of our administrative tool for the Portfolio database, our real-world example of using SQL. Even though we plan to have individual users register themselves to use the database and create their own portfolio records, administrators will also need to enter these records on occasion. In this exercise, we will add forms to allow the creation, update, and deletion of these records. While we will not be working with a view in this exercise, you will get lots of practice with embedded SQL statements.

Step-by-Step

1. Open DeleteMarked.vbp.

2. Save the project as InsertNonCritical.vbp.

3. Right-click the project in the Project Explorer, select Add from the menu, and choose to add a form.

4. Select DeletingData.frm in the Existing tab and click Open.

5. Right-click on DeletingData.frm and save it as InsertNonCritical.frm.

6. Change the form's Name property to frmInsertNonCritical.

7. Make the form look like this:

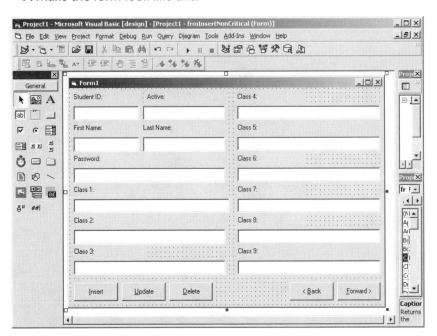

8. Make sure that you name each of the text boxes after its label. For example, txtStudentID, txtFName, txtClass1, and so on.

9. Add these lines to the General section of the form:

```
Option Explicit


'For the ADO connection
Dim mcnnGlobalDatabase As New ADODB.Connection
Dim mcmdGlobalDatabase As New ADODB.Command
Dim mrstGlobalDatabase As New ADODB.Recordset

Dim mcnnGlobalDatabase2 As New ADODB.Connection
Dim mcmdGlobalDatabase2 As New ADODB.Command
Dim mrstGlobalDatabase2 As New ADODB.Recordset
```

> **Create connection objects to handle lookups**

> **Create connection objects to manage the recordset presentation**

10. Make the form's load event look like this:

> **Connect to the database**

```
Private Sub Form_Load()
    With mcnnGlobalDatabase
        .ConnectionString = "Provider=SQLOLEDB.1;Persist Security
            Info=False;User ID=sa;Initial Catalog=Portfolio;Data
            Source=192.168.42.252;Command Timeout = 30;"
        .CursorLocation = adUseClient
        .Open
    End With

    With mcmdGlobalDatabase
        .ActiveConnection = mcnnGlobalDatabase
        .CommandType = adCmdText
        .CommandText = "select * from student"
    End With

    Set mrstGlobalDatabase = mcmdGlobalDatabase.Execute

    txtStudentID.Text
        =rstGlobalDatabase.Fields("Student_ID").Value
    txtActive.Text = mrstGlobalDatabase.Fields("Active").Value
    txtFName.Text = mrstGlobalDatabase.Fields("First_Name").Value
    txtLName.Text = mrstGlobalDatabase.Fields("Last_Name").Value
    txtPassword.Text =
        mrstGlobalDatabase.Fields("Password").Value

    With mcnnGlobalDatabase2
        .ConnectionString = "Provider=SQLOLEDB.1;Persist Security
            Info=False;User ID=sa;Initial Catalog=Portfolio;Data
            Source=192.168.42.252;Command Timeout = 30;"
        .CursorLocation = adUseClient
        .Open
```

> **Select the set of all students**

> **Display the current record**

> **Connect to the database**

```
End With

With mcmdGlobalDatabase2
    .ActiveConnection = mcnnGlobalDatabase2
    .CommandType = adCmdText
    .CommandText = "select * from Class_Student where
        Student_ID = " &
        mrstGlobalDatabase.Fields("Student_ID").Value
End With

Set mrstGlobalDatabase2 = mcmdGlobalDatabase2.Execute

mrstGlobalDatabase2.MoveFirst

If Not mrstGlobalDatabase2.EOF Then
    txtClass1.Text =
        mrstGlobalDatabase2.Fields("Class_ID").Value
    mrstGlobalDatabase2.MoveNext
End If
If Not mrstGlobalDatabase2.EOF Then
    txtClass2.Text =
        mrstGlobalDatabase2.Fields("Class_ID").Value
    mrstGlobalDatabase2.MoveNext
End If
If Not mrstGlobalDatabase2.EOF Then
    txtClass3.Text =
        mrstGlobalDatabase2.Fields("Class_ID").Value
    mrstGlobalDatabase2.MoveNext
End If
If Not mrstGlobalDatabase2.EOF Then
    txtClass4.Text =
        mrstGlobalDatabase2.Fields("Class_ID").Value
    mrstGlobalDatabase2.MoveNext
End If
If Not mrstGlobalDatabase2.EOF Then
    txtClass5.Text =
        mrstGlobalDatabase2.Fields("Class_ID").Value
    mrstGlobalDatabase2.MoveNext
End If
If Not mrstGlobalDatabase2.EOF Then
    txtClass6.Text =
        mrstGlobalDatabase2.Fields("Class_ID").Value
    mrstGlobalDatabase2.MoveNext
End If
If Not mrstGlobalDatabase2.EOF Then
    txtClass7.Text =
        mrstGlobalDatabase2.Fields("Class_ID").Value
    mrstGlobalDatabase2.MoveNext
End If
If Not mrstGlobalDatabase2.EOF Then
    txtClass8.Text =
        mrstGlobalDatabase2.Fields("Class_ID").Value
```

Lookup the class information for the student in the current record

Display the class information

11

```
            mrstGlobalDatabase2.MoveNext
        End If
        If Not mrstGlobalDatabase2.EOF Then
            txtClass9.Text =
                mrstGlobalDatabase2.Fields("Class_ID").Value
            mrstGlobalDatabase2.MoveNext
        End If
        End If
End Sub
```

11. Add this procedure to the form using Tools I Add Procedure:

```
Public Sub RefreshData()
    With mcmdGlobalDatabase
        .CommandType = adCmdText                    ◄─── Refresh the student recordset
        .CommandText = "select * from student"
    End With

    Set mrstGlobalDatabase = mcmdGlobalDatabase.Execute
                                                      Refresh the
                                                      display fields
    If Not (mrstGlobalDatabase.BOF And mrstGlobalDatabase.EOF) Then ↙
        txtStudentID.Text = mrstGlobalDatabase.Fields("Student_ID").Value
        txtActive.Text = mrstGlobalDatabase.Fields("Active").Value
        txtFName.Text = mrstGlobalDatabase.Fields("First_Name").Value
        txtLName.Text = mrstGlobalDatabase.Fields("Last_Name").Value
        txtPassword.Text = mrstGlobalDatabase.Fields("Password").Value

        With mcmdGlobalDatabase2                     ◄─── Refresh class information
            .CommandType = adCmdText
            .CommandText = "select * from Class_Student where Student_ID =
                " & mrstGlobalDatabase.Fields("Student_ID").Value
        End With

        Set mrstGlobalDatabase2 = mcmdGlobalDatabase2.Execute

        mrstGlobalDatabase2.MoveFirst               ◄─── Refresh class display fields

        If Not mrstGlobalDatabase2.EOF Then
            txtClass1.Text = mrstGlobalDatabase2.Fields("Class_ID").Value
            mrstGlobalDatabase2.MoveNext
        End If
        If Not mrstGlobalDatabase2.EOF Then
            txtClass2.Text = mrstGlobalDatabase2.Fields("Class_ID").Value
```

```
                mrstGlobalDatabase2.MoveNext
            End If
            If Not mrstGlobalDatabase2.EOF Then
                txtClass3.Text = mrstGlobalDatabase2.Fields("Class_ID").Value
                mrstGlobalDatabase2.MoveNext
            End If
            If Not mrstGlobalDatabase2.EOF Then
                txtClass4.Text = mrstGlobalDatabase2.Fields("Class_ID").Value
                mrstGlobalDatabase2.MoveNext
            End If
            If Not mrstGlobalDatabase2.EOF Then
                txtClass5.Text = mrstGlobalDatabase2.Fields("Class_ID").Value
                mrstGlobalDatabase2.MoveNext
            End If
            If Not mrstGlobalDatabase2.EOF Then
                txtClass6.Text = mrstGlobalDatabase2.Fields("Class_ID").Value
                mrstGlobalDatabase2.MoveNext
            End If
            If Not mrstGlobalDatabase2.EOF Then
                txtClass7.Text = mrstGlobalDatabase2.Fields("Class_ID").Value
                mrstGlobalDatabase2.MoveNext
            End If
            If Not mrstGlobalDatabase2.EOF Then
                txtClass8.Text = mrstGlobalDatabase2.Fields("Class_ID").Value
                mrstGlobalDatabase2.MoveNext
            End If
            If Not mrstGlobalDatabase2.EOF Then
                txtClass9.Text = mrstGlobalDatabase2.Fields("Class_ID").Value
                mrstGlobalDatabase2.MoveNext
            End If
        End If
    End If

End Sub
```

12. Insert these lines into the Update button's click event:

```
Private Sub cmdUpdate_Click()
    'For the ADO connection
    Dim cnnMyDatabase As New ADODB.Connection
    Dim cmdMyDatabase As New ADODB.Command
    Dim rstMyDatabase As New ADODB.Recordset

    If txtStudentID <> "" Then
```

11

```
With cnnMyDatabase
    .ConnectionString = "Provider=SQLOLEDB.1;Persist Security
    Info=False;User ID=sa;Initial Catalog=Portfolio;Data
        Source=192.168.42.252;Command Timeout = 30;"
    .Open
End With

With cmdMyDatabase
    .ActiveConnection = cnnMyDatabase
    .CommandType = adCmdText
    .CommandText = "update Student set Student_ID = " & _
        txtStudentID.Text & _
        ", First_Name = '" & txtFName.Text & "', _
        Last_Name = '" & _
        txtLName.Text & _
        "', Password = '" & txtPassword.Text & "', _
        Active = " & _
        txtActive.Text & " where Student_ID = " &
        txtStudentID.Text
End With

Set rstMyDatabase = cmdMyDatabase.Execute

cmdMyDatabase.CommandText = "delete from Class_Student where
    Student_ID = " & txtStudentID.Text

Set rstMyDatabase = cmdMyDatabase.Execute

If txtClass1.Text <> "" Then
    cmdMyDatabase.CommandText = "insert into Class_Student
        (Class_ID, Student_ID) " & _
        "values((select Class_ID from Class where _
        Class_Name = '" & _
        txtClass1.Text & "'), " & txtStudentID.Text & ")"
    Set rstMyDatabase = cmdMyDatabase.Execute
End If
If txtClass2.Text <> "" Then
    cmdMyDatabase.CommandText = "insert into Class_Student
        (Class_ID, Student_ID) " & _
        "values((select Class_ID from Class where _
        Class_Name = '" & _
        txtClass2.Text & "'), " & txtStudentID.Text & ")"
```

Update student information

Delete class information for this student

Insert class information for this student

```
        Set rstMyDatabase = cmdMyDatabase.Execute
    End If
    If txtClass3.Text <> "" Then
        cmdMyDatabase.CommandText = "insert into Class_Student
            (Class_ID, Student_ID) " & _
            "values((select Class_ID from Class where _
            Class_Name = '" & _
            txtClass3.Text & "'), " & txtStudentID.Text & ")"
        Set rstMyDatabase = cmdMyDatabase.Execute
    End If
    If txtClass4.Text <> "" Then
        cmdMyDatabase.CommandText = "insert into Class_Student
            (Class_ID, Student_ID) " & _
            "values((select Class_ID from Class where _
            Class_Name = '" & _
            txtClass4.Text & "'), " & txtStudentID.Text & ")"
        Set rstMyDatabase = cmdMyDatabase.Execute
    End If
    If txtClass5.Text <> "" Then
        cmdMyDatabase.CommandText = "insert into Class_Student
            (Class_ID, Student_ID) " & _
            "values((select Class_ID from Class where _
            Class_Name = '" & _
            txtClass5.Text & "'), " & txtStudentID.Text & ")"
        Set rstMyDatabase = cmdMyDatabase.Execute
    End If
    If txtClass6.Text <> "" Then
        cmdMyDatabase.CommandText = "insert into Class_Student
            (Class_ID, Student_ID) " & _
            "values((select Class_ID from Class where _
             Class_Name = '" & _
            txtClass6.Text & "'), " & txtStudentID.Text & ")"
        Set rstMyDatabase = cmdMyDatabase.Execute
    End If
    If txtClass7.Text <> "" Then
        cmdMyDatabase.CommandText = "insert into Class_Student
            (Class_ID, Student_ID) " & _
            "values((select Class_ID from Class where _
            Class_Name = '" & _
            txtClass7.Text & "'), " & txtStudentID.Text & ")"
        Set rstMyDatabase = cmdMyDatabase.Execute
    End If
    If txtClass8.Text <> "" Then
```

11

```
              cmdMyDatabase.CommandText = "insert into Class_Student
                  (Class_ID, Student_ID) " & _
                  "values((select Class_ID from Class where _
                  Class_Name = '" & _
                  txtClass8.Text & "'), " & txtStudentID.Text & ")"
              Set rstMyDatabase = cmdMyDatabase.Execute
          End If
          If txtClass9.Text <> "" Then
              cmdMyDatabase.CommandText = "insert into Class_Student
                  (Class_ID, Student_ID) " & _
                  "values((select Class_ID from Class where _
                  Class_Name = '" & _
                  txtClass9.Text & "'), " & txtStudentID.Text & ")"
              Set rstMyDatabase = cmdMyDatabase.Execute
          End If

          RefreshData

      Else
          MsgBox "No data to update!"
      End If

End Sub
```

13. Insert these lines into the Insert button's click event:

```
Private Sub cmdInsert_Click()

    'For the ADO connection
    Dim cnnMyDatabase As New ADODB.Connection
    Dim cmdMyDatabase As New ADODB.Command
    Dim rstMyDatabase As New ADODB.Recordset


    If txtStudentID <> "" Then
        With cnnMyDatabase
            .ConnectionString = "Provider=SQLOLEDB.1;Persist Security
```

```
                    Info=False;User ID=sa;Initial Catalog=Portfolio;Data
                    Source=192.168.42.252;Command Timeout = 30;"
            .Open
    End With

    With cmdMyDatabase
            .ActiveConnection = cnnMyDatabase         ┌─────────────────────────────┐
            .CommandType = adCmdText                  │ Insert student information   │
            .CommandText = "insert into Student (Student_ID, _
                First_Name,
                Last_Name, Password, Active) " & _
                "values(" & txtStudentID.Text & ", '" & _
                 txtFName.Text & "', '" & txtLName.Text & _
                "', '" & txtPassword.Text & "', " & _
                txtActive.Text & ")"
    End With

    Set rstMyDatabase = cmdMyDatabase.Execute     ┌──────────────────────────────┐
                                                  │ Insert class information      │
                                                  │ for the new student           │
    If txtClass1.Text <> "" Then                  └──────────────────────────────┘
        cmdMyDatabase.CommandText = "insert into Class_Student
            (Class_ID, Student_ID) " & _
            "values((select Class_ID from Class where _
             Class_Name = '" & _
            txtClass1.Text & "'), " & txtStudentID.Text & ")"
        Set rstMyDatabase = cmdMyDatabase.Execute
    End If
    If txtClass2.Text <> "" Then
        cmdMyDatabase.CommandText = "insert into Class_Student
            (Class_ID, Student_ID) " & _
            "values((select Class_ID from Class where _
            Class_Name = '" & _
            txtClass2.Text & "'), " & txtStudentID.Text & ")"
        Set rstMyDatabase = cmdMyDatabase.Execute
    End If
    If txtClass3.Text <> "" Then
        cmdMyDatabase.CommandText = "insert into Class_Student
            (Class_ID, Student_ID) " & _
            "values((select Class_ID from Class where _
```

11

```
                Class_Name = '" & _
                txtClass3.Text & "'), " & txtStudentID.Text & ")"
            Set rstMyDatabase = cmdMyDatabase.Execute
      End If
      If txtClass4.Text <> "" Then
            cmdMyDatabase.CommandText = "insert into Class_Student
                (Class_ID, Student_ID) " & _
                "values((select Class_ID from Class where _
                Class_Name = '" & _
                txtClass4.Text & "'), " & txtStudentID.Text & ")"
            Set rstMyDatabase = cmdMyDatabase.Execute
      End If
      If txtClass5.Text <> "" Then
            cmdMyDatabase.CommandText = "insert into Class_Student
                (Class_ID, Student_ID) " & _
                "values((select Class_ID from Class where
                Class_Name = '" & _
                txtClass5.Text & "'), " & txtStudentID.Text & ")"
            Set rstMyDatabase = cmdMyDatabase.Execute
      End If
      If txtClass6.Text <> "" Then
            cmdMyDatabase.CommandText = "insert into Class_Student
                (Class_ID, Student_ID) " & _
                "values((select Class_ID from Class where _
                Class_Name = '" & _
                txtClass6.Text & "'), " & txtStudentID.Text & ")"
            Set rstMyDatabase = cmdMyDatabase.Execute
      End If
      If txtClass7.Text <> "" Then
            cmdMyDatabase.CommandText = "insert into Class_Student
                (Class_ID, Student_ID) " & _
                "values((select Class_ID from Class where _
                Class_Name = '" & _
                txtClass7.Text & "'), " & txtStudentID.Text & ")"
            Set rstMyDatabase = cmdMyDatabase.Execute
      End If
      If txtClass8.Text <> "" Then
            cmdMyDatabase.CommandText = "insert into Class_Student
                (Class_ID, Student_ID) " & _
                "values((select Class_ID from Class where _
```

```
                Class_Name = '" & _
          ·     txtClass8.Text & "'), " & txtStudentID.Text & ")"
            Set rstMyDatabase = cmdMyDatabase.Execute
        End If
        If txtClass9.Text <> "" Then
            cmdMyDatabase.CommandText = "insert into Class_Student
                (Class_ID, Student_ID) " & _
                "values((select Class_ID from Class where _
                Class_Name = '" & _
                txtClass9.Text & "'), " & txtStudentID.Text & ")"
            Set rstMyDatabase = cmdMyDatabase.Execute
        End If


        RefreshData
    Else
        MsgBox "No data to insert!"
    End If
End Sub
```

14. Insert these lines into the Delete button's click event:

```
Private Sub cmdDelete_Click()
    'For the ADO connection
    Dim cnnMyDatabase As New ADODB.Connection
    Dim cmdMyDatabase As New ADODB.Command
    Dim rstMyDatabase As New ADODB.Recordset

    If txtStudentID <> "" Then
        With cnnMyDatabase
            .ConnectionString = "Provider=SQLOLEDB.1;Persist Security
                Info=False;User ID=sa;Initial Catalog=Portfolio;Data
                Source=192.168.42.252;Command Timeout = 30;"
            .Open
        End With

        With cmdMyDatabase
            .ActiveConnection = cnnMyDatabase
            .CommandType = adCmdText                     ┌─ Delete class information
            .CommandText = "delete from Class_Student " & _
```

11

```
                    "where Student_ID = " & txtStudentID.Text
         End With
```

┌──────────────────┐
│ **Delete student** │
│ **information**   │
└──────────────────┘

```
         Set rstMyDatabase = cmdMyDatabase.Execute

         cmdMyDatabase.CommandText = "delete from Student " & _
             "where Student_ID = " & txtStudentID.Text

         RefreshData
    Else
         MsgBox "No record to delete!"
    End If

End Sub
```

15. Insert these lines into the Forward button's click event:

```
Private Sub cmdForward_Click()
    If Not (mrstGlobalDatabase.BOF And mrstGlobalDatabase.EOF) Then
         mrstGlobalDatabase.MoveNext
```

┌─────────────────────────────────┐
│ **Move to the next record and** │
│ **redisplay student information** │
└─────────────────────────────────┘

```
         txtStudentID.Text = _
             mrstGlobalDatabase.Fields("Student_ID").Value
         txtActive.Text = mrstGlobalDatabase.Fields("Active").Value
         txtFName.Text = mrstGlobalDatabase.Fields("First_Name").Value
         txtLName.Text = mrstGlobalDatabase.Fields("Last_Name").Value
          txtPassword.Text = _
             mrstGlobalDatabase.Fields("Password").Value

         mcmdGlobalDatabase2.CommandText = "select * from " _
             "Class_Student " & _
             where Student_ID = " & _
             mrstGlobalDatabase.Fields("Student_ID").Value
```

┌──┐
│ **Get class information for this record** │
└──┘

```
         Set mrstGlobalDatabase2 = mcmdGlobalDatabase2.Execute

         mrstGlobalDatabase2.MoveFirst
```

┌────────────────────┐
│ **Display the class** │
│ **information**   │
└────────────────────┘

```
         If Not mrstGlobalDatabase2.EOF Then
             txtClass1.Text = _
             mrstGlobalDatabase2.Fields("Class_ID").Value
             mrstGlobalDatabase2.MoveNext
         End If
         If Not mrstGlobalDatabase2.EOF Then
             txtClass2.Text = _
             mrstGlobalDatabase2.Fields("Class_ID").Value
             mrstGlobalDatabase2.MoveNext
         End If
```

```
            If Not mrstGlobalDatabase2.EOF Then
                txtClass3.Text = _
                mrstGlobalDatabase2.Fields("Class_ID").Value
                mrstGlobalDatabase2.MoveNext
            End If
            If Not mrstGlobalDatabase2.EOF Then
                txtClass4.Text = _
                mrstGlobalDatabase2.Fields("Class_ID").Value
                mrstGlobalDatabase2.MoveNext
            End If
            If Not mrstGlobalDatabase2.EOF Then
                txtClass5.Text = _
                 mrstGlobalDatabase2.Fields("Class_ID").Value
                mrstGlobalDatabase2.MoveNext
            End If
            If Not mrstGlobalDatabase2.EOF Then
                txtClass6.Text = _
                 mrstGlobalDatabase2.Fields("Class_ID").Value
                mrstGlobalDatabase2.MoveNext
            End If
            If Not mrstGlobalDatabase2.EOF Then
                txtClass7.Text = _
                mrstGlobalDatabase2.Fields("Class_ID").Value
                mrstGlobalDatabase2.MoveNext
            End If
            If Not mrstGlobalDatabase2.EOF Then
                txtClass8.Text = _
                mrstGlobalDatabase2.Fields("Class_ID").Value
                mrstGlobalDatabase2.MoveNext
            End If
            If Not mrstGlobalDatabase2.EOF Then
                txtClass9.Text = _
                 mrstGlobalDatabase2.Fields("Class_ID").Value
                mrstGlobalDatabase2.MoveNext
            End If
        End If
End Sub
```

11

16. Insert these lines into the Back button's click event:

```
Private Sub cmdBack_Click()
    If Not (mrstGlobalDatabase.BOF And mrstGlobalDatabase.EOF) Then
        mrstGlobalDatabase.MovePrevious    ◄── Move to the previous record and
                                               display student information
        txtStudentID.Text =
mrstGlobalDatabase.Fields("Student_ID").Value
        txtActive.Text = mrstGlobalDatabase.Fields("Active").Value
```

```
txtFName.Text = mrstGlobalDatabase.Fields("First_Name").Value
txtLName.Text = mrstGlobalDatabase.Fields("Last_Name").Value
txtPassword.Text = mrstGlobalDatabase.Fields("Password").Value

mcmdGlobalDatabase2.CommandText = "select * " & _
    from Class_Student where Student_ID = " & _
    mrstGlobalDatabase.Fields("Student_ID").Value
```

**Get class
information
for this
record**

```
Set mrstGlobalDatabase2 = mcmdGlobalDatabase2.Execute

mrstGlobalDatabase2.MoveFirst
```

**Display the class
information**

```
If Not mrstGlobalDatabase2.EOF Then
    txtClass1.Text = _
    mrstGlobalDatabase2.Fields("Class_ID").Value
    mrstGlobalDatabase2.MoveNext
End If
If Not mrstGlobalDatabase2.EOF Then
    txtClass2.Text = _
    mrstGlobalDatabase2.Fields("Class_ID").Value
    mrstGlobalDatabase2.MoveNext
End If
If Not mrstGlobalDatabase2.EOF Then
    txtClass3.Text = _
    mrstGlobalDatabase2.Fields("Class_ID").Value
    mrstGlobalDatabase2.MoveNext
End If
If Not mrstGlobalDatabase2.EOF Then
    txtClass4.Text = _
     mrstGlobalDatabase2.Fields("Class_ID").Value
    mrstGlobalDatabase2.MoveNext
End If
If Not mrstGlobalDatabase2.EOF Then
    txtClass5.Text = _
    mrstGlobalDatabase2.Fields("Class_ID").Value
    mrstGlobalDatabase2.MoveNext
End If
If Not mrstGlobalDatabase2.EOF Then
    txtClass6.Text = _
    mrstGlobalDatabase2.Fields("Class_ID").Value
    mrstGlobalDatabase2.MoveNext
End If
If Not mrstGlobalDatabase2.EOF Then
    txtClass7.Text = _
     mrstGlobalDatabase2.Fields("Class_ID").Value
    mrstGlobalDatabase2.MoveNext
End If
If Not mrstGlobalDatabase2.EOF Then
    txtClass8.Text = _
    mrstGlobalDatabase2.Fields("Class_ID").Value
    mrstGlobalDatabase2.MoveNext
```

```
        End If
        If Not mrstGlobalDatabase2.EOF Then
            txtClass9.Text = _
            mrstGlobalDatabase2.Fields("Class_ID").Value
            mrstGlobalDatabase2.MoveNext
        End If
    End If
End Sub
```

17. Add a button that shows the form.

18. Advanced: Copy this form and modify it to add teachers to the Teacher table and the Class_Teacher table.

☑ Mastery Check

1. Give the purpose of a view.

2. Why might you use an updatable view?

3. In an updatable view, what does using WITH CHECK OPTION accomplish?

4. Can you use a UNION in a view?

5. In the SQL Server view builder, what happens if you end your query with a semicolon?

6. Can you use a CASE in a view?

7. What happens if you do not provide a column list in a view?

8. How many subqueries can you use in a view?

9. Is it wise to create views that reference other views?

10. What restriction characterizes updatable views?

Module 12

Building Stored Procedures

Goals

- Understand the role of stored procedures
- Learn how to create a stored procedure
- Learn how to call a stored procedure
- Understand how to use the results returned by a stored procedure

Up to this point, when we talked about using a SQL statement to return data from our database, we have spoken about writing a SELECT statement. That SELECT statement goes into a command object, which is attached to a connection object, and the execution of the command attached to the connection is returned into a recordset object. We have not thought much about how the way we have framed these steps affects the speed and efficiency of our interaction with the database. Let's take a look at some of the issues involved.

To begin, the style of interaction we have been advocating is completely under our control. We work at our client machines, the connection is defined and processed on our client machine, the command is created and processed on our client machine, and the recordset is manipulated on our client machine. Our client computer, therefore, determines much about how efficient our interaction with the database happens to be. For example, the query tool we use to run the query against the database must compile the query. Any query optimization that takes place must happen within our query tool. If our tool is good at optimization, so much the better. If our query tool is not so good at optimization, then our query tool becomes a bottleneck, possibly the slowest link in the set of links and steps that ultimately returns the data to us.

Retaining control of the query process at the client machine can introduce other kinds of speed bottlenecks. Much of the work is done by the client CPU, which is much more likely to be slow than a server CPU. Furthermore, servers are likely to have multiple CPUs to share the processing effort, while client computers typically do not. The database software running on the server is more likely than the client software to have a sophisticated compiler that will be more efficient than the client's SQL compiler. Server query optimization routines are tied directly to the type of hardware available on the server, and they are always more efficient than any type of optimization undertaken client side by a client's compiler. As a result, the server is likely to be able to compile and execute queries more efficiently than the client computer ever can. In addition, when a server executes a stored procedure, it caches the execution plan for that procedure. (The execution plan is the fully optimized form of the query.) If you reuse the stored procedure before its execution plan ages out of the cache, you do not need to compile and optimize the query again. You just reuse the execution plan already prepared.

Note

In discussing the efficiency of choosing the location for processing, we have to note that much depends on the client software and the database you are using. Some client development systems, notably Gupta's SQL Windows development environment, allow compiling a SQL statement at the client. Others pass the statement on to the server for compilation and optimization. Final query optimization always takes place at the server, but some clients may be able to undertake some optimization themselves.

If you are beginning to wonder whether we are trying to make the case that the database server should do as much processing of our queries as possible, you are right. But there are many more reasons for allowing the server to handle queries than just the possible improvements in database performance and client program performance. Consider the effort it takes to maintain queries. As we build the portfolio program, we are building a set of queries that we know we will use over and over again. Any client that accesses the database will use these procedures, and these clients will be spread throughout the school district. Any given school is likely to have at least 30 workstations that access the database. Every principal's office is going to have one as well. What if we need to add a column to a table to accommodate the special needs of a district two years after installation of the system? If our queries reside in the client program, we have to redistribute the client to all of the computers where it is installed. This is an arduous task. If we had the queries relating to that table on the database server only, we would simply change the query in one place and avoid redistribution of the client program.

In addition to simplifying query maintenance, storing queries at the server also helps with intellectual property issues. Any business invests thousands of work hours in devising appropriate procedures for operating the company. Some of these procedures are logistical, as in determining the cheapest method of delivering 18 training PCs to a training site. Others are mathematical, as in choosing the means of calculating interest rates on overdue accounts. Others are proprietary, as in selecting the method of storing portfolio materials effectively, and retrieving them efficiently. All of these types of procedures collectively can be called business rules. Many of them will be considered trade secrets, something you really would prefer that your competitors not understand. You want

12

to capitalize on your business rules to remain ahead of your competitors. Keeping as many such rules as practicable secure on your server in SQL queries allows you to carry out your business without divulging how you do business. Clients can get the results of your proprietary way of doing business when they interact with your database server. They don't have to know how you tracked their package from your shipping point to their doorstep and allowed them to watch it move every step of the way.

Query procedures stored at the database server are called *stored procedures*. Stored procedures can easily be invoked by any client using built-in features of SQL and SQL databases. The average database program consists of a client that has connection objects that link to the database and command objects that contain calls to stored procedures. The general trend in database programming is to lend out the client program as much as possible, and to rely on the database server to undertake much of the processing traditionally associated with the computer program that runs on your PC.

Editing the Procedure

We are going to begin in this module by building straightforward, simple stored procedures. In the next three modules, we are going to elaborate on building stored procedures and show you how to make them much more complex. You will find throughout this exploration of what you can do in stored procedures that you can accomplish a lot of programming in SQL rather than in the procedural or object-oriented language you use to build your client program.

Let's begin by selecting one of the queries we have already created for our portfolio program. For the time being, we will focus on SELECT statements. Here is the procedure we used to get the school recordset:

```
SELECT * FROM school
```

You will find this SQL statement in the properties for the data control on frmSchools.

This SQL statement would do well as a stored procedure. It returns every column and every row from the School table. However, for use as a stored procedure, this query should be a little more explicit. When you come back to maintain this query in the future, the last thing you want is to wonder what * means. Is that three columns, four columns, or what? In addition, you want to lay the query out using white space so that it is readable. You want to be able to locate the columns returned easily, as well as the syntax elements that appear. Figure 12-1 shows a common way to lay out stored procedures. Note the use of capitals for the SQL keywords, vertical lists for the list of columns, and the isolation of keywords to the left sides of lines. This style makes dealing with stored procedures easier in any database.

Here is the properly formatted code for the stored procedure that will select a recordset of schools from the database:

```
SELECT School_ID,
       School_Name,
       Active
FROM School
```

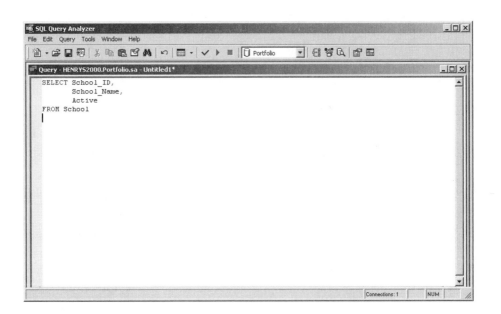

Figure 12-1   Laying out the stored procedure code in Query Analyzer

12

Using tools like Query Analyzer, you can develop and test queries for stored procedures easily. We need to emphasize a couple of points about such tools. First, almost all of them support color coding of SQL statements. Keywords appear in blue, strings in red, functions in purple, and so on. Because of this color coding, you may not want to follow a formatting style, because the color coding easily allows you to spot the syntax elements when reading the query. Resist this temptation. About the time you rely on the color coding, you will have to switch to an editor that does not support it. In addition, the redundancy of color coding and formatting helps tremendously to show the nature of the statement. A misalignment in the code can be a glaring clue, along with the color, that you have omitted a word, a parenthesis, or something similar.

Second, speed counts in developing queries. As you run your queries, watch the execution times in the lower-left corner of the window. You want your queries to return quickly. When they don't, you need to think of ways to improve the return time. Try an alternative way of stating the query in SQL. (We will look at some such methods as we work on stored procedures.) Try using a subquery rather than a view of the values the query depends on. Try to find ways to offload some of the query processing to a stored procedure that is scheduled to run overnight. Do what it takes to keep response time as low as possible.

Using Create Procedure

Now that we have our query, we need to make it into a stored procedure. The statement for doing so is CREATE PROCEDURE, and it has the following basic syntax:

```
CREATE PROCEDURE name[;int_number] AS sql_query
```

Name stands for the procedure name. If you include the semicolon and an integer, you are creating a group of stored procedures that have the same root name and that are uniquely distinguished by the number attached to them. A series of order entry procedures might be named OrderEntry;1, OrderEntry;2, and OrderEntry;3, for example. This naming convention does not allow you to name the procedures in self-documenting ways, but it does allow you to drop all the order entry procedures at once by using only the root name in the DROP statement. *Sql_query* is, of course, the query we have just edited.

Our CREATE PROCEDURE statement for the stored procedure we are working on looks like this:

```
CREATE PROCEDURE selFrmSchoolAdodc1

AS

SELECT School_ID,
       School_Name,
       Active
FROM School
```

Note the naming convention we used. The first three lowercase characters identify the verb used in the query. We know this is a SELECT query when we look at the name. The next three characters identify the type of programming element this query is associated with. Since the query is part of a form, the abbreviation Frm is used. The next few characters in the query identify the name of the programming element related to the query. If we had to trace this query back to our program, we would know immediately to look at frmSchool. The final element in the query is the name of the control or procedure in which the query is used.

Hint

This naming convention will not work for every program. For example, when queries are related to a set of reports, it is common practice to use the name of the report in the stored procedure name. Once you know the name of the report, you should be able to rely on other naming conventions to locate the code that relates to building the report.

You may be thinking that names could get awfully long using this convention. This statement is true. However, the typing of a few characters while creating the program can save endless headaches later in the life cycle of a program. It is frightening to look at a long list of stored procedures that have to be changed and to have no idea how to find them in the program code. Type those characters now. You will appreciate having done so later.

12

Hint

When more than one program accesses a database, it is useful to append a program identifier to stored procedure names. You can easily tell which program's code you need to examine if you do so.

We have one more detail to note. If you examine the stored procedure we just created by right-clicking it in the Enterprise Manager and examining its properties, you will see this SQL code:

```
CREATE PROCEDURE selFrmSchoolAdodc1

AS

SELECT School_ID,
       School_Name,
       Active
FROM School

GO
```

Note the GO statement. This statement signals that the batch of statements preceding it (as far back as the last GO or the beginning of the code, whichever applies) should execute *now*. Think of GO as a marker that initiates execution. SQL Server 2000 appends this statement for you when you create the procedure. Note, however, that using GO in stored procedures is not supported by all SQL databases. You may find that it works at the end of the stored procedure, but that you receive syntax errors if you use it elsewhere.

Note

The Keyword GO identifies the termination of a batch. A batch is a statement or statements that are submitted to the compiler. Their syntax is checked together. It is essentially a network round trip from the client delivering this set of statements for execution and returning to collect the next batch of statements.

1-Minute Drill

- **Why use a special statement layout when creating stored procedures?**

- **What gives a stored procedure a speed advantage?**

- **What do you sacrifice when you use a number in a query name?**

Hint
To drop a procedure, use DROP PROCEDURE *procedureName*.

StoredSelects.sql

Project 12-1: Convert Queries

Now that we have examined how to convert a select query to a stored procedure, it is time to convert all of the queries we have used so far to stored procedures. We need to find all the SELECT queries in the program and convert them. Take the following steps.

Step-by-Step

1. Check through the portfolio administration program to find all the SELECT queries.

2. Edit these queries in the Query Analyzer to make them proper stored procedures.

3. Add the CREATE PROCEDURE statement at the head of each query.

4. Run the statement to create the stored procedure.

- To improve readability of the code and your ability to recognize syntax errors.
- Stored procedures run on the server, which is typically faster and better optimized for compiling queries. The execution plan for the stored procedure also gets cached in memory, so that reuse before the plan ages out of the cache means that the procedure need not be compiled and optimized again.
- You cannot give each query a self-documenting name.

12

Calling the Procedure

To use a stored procedure, you have to be able to call it. You need a means of informing the server that you wish to use one of its procedures and that you would like it to return the results to you. Exactly how you so inform the server and receive the results depends on the context you are in.

If you are in a query tool, the tool itself will handle receiving the results of the recordset. You need only use a statement like this to ask the server to execute a stored procedure for you:

```
EXEC selFrmSchoolAdodc1
```

The EXEC statement asks the server to execute the procedure and to return the results to the program that issued the EXEC. In the Query Analyzer, you see the results of the query in the lower pane of your connection window.

If, however, you want to return the results to a program, you need a means of catching the results. If you are using a data control, the data control itself will set up the objects it needs to collect the recordset. You simply need to place the EXEC statement in its RecordSource property. If you are using ADO objects or similar objects, your command object can issue the EXEC and receive the results. The EXEC statement goes into the command object's CommandText property. You need to assign what the command object returns to a recordset object so that you can use the results. This action happens when you execute the command object, as in the following statement:

```
Set rstRecordset = cmdSQLStatement.Execute
```

Using the Results

You can use the results of a stored procedure exactly as you can use any recordset. Once the recordset returns, it behaves the same way as any other recordset. Here are some of your options in using the recordset:

- Viewing it in a tool like the Query Analyzer

- Assigning the recordset to the Recordset property of a data control

- Assigning the values associated with the current record to a set of controls that will display the data

- Creating buttons that will allow you to move forward and backward within the recordset and update the values of the controls that display the current record

- Attaching the recordset to a grid control that accepts a recordset as a property to allow display of the records

We have already demonstrated many of these options in the programming exercises. The main point is that once you have the recordset in hand, it behaves the same way. From your point of view as a consumer of the returned data, which computer actually crunches the query makes absolutely no difference. You see the same thing at your end.

Ask the Expert

Question: Do you really need the GO at the end of a stored procedure?

Answer: No, not really, for most databases. A stored procedure without the GO will probably run just fine. With some databases, you may actually receive an error if you try to use it instead of letting the database terminate the procedure for you.

12

Question: I have a friend who says I should use RETURN instead of GO.

Answer: You can use RETURN instead of GO to end a stored procedure. When SQL encounters RETURN in the flow of execution, it stops executing SQL code. Any statements after RETURN in the procedure will not execute. RETURN ends execution of the stored procedure, no matter whether you intended for other logic to apply.

Because of this behavior, GO is a somewhat more benign ending than RETURN. GO tells the database how many statements to execute in the batch of statements, those statements execute with the logic you embedded in them, and then the procedure ends. If you misplace a RETURN, thinking that it will act like GO, you may encounter some unexpected results.

RETURN does, however, cause the procedure to send a value back to the calling program, whatever the calling program may be written in and wherever the calling program may reside. If no value follows RETURN on the same line, the value 0 is passed back to the calling program. You want to use RETURN instead of GO if you need a value to pass back to the caller.

StoredProcs.vbp

Project 12-2: Convert Queries to Stored Procedures

In this programming exercise, we are going to convert our SELECT queries to stored procedures. Now that the procedures are loaded into the database, we can invoke them using EXEC. Take the following steps.

Step-by-Step

1. Search the portfolio administration program for SELECT.

2. For each SELECT you find, convert the command text to an EXEC of the correct stored procedure. (Two procedures must wait until Module 13.)

3. Review all data controls and their properties.

4. Where a data control uses a SELECT, convert it to an EXEC of the appropriate stored procedure.

☑ Mastery Check

1. Give the purpose of a stored procedure.

2. Under what circumstances might it be preferable to execute as much SQL processing on the client side as possible?

3. What SQL statement cannot be used in a stored procedure?

4. With what tools should you create the query for the stored procedure?

5. What SQL statement actually creates a stored procedure?

6. What do you gain if you include numbers in stored procedure names?

7. Is GO always preferred over RETURN to end a stored procedure?

8. How do you invoke a stored procedure?

9. How should you name stored procedures?

10. What is the white space used for in laying out a stored procedure in the editor?

12

Module 13

Programming in Stored Procedures

Goals

- Understand how to use variables
- Learn how to use flow control
- Understand the use of return values
- Learn how to raise errors

Having created stored procedures that implement basic SQL statements, you know how to call a server-side procedure that can insert, update, delete, or select data. In this module, we want to extend your knowledge of stored procedures to add capabilities. The real power of stored procedures goes beyond just inserting, updating, deleting, or selecting. SQL contains some powerful and practical programming capabilities. Because of these capabilities, you can create sophisticated database maintenance programs that you can call from the client and that will run on the server.

Consider this example. You are contracting with a company that needs to extract financial information from its database three times per day. In the morning, the company wants to see the overnight totals for sales from the previous day. At midday, they want to see the same totals computed for the current day. At the close of business, they would like to see total sales to that point during the day and a comparison to the previous day's sales to the same point in time. (Remember, in the world of e-commerce, sales go on for 24 hours.) You can obviously write three stored procedures and write a client program that will invoke the appropriate stored procedure at the correct time. This solution is the sort of solution we have prepared you to create at this point.

Consider the problems associated with such a solution, however. What guarantee do you have that the client PC will be up and running at the appropriate times? How confident are you of the scheduling software you run on the client PC? What happens if a user closes the scheduler, your client program, or both? Are you certain that the time at the client PC will always be synchronized properly with the time at the server? What happens if the network connection between the client and the server drops unexpectedly?

If you suspect that we are building the case for putting all of the logic associated with this solution on the server, you have indeed caught our drift. When you think of client/server interactions, either two-tiered or *n*-tiered, you have to remember what clients are good for and what servers are good for. Clients are good for interacting with users, for retrieving information, and for allowing the user to manipulate that information. Client PCs are not always up, because users have access to the power switch. Programs are not guaranteed to be running on the client, because users can exit the programs. When you think of clients, you want to think in terms of user interaction and data retrieval at the request of the user. Counting on clients for mission-critical tasks is unwise. If the user is not supposed to be in direct control of the task, it does not belong on a client PC.

Servers, on the other hand, have much more stable environments for mission-critical tasks. First, servers are typically up and running. If they are down, the business is usually shut down. Second, servers are under the care of system administrators, who are trained to keep the servers running in a healthy state. Because they are under such care, servers can easily execute scheduled programs. Third, servers usually have more resources to devote to execution of complex procedures. Because of these resources, servers are usually faster at handling a given process than are client PCs.

Our goal is to teach you the SQL techniques that allow you to create server-side programs of the type we have just described. We will use one table in the Pubs database to provide the data, and we will keep our SQL data retrieval statements simple so that we can focus more effectively on the techniques we are introducing. But when you are finished with this module, you will have constructed a stored procedure that will perform the described calculations and return the data requested.

Using Variables

To build the types of procedures we have been talking about, you need to be able to use variables. *Variables* are, as in any other programming language, named storage locations. You can assign a value to them, or you can set them to a constant value. In our case, we are going to need constant values for three times of day: the cutoff for doing the overnight run of the procedure, the cutoff for doing the midday run, and the cutoff for the close-of-business run. We can simply enter these times into any of our statements if we want to, but placing them in variables allows us to name the cutoffs appropriately when we name the variables, and to change the cutoffs if we need to later by changing a value at one location instead of perhaps 30 scattered throughout the code.

To use variables, you must first declare them in your stored procedure. The customary place for declaring variables is at the top of the stored procedure's code. The method for declaring a variable is to use the

13

DECLARE keyword followed by the variable name followed by the data type. The following lines are examples:

```
DECLARE @OverNight datetime
DECLARE @MidDay datetime
DECLARE @CloseOfBusiness datetime
```

Hint

The at sign (@) has a special meaning in variable names. Those variable names beginning with one at sign are local to the stored procedure. Those beginning with two at signs (@@) are global and available to any stored procedure running on the server.

You may be wondering whether you can declare more than one variable on a single line. The answer is that you can, and here is the appropriate convention for doing so:

```
DECLARE @OverNight datetime, @MidDay datetime, @CloseOfBusiness datetime
```

Note that each variable name must be paired with its data type. Also note that default values are not set using the DECLARE statement.

So how do we get our default values into our variables? We have two options. You can use SELECT, as in the following statement:

```
SELECT @OverNight = '4:00 am'
```

SELECT is perhaps the more common way that you will see assignments taking place, because you can be certain that it has been implemented in all SQL databases that you might encounter. Later standards offered the SET statement as a means to set a variable's value. SET statements look like this:

```
SET @OverNight = '4:00 am'
```

What is the difference? Basically, at this point, there is very little difference. SET allows you to assign a value that is the result of a query, as in the following:

```
SET @SalesTotal = (SELECT SUM(Qty) FROM Sales WHERE Title_ID = 'BU1032')
```

In this SET statement, the SELECT sums the values in the Qty column and returns one and only one value, which is then assigned to the variable. But so does SELECT. This form of the statement looks like this:

```
SELECT @SalesTotal = (SELECT SUM(Qty) FROM Sales WHERE Title_ID = 'BU1032')
```

However, when we take up cursors in Module 15, there will be a difference. SET allows you to work with cursors and variables, whereas SELECT does not. We will postpone discussion of this feature to Module 15. For now, let's take a quick review of what we have learned so far.

Hint

The SELECT statement in the last example will serve as the prototype for the SELECT statement that we will use to sum sales totals.

1-Minute Drill

- **What about servers makes them better suited to running database procedures?**
- **How do you declare a variable?**
- **How do you assign a value to a variable?**

Using Flow Control

Now that we have a means of establishing constants for our times, and a means of using variables just as you would in any other programming language, we need to take up the topic of flow control. We need to be able to recognize when to run each totaling action against the database.

- **The server is more likely to be up, more likely to allocate appropriate resources to complete the task, and more likely to have appropriate scheduling software.**
- **DECLARE @*VariableName***
- **SELECT @VariableName = Value or SET @VariableName = Value**

13

We have a way of representing the times; now we need a way to represent the decision.

Representing decisions is the purpose of flow control statements. SQL offers two types of flow control:

● IF . . . ELSE

● Loop structures implemented on a database-specific basis

All databases support IF . . . ELSE. Some databases support the LOOP statement and the FOR statement. Others support the WHILE statement. We will get into the intricacies of looping in a few paragraphs. For now, let's look at the IF . . . ELSE statement.

IF allows you to test a condition, and then to execute one statement or a set of statements if the condition is true. The basic syntax is the following:

```
IF condition
    BEGIN
        Statements
    END
ELSE
    BEGIN
        Statements
    END
```

Condition is any SQL expression that can evaluate to True or False. *Statements* are any valid SQL statements. BEGIN and END demarcate blocks of statements that must run in sequence as a unit. The BEGIN/END block states the following: All statements between these markers are subject to the condition specified by the preceding IF or ELSE statement.

To set up the first condition for our stored procedure, we need to see if the current time is greater than or equal to the overnight cutoff time. If the condition is true, we run the SUM statement for the previous 24 hours. The statement block for this condition looks like this:

```
IF DATEPART(hh, GETDATE()) < DATEPART(hh, @OverNight)
    AND DATEPART(dd, GETDATE()) = DATEPART(dd, @OverNight)
    BEGIN
        SELECT SUM(Qty) FROM Sales WHERE ord_date BETWEEN GETDATE()
            AND DATEADD(d, -1, GETDATE())
    END
```

Note the logic here. If the current datetime stamp is less than our cutoff (and the day is the same), we run the statement. The statement selects the sum of sales quantities for each sales transaction from the Sales table. Note that the value we place in @OverNight needs to be a datetime value that contains an hour value extractable by DATEPART(). In addition, we are assuming the use of a twenty-four-hour clock, so that we can easily distinguish between morning and evening. Also note that ord_date needs to contain more than just a date. It should contain both the date and the time. Our data entry application, therefore, should make sure to use GETDATE() to set this field. Finally, we must assume that we are launching the stored procedure before our cutoff time, but very close to it.

Note

We are avoiding as many complicating details here as we can. You may want more precision than pulling the hour out of the two time values may offer. If so, you can use nested IF statements to test for additional parts of the date. Or you can set a variable to the value of GETDATE(), and use DATEPART() to pull elements that you concatenate into a string. You can then compare the time string that you placed in the variable to @OverNight.

The remaining two conditions use very similar logic. They should look like the following code fragment:

```
IF DATEPART(hh, GETDATE()) < DATEPART(hh, @MidDay)
   AND DATEPART(dd, GETDATE()) = DATEPART(dd, @MidDay)
   BEGIN
       SELECT SUM(Qty) FROM Sales WHERE ord_date BETWEEN DATEPART(hh,
           @OverNight) AND DATEPART(hh, GETDATE())
           AND DATEPART(mm, ord_date) = DATEPART(mm, GETDATE())
           AND DATEPART(dd, ord_date) = DATEPART(dd, GETDATE())
           AND DATEPART(yyyy, ord_date) = DATEPART(yyyy, GETDATE())
   END
IF DATEPART(hh, GETDATE()) < DATEPART(hh, @CloseOfBusiness)
   AND DATEPART(dd, GETDATE()) = DATEPART(dd, @CloseOfBusiness)
   BEGIN
       SET @DayCurrentSales = SELECT SUM(Qty) FROM Sales WHERE ord_date
           BETWEEN DATEPART(hh, @OverNight) AND DATEPART(hh, GETDATE())
           AND DATEPART(mm, ord_date) = DATEPART(mm, GETDATE())
           AND DATEPART(dd, ord_date) = DATEPART(dd, GETDATE())
           AND DATEPART(yyyy, ord_date) = DATEPART(yyyy, GETDATE())
       SET @DayPreviousSales = SELECT SUM(Qty) FROM Sales WHERE ord_date
           BETWEEN DATEPART(hh, @OverNight) AND DATEPART(hh, GETDATE())
```

13

```
      AND DATEPART(mm, ord_date) = DATEPART(mm, DATEADD(d, -1,
      GETDATE()))AND DATEPART(dd, ord_date) = DATEPART(dd, DATEADD(d,
      -1, GETDATE())) AND DATEPART(yyyy, ord_date) = DATEPART(yyyy,
      DATEADD(d, -1, GETDATE()))
END
```

The date math here seems complex, but it really is not. In the first IF block, we extract the hour value from @OverNight and GETDATE() to determine the hour range to select. The use of BETWEEN allows us to select times between these two hours. The remaining conditions make sure that ord_date has the same month, the same day, and the same year as the current date. In the second IF block, we perform the same logic, except that in the second SELECT statement we use DATEADD() to subtract one day from the current date. We therefore get the values for the day previous.

We mentioned that you can use loops to control flow in SQL. That statement is true, but the types of loops you may use vary widely. If you are used to Oracle, you are familiar with an unconditional LOOP statement and with a FOR LOOP statement. Other databases do not support these loop structures. SQL Server supports only a WHILE loop. As a result, we will explore a loop structure that is reasonably common to all databases, and let you investigate your particular database's implementation of loops through its documentation.

To give you a sense of how implementations vary, here is a common loop structure written for Oracle:

```
DECLARE LOOPCOUNTER NUMBER;
BEGIN
    LOOPCOUNTER := 0
    WHILE (LOOPCOUNTER <5) LOOP
        LOOPCOUNTER := LOOPCOUNTER + 1;
    END LOOP;
END;
```

Note the use of semicolons to end SQL statements, and note that the LOOP statement begins with LOOPCOUNTER := 0 and ends with END LOOP. Also note the use of a specialized assignment operator (:=). Also note that the at sign (@) does not begin the variable.

Here is the same loop written for SQL Server 2000:

```
DECLARE @LOOPCOUNTER NUMERIC
SELECT @LOOPCOUNTER = 1
```

```
WHILE (@LOOPCOUNTER <5)
BEGIN
    SELECT @LOOPCOUNTER = @LOOPCOUNTER + 1
END
```

Here the at sign (@) is in use, semicolons do not terminate the statements, and SELECT is used to assign values to variables. (SET could also be used.)

Both of these loops accomplish the same do-nothing task. The loop executes four times and increments the value of the counter by 1 in each pass. After the counter reaches the value of 5, the loop exits. Such loop structures, with minor variations, are likely to be implemented on your database.

Let's make a loop do some simple work. Suppose we want to make sure that our procedure executes only within ten minutes of our overnight cutoff time. We want it to exit if it somehow gets started earlier or later. The following loop structure will get the job done:

```
WHILE (DATEPART(mi, GETDATE())
    BETWEEN DATEPART(mi, DATEADD(mi, -10, @OverNight))
    AND DATEPART(mi, @OverNight)
    AND DATEPART(mm, @OverNight) = DATEPART(mm, GETDATE())
    AND DATEPART(dd, @OverNight) = DATEPART(dd, GETDATE()))
BEGIN
    Place IF statements here
    BREAK
END
```

This loop executes only when the minutes value (signified by "mi") extracted from GETDATE() is between the minutes value extracted from @OverNight and ten minutes before @OverNight. We use the same logic we used in our IF procedures to make sure that the condition applies to the same day and the same time. We check the day portions of GETDATE() and @OverNight to make sure they are equal. We do have to be careful about when we set @OverNight. Its value and the one for ten minutes before should not cross an hour boundary. If they do, BETWEEN will not see the interval correctly.

We've placed a tag in this loop to indicate where the IF statements would go, just to reduce the clutter while we talk about loops. The BREAK statement unconditionally exits the loop after the IF statements execute, making sure that we run our calculation only once.

13

1-Minute Drill

● **Why use a BREAK statement in a loop?**

● **What does an IF statement do?**

● **How do you get a statement block to execute if the IF condition is False?**

Returning Values

As you look at the stored procedure we are creating so far, you might notice that we have not done all the math. We have not calculated the difference between yesterday's sales and today's sales. You might also notice that, while we select the values, they are generally inaccessible. We will fix both problems by using return values.

Return values are values sent back from the stored procedure to the calling procedure. Only one value can be sent back this way. Since our stored procedure needs to return only one result, this limitation does not present a problem. To send a return value back to the calling procedure, use the RETURN statement. It has one of these two forms:

```
RETURN
RETURN expression
```

If you use the first form of the statement, RETURN always returns the value of 0. If you use the second form of the statement, RETURN returns the value of the SQL expression that follows the keyword.

● To prevent the loop from executing more times than you desire it to.
● It governs whether the next statement block executes. The block executes if the IF condition is True.
● Use a corresponding ELSE statement.

Hint

Most databases have an internal global variable that holds the error number of any error generated. In SQL Server, for example, this global variable is @@error. The variable holds a value of 0 if no error has occurred; it holds the error number otherwise. The value in the variable is the error code for the last statement run. This variable is a useful value to return to the calling procedure, unless you must calculate and return another value.

In our case, we need to return our calculated results. Here are our IF statements with the RETURN statements inserted:

```
IF DATEPART(hh, GETDATE()) < DATEPART(hh, @OverNight)
   AND DATEPART(dd, GETDATE()) = DATEPART(dd, @OverNight)
   BEGIN
       SET @OverNightSales = SELECT SUM(Qty) FROM Sales
           WHERE ord_date BETWEEN GETDATE()
           AND DATEADD(d, -1, GETDATE())
   END
IF DATEPART(hh, GETDATE()) < DATEPART(hh, @MidDay)
   AND DATEPART(dd, GETDATE()) = DATEPART(dd, @MidDay)
   BEGIN
       SET @MidDaySales = SELECT SUM(Qty) FROM Sales
           WHERE ord_date BETWEEN DATEPART(hh,
           @OverNight) AND DATEPART(hh, GETDATE())
           AND DATEPART(mm, ord_date) = DATEPART(mm, GETDATE())
           AND DATEPART(dd, ord_date) = DATEPART(dd, GETDATE())
           AND DATEPART(yyyy, ord_date) = DATEPART(yyyy, GETDATE())
       RETURN @MidDaySales
   END
IF DATEPART(hh, GETDATE()) < DATEPART(hh, @CloseOfBusiness)
   AND DATEPART(dd, GETDATE()) = DATEPART(dd, @CloseOfBusiness)
   BEGIN
       SET @DayCurrentSales = SELECT SUM(Qty) FROM Sales WHERE ord_date
           BETWEEN DATEPART(hh, @OverNight) AND DATEPART(hh, GETDATE())
           AND DATEPART(mm, ord_date) = DATEPART(mm, GETDATE())
           AND DATEPART(dd, ord_date) = DATEPART(dd, GETDATE())
           AND DATEPART(yyyy, ord_date) = DATEPART(yyyy, GETDATE())
       SET @DayPreviousSales = SELECT SUM(Qty) FROM Sales WHERE ord_date
           BETWEEN DATEPART(hh, @OverNight) AND DATEPART(hh, GETDATE())
           AND DATEPART(mm, ord_date) = DATEPART(mm, DATEADD(d, -1,
           GETDATE()))AND DATEPART(dd, ord_date) = DATEPART(dd, DATEADD(d,
           -1, GETDATE())) AND DATEPART(yyyy, ord_date) = DATEPART(yyyy,
           DATEADD(d, -1, GETDATE()))
       RETURN @DayCurrentSales - @DayPreviousSales
   END
```

13

Note

We have used variables to collect and store the values returned by the SELECT statements.

To obtain the return value from a stored procedure, use this EXEC statement as a template:

```
EXEC @SomeVariable = StoredProcedureName
```

1-Minute Drill

● **What is a good value to return from a stored procedure?**

● **What does RETURN with no argument return?**

● **Can you do math in a RETURN statement?**

Raising Errors

We've seen how to return an error number from a stored procedure. However, if an error occurs, you might want to return it to the calling program independently of the return value of your stored procedure. It would be very convenient if your application's error handling code could receive the error and report it just like any other error.

Each SQL database provides a mechanism for returning errors. However, the exact methodology is implementation specific. We will use SQL Server as an example of how SQL databases implement such error handling mechanisms, and point you to the documentation for your database to find out exactly how your database implements this functionality.

● **@@error**
● **0**
● **Yes**

In SQL Server, you use the RAISEERROR statement to return an error. It has this syntax:

```
RAISEERROR ({msg_num or msg_str}, severity_num, state[, argument1 [, argument2]])
    [WITH options]
```

You must provide a message number or message string. You must also provide a number that represents a severity level. Valid numbers are 0 through 25, with the severity increasing as the number increases. Your documentation will help you to decipher the exact meaning of severity levels. In general, you as a user can use error severity levels of 0 through 19. System administrators can also use levels 20 through 25. You have to be aware, however, that some severity numbers are reserved for certain purposes, as shown in Table 13-1.

State is an arbitrary number between 1 and 127 that represents the state of the system at the time the error was raised. Since the number is arbitrary, you can define its meaning for yourself.

Severity Number	Meaning
10	Status information
17	Insufficient resources
18	Nonfatal error internal to SQL Server
19	Fatal error internal to SQL Server
20	Fatal error in current process; database undamaged
21	Fatal error in current database; database undamaged
22	Table integrity is suspect; run the statement DBCC CHECKDB in the Query Analyzer
23	Database integrity is suspect; run the statement DBCC CHECKDB in the Query Analyzer
24	Hardware error; you may need to reload the database or repair hardware

Table 13-1   **Reserved Severity Level Numbers**

13

To raise an error using an error number, use this statement as a model:

```
RAISEERROR (50025, 1, 1)
```

This statement raises error number 50025. SQL Server reserves error numbers 1 through 50000 for itself. Error numbers above 50000 represent user-defined errors. The severity level is 1, and the state number is 1. In general, this would represent an informational error. You should increase the severity level for more damaging errors, and change the state level to reflect a meaning that you define, if you so desire.

Hint

State levels are numbers that you use to communicate with yourself about the status of your stored procedure. You can use them, for example, to indicate which RAISEERROR statement raised the error.

To raise an error that has a string message, use the following form of RAISEEROR as a model:

```
RAISEERROR ('This is a user defined error.', 1, 1)
```

To include additional information in your error string, you can use substitution parameters. For example, the following statement inserts the error number in the string:

```
RAISEERROR ('This is a user defined error number %d.', 1, 1, 50025)
```

Substitution parameters represent placeholders. Following the main part of the statement, you place the values to substitute in a comma-separated list. The first value in the list substitutes for the first parameter, the second value for the second parameter, and so forth. The percent sign (%) signifies that the next character represents a substitution point. The characters following the percent sign represent the data type of the substituted value, as shown in Table 13-2.

As the last part of your statement, you may use an option keyword. You have the following options:

Substitution Code	Data Type
d or I	Signed integer
O	Unsigned octal
P	Pointer
S	String
U	Unsigned integer
x or X	Unsigned hexadecimal

Table 13-2   Data type of the substituted value

- **LOG** Write the error to the database log.

- **NOWAIT** Send the message with no delay to the client.

- **SETERROR** Set the value of @@error to the message number or message string you provided.

Project 13-1: Assemble the Stored Procedure

StoredProcedure.sql It's time to assemble the stored procedure we have been building. Using the Query Analyzer, assemble all the statements we have been using and add a CREATE PROCEDURE.

Step-by-Step

1. Create DECLARE statements for all the variables used.

2. Add the SET statements to set the values of the constants.

3. Add the WHILE statement for the loop.

4. Add the IF statements to do the bulk of the work.

5. Add the CREATE PROCEDURE statement at the head of the file.

6. Run these commands to create the procedure.

13

☑ *Mastery Check*

1. What flow control options do you have in SQL?

2. What kind of loops does SQL provide?

3. What statement raises an error?

4. What global variable holds the last error?

5. How do you get a value out of a stored procedure?

6. What must you include in a RAISEERROR statement?

7. What value does RETURN return by default?

8. How do you obtain the return value from a stored procedure?

9. What does %d mean in an error string?

10. How are substitution parameters matched with substitution codes in an error string?

Module 14

Using Parameters

Goals

- Learn how to create parameters for stored procedures
- Learn how to pass values into a stored procedure
- Learn how to receive values back from a stored procedure
- Practice programming with stored procedures and parameters in Visual Basic

In Module 13, we showed you how to return values from a stored procedure and how to raise errors. You were able to get feedback from the procedure we created if an error occurred. Errors are passed back to your database programs through the normal error handling procedures associated with the programming language you use. We could only use return values, however, if we set a SQL variable equal to the return value of the stored procedure. Therefore, we could only work with return values within SQL. We could not get the return value back to a program that the user might have for data entry.

In this module, we will examine how to pass information to your stored procedures and how to get information back from SQL to your database program. The construct used to pass information back and forth is a *parameter*. As a programmer, you are probably already familiar with parameters to functions. Depending on your background, you may be familiar with both input parameters and output parameters. *Input parameters* are values you pass to the function. *Output parameters* are values the function passes back. Output parameters are usually separate from a function's return value.

Let's take a brief look at the use of parameters in programming. We will limit ourselves to functions because we want to be able to distinguish the roles of input parameters, output parameters, and return values. Most programming languages have a function that counts the characters in a string. In Visual Basic, this function is the Len() function. The classic use of Len() is in a statement like the following:

```
intReturnValue = Len(strInputParameter)
```

Len() has one input parameter, the string whose length you would like to know. You pass this string to the function as the input parameter in parentheses, and Len() undertakes its processing to count the number of characters in the string. Len() has a return value, which is the number of characters.

Note

In working with functions, you may be more used to calling parameters *arguments*.

When you think of parameters for stored procedures, you have exactly the same situation. You can define a variable in your stored procedure that serves to catch the value of the parameter you pass. Your procedure undertakes its processing. If you choose to have a return value, you can pass the result of the stored procedure's processing back to the stored procedure as a return value. With a few tricks that we'll examine shortly, you can receive that return value into your program as the value of a variable. The ActiveX Data Objects have a facility that will collect the return value for you. You just need to know how to set ADO up to receive parameters to do so.

Visual Basic functions typically work with input parameters and return values. You pass one or many parameters, the function undertakes its processing, and it returns the result of its processing. If you have ever worked with Windows API calls, you see the use of output parameters frequently. Consider the function GetCurrentDirectory() in the Windows API. It retrieves the current directory name. If you declare it for use in Visual Basic, you discover that you must use the function in the following manner:

```
IntReturnValue = GetCurrentDirectory(intBufferLength, strBuffer)
```

The return value of this function is either 0 or the number of characters written to the buffer. Here you may wish to pause. Why isn't the return value the name of the directory? What does "written to the buffer" mean? Isn't strBuffer an input parameter? Actually, intBufferLength is the only input parameter. The function needs to know how many bytes it can write to strBuffer before it hits an overflow condition, which would produce an error. GetCurrentDirectory() uses this value to limit the number of characters it will retrieve. Because of this limit, you want to be sure that you pass it a value that represents the expected length of the current directory name.

The return value tells you how many characters were actually written to the buffer. This value allows you to evaluate whether the function was successful without the overhead of a full string comparison, as in the following conditional:

```
If strBuffer = "MyDirectory" Then
```

14

In this comparison, to find out if we received data, we must compare strBuffer to "MyDirectory" byte by byte. Potentially, you might have to make 11 comparisons to find out if you received the correct current directory. With the approach implemented by GetCurrentDirectory(), if 0 bytes came back, you know the function failed. You compare one byte to another byte. You need only conduct the more expensive comparison if you got data of the expected length.

What is strBuffer? Technically in Visual Basic, it is a string variable. From the operating system's perspective, it is a named storage location that represents a span of physical memory. This physical memory is where the name of the current directory is written during function processing. Your program can then access this storage location any time it wishes to know what the current directory is. The essence of output parameters is that they are storage locations accessible both to the caller and to the function code. Any data placed there is accessible both to the function and to the program that called it. The buffer is like a mailbox for passing messages. The function deposits some data; the calling program can retrieve it at will.

With SQL, the same sort of routine is available. If you mark a parameter as an output parameter, the parameter is allocated memory for storage. The value is placed at that location, and the address of that location is made available to the calling program. If processing is running on the database server, memory is allocated on the database server. If processing is running on the client computer, memory is allocated there. Database APIs, like the ODBC API we introduced you to in Module 1, have the capability to allocate and read the memory for output parameters. If they need to move the data across the network from one machine to another, they have that capability as well. The ActiveX Data Objects that we have used for programming client access to our database have the ability to receive and store parameter values.

Note

The process of moving data across the network from one machine to another is called *marshaling*.

Creating Parameters

To take full advantage of parameters, you have to be able to create them in two locations, both at the stored procedure that will receive the parameters and at the program that will call the stored procedure. To create a parameter at a stored procedure, you provide a list of variables following the procedure name and before the AS in a CREATE PROCEDURE statement. A CREATE PROCEDURE with parameters looks like this:

```
CREATE PROCEDURE myProc
@ParameterIN        varchar(20),
@ParameterOut       int      OUTPUT
AS

Insert SQL statements for the stored procedure here
```

Note that you are adding the same information for a variable declaration to the CREATE PROCEDURE statement. You just don't include the DECLARE keyword itself. Input parameters require no special keyword for their definition. Output parameters require that the OUTPUT keyword be included in the parameter's definition, as the code fragment shows. The list of parameters in a stored procedure is a comma-separated list.

To create parameters on the program side, you use the ADO command object. This object maintains a collection of parameters that it can pass to a stored procedure and receive from a stored procedure. Once you have the command object built, you need to use statements like the following to add parameters:

```
'To build an input parameter
Set prmInput = cmdCommand.CreateParameter("MyInputParameter", adVarChar,
    adParamInput, 20, "ParameterValue")
cmdCommand.Parameters.Append prmInput
'To build an output parameter
Set prmOutput = cmdCommand.CreateParameter("MyOutputParameter", adInteger,
    adParamOutput, 4)
cmdCommand.Parameters.Append prmOutput
'To build an input parameter
Set prmReturn = cmdCommand.CreateParameter("MyReturnParameter", adInteger,
    adParamReturnValue, 4)
cmdCommand.Parameters.Append prmReturn
```

14

In general, the set statement uses the CreateParameter method on the command object to create a parameter with the attributes passed between the parentheses. All of these attributes are optional. They are:

- **Name** A string that gives the parameter a name that you can use to refer to it later.

- **Type** The data type of the parameter. ADO defines constants for these data types that match with the SQL data types in use. These constants are adBigInt, adBinary, adBoolean, adBSTR (for Unicode strings), adChapter, adChar, adCurrency, adDBDate, adDBTimeStamp, adDecimal, adDouble, adEmpty, adError, adFileTime, adGUID, adInteger, adLongVarBinary, adLongVarChar, adLongVarWChar, adNumeric, adSingle, adSmallInt, adTinyInt, adUnsignedBigInt, adUnsignedInt, adUnsignedSmallInt, adUnsignedTinyInt, adVarBinary, adVarChar, adVarNumeric, adVarWChar (for null-terminated Unicode strings), and adWChar (null-terminated Unicode strings).

- **Direction** The direction of the parameter. Possible values are adParamInput, adParamOutput, adParamInputOutput (indicating the parameter will both pass values in and receive values), adParamReturnValue, and adParamUnknown.

- **Size** An integer indicating the number of characters or bytes that the parameter uses.

- **Value** The value of the parameter. You use this attribute to set a value at the time of creation.

In the examples preceding, we created an integer output parameter with the name MyOutputParameter. It has a size of 4 because the integer data type used four bytes of storage. We did not assign it an initial value at the time of creation. We also created an input parameter with the name MyInputParameter. It is a VarChar and its size is 20, the maximum number of characters we allow it to hold. We gave it the initial value of "ParameterValue," a fourteen-character string. We also created a return value parameter named MyReturnParameter. It is an integer data type with a size of four bytes. We did not set its initial value.

Hint

Your parameter data types in the parameters collection need to match the data types you use in your stored procedure.

Passing Values

Now that you can create parameters, to use them at all you need to be able to pass values to them when you run a stored procedure. In SQL, you can pass values in an EXECUTE statement by listing the values for the parameters in the correct order after the name of the stored procedure. The following example demonstrates this method:

```
EXECUTE ProcedureName 'InputValue1', 'InputValue2'
```

Multiple parameters are separated by commas in the list. You can also explicitly list the names of the parameter variables in the list, as in this example:

```
EXECUTE ProcedureName @Parameter1 = 'InputValue1', @Parameter2 =
    'InputValue2'
```

You can use default parameter values in a stored procedure. To do so, simply include values in the CREATE PROCEDURE statement, as in the following:

```
CREATE PROCEDURE myProc
@ParameterIn        varchar(20) = 'ThisValue',
@ParameterOut       int      OUTPUT
AS

Insert SQL statements for the stored procedure here
```

When you use a stored procedure with default values defined, the stored procedure uses the default value if you pass no value for the input parameter that has the value defined. You can also use the DEFAULT keyword to explicitly identify that you want to use the default value, as in these EXECUTE statements:

```
EXECUTE ProcedureName DEFAULT, 'InputValue2'
EXECUTE ProcedureName @Parameter1 = 'InputValue1', @Parameter2 =
    DEFAULT
```

From a client program, you have two methods of passing parameters. In the first, you concatenate the parameters into the string that makes up

14

the command object's CommandText property. This is the method you should use if you do not wish to create a collection of input parameters using the command object. Assuming that you have declared the variable strInputValue, you can pass the parameter to the stored procedure using syntax like the following:

```
cmdCommand.CommandText = "Exec myProc " & strInputValue
```

If you need to pass more than one parameter, separate the parameter values with commas. Such a CommandText string passing three values would look like this:

```
cmdCommand.CommandText = "Exec myProc " & strInputValue & ", " & _
    strParam2 & ", " & strParam3
```

Parameters go in the CommandText string in the exact same order as they appear in the parameter list in the stored procedure.

If you have created a collection of input parameters, you do not need to concatenate parameter values into the CommandText string. Instead, make sure that you have created your parameters in the same order that they appear in the stored procedure. The first input parameter appended to the collection needs to be the first parameter in the parameter list for the stored procedure, the second appended to the collection needs to be the second to appear in the stored procedure's parameter list, and so forth. Do not set the command type to adCommandText. Instead, set it to adCmdStoredProc. Set the CommandText property to the name of the stored procedure, and execute the command. Your command object locates the stored procedure and executes it, passing the parameters in for you. One way to imagine the process is that the command object creates the SQL EXECUTE statement for you on the fly, placing the parameters in the statement in the correct order with the correct syntax.

ADO and SQL provide no inherent advantage to either method of executing stored procedures. If you need to use output parameters, however, or want to collect a return value, you should use the parameters collection. It is the most efficient means of retrieving information from a stored procedure into your program.

1-Minute Drill

● **How do you define a parameter in a stored procedure?**

● **What does an input parameter do?**

● **What do output parameters do?**

Project 14-1: Add Parameters

StoredProcParams.sql

Take the stored procedure you created in Module 13 and add parameters to it. You need one parameter for each of the three time constants the stored procedure uses. Once you make the conversion, you can pass in the time values from the calling procedure.

Step-by-Step

1. Convert the DECLARE statements into a parameter list.

2. Remove the SET statements that set the values.

3. Verify that all references to these three values are still correct and do not alter the values of the three variables. (If you leave in code that alters their values, then the values you pass it won't be the values used in processing the query.)

4. Drop the old procedure.

5. Execute the new CREATE PROCEDURE statement to create the parameterized version of the stored procedure.

Using the Results

If your query has a return value and/or output parameters, you can collect those results for use later in processing. Collecting the results within SQL

● **Place the information that you would place in a DECLARE statement between the procedure name and AS in the CREATE PROCEDURE statement.**
● **Input parameters provide values to the stored procedure for use in its processing.**
● **Output parameters receive values that result from the stored procedure's execution.**

14

is no difficult problem. To collect a return value, add a variable to the EXECUTE statement that receives the return value, as in the following:

EXECUTE @ReturnValue = MyStoreProcedure

To collect an output parameter, include the parameter on the parameter list and use the OUTPUT keyword, as in this EXECUTE statement:

```
EXECUTE @ReturnValue = MyStoredProcedure @OutputParameter =
    @ReceivedValue OUTPUT
```

The first value following the procedure name, @OutputParameter, is the name of the parameter variable defined in the stored procedure. The variable name to the left of the equal sign, @ReceivedValue, is the variable that receives the output value from the stored procedure. This receive variable gets defined in the calling procedure. You are passing the value of a variable defined in the stored procedure to a variable defined outside the stored procedure.

In a program, collecting output values is very straightforward, but there is one trick that will cause you problems if you are not paying attention. To receive a return value or an output parameter, use the Parameters collection. Define a return value parameter and an output parameter as we demonstrated earlier in this module. Next, execute the command. So far, the basic code for this operation looks like this:

```
'To build an output parameter
Set prmOutput = cmdCommand.CreateParameter("MyOutputParameter", adInteger,
    adParamOutput, 4)
cmdCommand.Parameters.Append prmOutput
'To build an input parameter
Set prmReturn = cmdCommand.CreateParameter("MyReturnParameter", adInteger,
    adParamReturnValue, 4)
cmdCommand.Parameters.Append prmReturn
'To execute the command
cmdCommand.CommandText = "MyStoredProcedure"
cmdCommand.CommandType = adStoredProcedure
Set rstRecordset = cmdCommand.Execute
```

When the command finishes executing, the return parameter and the output parameter in the Parameters collection will contain the values received from the stored procedure. The trick is knowing when the command has finished executing. Formally, command execution ends when the last record for the recordset is marshaled across the network connection to your client program. ADO, however, makes the recordset object available to you for use before the final record returns. The reason for this behavior is that you can begin to use a large recordset while the data is still marshaling. For example, when you display records for browsing, you need the first record for the display immediately, but you can wait for the hundredth record until the user scrolls that far through the list of records. In most cases, the record will have arrived before the screen display needs it. Performance in the client program will appear to be faster, because the user will be able to interact with the data immediately, rather than waiting for all the records to arrive. If the user requests a record that has not yet arrived, the user has to wait until it arrives. Under most circumstances, however, users will notice few, if any, delays.

ADO does not include a flag that tells you when the recordset has completely returned. Because of this fact, you cannot tell when your output or return parameters will be available. To guarantee their availability, you must close the recordset, using a statement like the following:

> **Hint**
>
> If you Dim your recordset object WithEvents, you will receive the FetchComplete event when the recordset is populated. You can rely on this event to tell you when your parameters are available.

```
rstRecordset.Close
```

Having closed the recordset, you can access parameters in one of two ways. If you named your parameters, you can access them by name, as in the following statement:

```
intReturn = cmdCommand("MyReturnParameter")
strOutput = cmdCommand("MyOutputParameter")
```

If you did not name your parameters, you may access them using their zero-based index numbers in the Parameters collection, as in these statements:

```
intReturn = cmdCommand(1)
strOutput = cmdCommand(0)
```

> **Hint**
>
> If you need to gain access to the recordset after you collect the parameters, you can open the recordset again using its Open method.

14

Ask the Expert

Question: Is there a limit on how many output parameters you can have?

Answer: You need to check your database documentation to see if there are any limits on the number of output parameters. In general, the answer is yes, but the limit is so large as to be irrelevant. SQL Server 2000 has a limit of 2,100 parameters, for example.

For practical purposes, you might ask yourself why you want to return so many values as output parameters. Especially when you are moving data across a network, you have some overhead associated with output parameters. If, for example, you want to use fifty output parameters on a stored procedure, you might find it more efficient to return a recordset containing the values, and then to manipulate the recordset to extract the values you need into variables. Remember, using most database APIs like the ActiveX Data Objects, you can't have access to the parameters until all the data has returned. With a large recordset coming back from a stored procedure that has several output parameters, you have the overhead of building and returning your recordset to work through before you incur the overhead associated with the parameters. Output parameters are most efficient for stored procedures that are intended to return a few values rather than a recordset.

Question: What happens if the data passed to a parameter variable does not match the data type of the parameter variable?

Answer: The answer to this question depends on the database you are using and the kind of data you are passing. If you try to pass an integer to a tinyint, you might get lucky and not receive an error, if the integer is within the range of values accepted by tinyint. If you exceed the value acceptable for tinyint, however, you will receive an overflow error or a type mismatch error.

Question: What are the most likely types of bugs that appear when you use parameters?

Answer: Common kinds of mistakes you can make with parameters are to place parameter values in the wrong order, to mismatch data types, to forget to pass a value to a parameter with no default value supplied, or to forget to pass a value to a stored procedure that does have a default value specified for the parameter, thus using a value you didn't intend to use.

☑ *Mastery Check*

1. What happens if you pass two parameter values to a stored procedure that has three input parameters and default values specified for all parameters?

2. What happens if you pass two parameter values to a stored procedure that has three input parameters and no default values specified for the parameters?

3. How do you add a parameter to the parameters collection?

4. How do you collect a return value from a stored procedure using SQL?

5. How do you specify that a parameter is an output parameter in SQL?

6. What happens if you create a parameter using the command object and you provide none of the optional arguments for CreateParameter?

7. How do you create an output parameter using CreateParameter?

8. Under ADO, when are parameter values made available to your program?

9. Is there a disadvantage to not naming parameters under ADO?

10. How are parameters matched between the ADO Parameters collection and the actual stored procedure?

Module 15

Using Cursors

Goals

- Learn how to declare cursors
- Learn how to manipulate cursors
- Examine how to search a cursor
- Learn how to update a cursor

When you work with a recordset in Visual Basic or another programming language, you have great flexibility in the way you can search and manipulate data. You can find each record, for example, that has Field23 set to "Examine Me" and check to see whether Field11 is less than 20 and Field12 is greater than 4. If Field11 and Field12 meet these conditions, you can set Field1 equal to "Success" if Field2 equals 75. You can also set Field40 equal to "Procedure" if Field8 does not equal "Henrietta." Imagine trying to accomplish this operation with UPDATE statements.

Sometimes you might wish for an equivalent kind of processing in SQL. You will encounter occasions where it will be useful to locate a specific record and to perform data changes on that record. The changes may be so complex, as we tried to show in the last paragraph, that using an UPDATE with a WHERE clause might not successfully find every record that meets the complex conditions that qualify the record for changes. Or the changes might be so complex that you don't want to trust yourself to frame the UPDATE statement. You would rather have the row in hand, examine its columns for the correct conditions, and make the changes before moving on to the next row.

SQL offers you the construct called a cursor that allows you to retrieve a recordset into the cursor. Once you have a named cursor, you can fetch rows from the cursor and work on the current row. If you compare a SQL cursor to ADO recordsets, you find several similarities. You can move from row to row in the cursor, just as you can in the recordset. You can access field values in the row, update field values in the row, or delete a row. The difference between cursors and a client-side recordset is that you perform the operation on the database server, not on the client PC. Because of the location where processing takes place, cursors do not require that data be marshaled across the network. If you can define all the work that you would do with an ADO recordset as a stored procedure using a cursor, you can accomplish the same work using server-side processing. You harness the processing power of the server, you accomplish the same work, and no data has to come across the network channel. Theoretically, you reduce the overhead associated with performing the work.

You need to be careful, however, about how you use cursors. Many SQL programmers see cursors as performance robbers, and under certain circumstances, this claim is true. Cursors work best when all the processing takes place on the server, and the stored procedure using the cursor can run to completion on the server without having to communicate with the client. Cursors are slow when you must use a cursor to generate a recordset that you are going to return to the client, especially when the client cannot continue processing until the recordset has returned.

Note

Part of the reason that cursors are slow is that they create and maintain temporary tables to facilitate the use of the cursor. Typically, a cursor creates a temporary table in the database TempDB to hold the rows associated with the cursor. Additional overhead may be necessary if the cursor recordset is large and the cursor populates asynchronously, providing initial access to the top of the recordset while the rest of the data loads.

Cursors do introduce overhead. A SELECT statement will return faster than a cursor onto the recordset defined by the SELECT statement. The raw select does not have to generate the data structures that will contain the records, the pointer to records, and similar constructs that allow you to navigate among the records in the cursor. If you have a choice between using a cursor and not using a cursor, in general, the solution without the cursor will be superior in terms of performance.

However, sometimes handing a data job off to the server is the perfect solution. You define the job as a stored procedure. The only client interaction required is to invoke the stored procedure. The procedure runs, and the task completes entirely as a server-side operation. Such tasks are perfect for cursors. At other times, the flexibility and accuracy that cursors offer outweigh the possible performance hit. The main point is that you can accomplish as much with server-side processing using cursors as you can on the client side using database APIs to move through the recordset. Choosing which is best requires trying out the solutions and verifying their performance. In this module, we will focus on showing you the cursor solution and suggesting ways to evaluate whether the cursor solution is the best for your situation.

Declaring Cursors

To use a cursor, you must first declare the cursor. Declaring the cursor is the process of letting the database know that you intend to use a cursor.

When you declare a cursor, you can specify options to define how the cursor behaves. The basic declaration of a cursor looks like this:

```
DECLARE curAuthor CURSOR FOR SELECT * FROM authors
```

The basic elements of the statement are the following:

1. The keyword DECLARE

2. A name for the cursor

3. The keywords CURSOR FOR, which identify that you are creating a cursor

4. A select statement

The cursor you declare acts as a window onto the resultset of the SELECT statement. Using the cursor by name, you can access individual records returned by the select statement, as we will see in the next section.

You have additional options that you may specify in the cursor declaration. For example, you can use the following form:

```
DECLARE curAuthor INSENSITIVE CURSOR FOR SELECT * FROM authors
```

The keyword INSENSITIVE causes the cursor to place a copy of the data returned in a table in TempDB. All operations on the data take place on this private copy of the data. You cannot use an insensitive cursor to update data. You can also use this form of the statement:

```
DECLARE curAuthor SCROLL CURSOR FOR SELECT * FROM authors
```

The SCROLL keyword indicates that you can scroll through the data backward and forward. If this option is not specified, you can only scroll to the next record; this type of cursor is known as a forward-only cursor.

You have two additional options with the declaration of a cursor. After the SELECT statement, you can specify two different approaches to using the cursor. One is illustrated in the following SQL statement:

> **Hint**
> Both SCROLL and INSENSITIVE can be used together.

```
DECLARE curAuthor CURSOR FOR SELECT * FROM authors FOR READ ONLY
```

Using this FOR phrase makes the cursor read-only. You can read the data, but you cannot change it. No UPDATE or DELETE statements in relation to this cursor will be processed. If you want to update fields in this cursor, however, you can use the following form:

```
DECLARE curAuthor CURSOR FOR SELECT * FROM authors FOR UPDATE phone
```

The FOR UPDATE phrase specifies which columns, in a comma-separated list, can be updated in the cursor. If you wish to execute UPDATE statements, you can specify which columns can be updated, including some and excluding others.

Note

Each database may specify extensions of the declaration of cursors. SQL Server, for example, allows you to specify whether the cursor is global to the SQL session in Query Analyzer or local to a block of statements. You can also specify whether the cursor is forward-only, read-only, updatable fast-forward, and several other options, using specialized keywords. SQL Server allows you very fine control over the nature of the cursor. Other databases offer varying degrees of control using cursor extensions.

After you declare a cursor, use the OPEN command to open it for use. This statement has the following self-obvious syntax:

```
OPEN curAuthor
```

The OPEN statement causes the query that defines the cursor's recordset to populate the cursor with data. You can then use the cursor to manipulate data.

Manipulating Cursors

To manipulate cursors, you first need to open the cursor. You open the cursor using the following statement:

```
OPEN curAuthor
```

15

This statement causes the cursor to instantiate and return its recordset. You can use the FETCH statement to get rows from the cursor into memory so that you can operate on them. Every cursor will respond to the following statement:

```
FETCH NEXT FROM curAuthor
```

This statement causes the next row to be available for operations. What this means is that the next row is brought into memory, and SQL establishes a pointer to it and all of its fields. What happens to the row depends on what your intentions are. For example, if you want to bring the values of certain columns into variables, you must first declare the variables in the procedure that will do the fetching. You can fetch specific fields into specific variables using the following statement:

```
FETCH NEXT FROM curAuthor INTO @au_id, @au_frame, @au_lname, @phone,
    @address, @city,
    @state, @zip, @contract
```

In this case, the values from the next row are placed in variables named after the columns in the table.

FETCH supports additional keywords that allow you to position the cursor with great flexibility. Using PRIOR in place of NEXT causes the previous row to be fetched rather than the next row. FIRST positions the cursor at the first row, and LAST positions the cursor at the last row in the recordset. The following statement fetches the eighth row from the beginning of the cursor:

```
FETCH ABSOLUTE 8 FROM curAuthor
```

While this statement positions the cursor eight rows forward from the current row:

```
FETCH RELATIVE 8 FROM curAuthor
```

Absolute and relative positioning allow the use of positive numbers to move toward the last record and negative numbers to move toward the first record, and you can use variables rather than entering the number directly.

One other manipulation of cursors is allowed in all databases. You can declare a variable to be of the CURSOR data type. You can assign a cursor to this variable, and you can pass that cursor to a stored procedure as a parameter. First, let's take a look at the mechanics of the process. Use a statement of this form to declare a cursor variable:

```
DECLARE @MyCursor CURSOR
```

Set the value of this variable using a statement like this:

```
SET @MyCursor = curAuthor
```

You can also set the value of a cursor variable by substituting the cursor definition for the name in the preceding statement, as in the following:

```
SET @MyCursor = CURSOR FOR SELECT * FROM authors FOR UPDATE phone
```

Assuming that you have a stored procedure that can accept a cursor as a parameter, pass the cursor using a statement of this type:

```
EXECUTE selAuthorList @MyCursor OUTPUT
```

The main reason for passing a cursor to a stored procedure is so that you can return a cursor filled with data as an output parameter. Inside the stored procedure, you use a SET statement to populate the cursor. When the stored procedure returns, the cursor variable retains a reference to the dataset. This trick is useful when you want to obtain a set of rows as the output of a stored procedure. We will look at how a stored procedure using such a cursor might look later in this module.

Hint

You can substitute a cursor variable for a cursor name anywhere you can use a cursor name.

15

1-Minute Drill

- **How do you declare a cursor?**
- **How do you set a cursor variable to contain a reference to a named cursor?**
- **If you need to pass a named cursor to a stored procedure, what must you do?**

Updating and Searching Cursors

You can use UPDATE and DELETE statements to change or delete rows within the cursor. A DELETE statement for our curAuthor cursor looks like this:

```
DELETE authors WHERE CURRENT OF curAuthor
```

Such a delete statement must mention the name of a table in the cursor immediately after the DELETE keyword. WHERE CURRENT OF specifies that the deletion will take place at the current position of the cursor named after these keywords.

An UPDATE statement is similar in nature, taking the following syntax:

```
UPDATE authors SET au_lname = NULL WHERE CURRENT OF curAuthor
```

As with DELETE, a table name referenced in the cursor must appear after the UPDATE keyword. The familiar SET phrase, the same as in any UPDATE statement, follows. WHERE CURRENT OF specifies that the UPDATE takes place at the current location of the cursor named after these keywords.

Often you need to search a cursor to determine where to update or delete rows. SQL provides a couple of constructs to assist you in

---

- **DECLARE cursorname [OPTIONS] CURSOR FOR select statement [FOR read-only or update options]**
- **SET @variablename = cursorname**
- **Set a cursor variable equal to the cursor name and pass the variable as a parameter to the stored procedure**

searching a cursor. The first is a global variable, @@FETCH_STATUS. Your database places a result code for the last fetch in this variable, 0 if the fetch was successful, –1 if the fetch failed or you attempted to fetch beyond the last record in the cursor, or –2 if the row you attempted to fetch is missing (as when you have already deleted the row). To begin the operation of searching a cursor, first declare the cursor and open it. Then fetch the first row. The following lines undertake this operation:

```
DECLARE @au_id varchar(11), @au_fname varchar(20), @au_lname varchar(40)
DECLARE curAuthor CURSOR FOR SELECT au_id, au_frame, au_lname FROM authors
OPEN curAuthor
FETCH NEXT FROM curAuthor INTO @au_id, @au_fname, @au_lname
```

Note that we have decided to fetch three columns from the authors table in the Pubs database. We have chosen to fetch the values into three variables named after the columns they represent so that we can easily examine the values. At the end of this code fragment, we have retrieved the first row and loaded the values into the variables. We are now ready to undertake the search operation.

To undertake a search, build a while loop based on the value of the fetch status. As long as fetch status is zero, we can assume there are more rows to examine in the cursor. If fetch status is nonzero, either we have a problem with the cursor or we have run out of rows. In either circumstance, it is time to stop searching. The basic construct for the search loop looks like this:

```
WHILE @@FETCH_STATUS = 0
BEGIN
Place statements that seek a match here
END
```

This logic is all we need to search all the rows in the cursor. To locate the record for the author whose last name is Stringer, use logic like the following:

```
WHILE @@FETCH_STATUS = 0
BEGIN
    IF @au_lname = 'Stringer'
        RETURN 99
    FETCH NEXT FROM curAuthor INTO @au_id, @au_fname, @au_lname
END
```

15

For this example, we are returning a value to indicate success, on the assumption that this code might appear in a stored procedure. You could also use the PRINT statement in SQL to print output to the screen. PRINT takes one argument, the string to print. It looks like this:

```
PRINT 'Message'
```

You might also take more complex actions, such as opening a cursor passed to the stored procedure as an output parameter and fetching the author's record into it. The code to do so would look something like this, assuming @PassedCursor is defined as a parameter to the stored procedure.

```
FETCH NEXT FROM curAuthor INTO @au_id, @au_frame, @au_lname
FETCH NEXT FROM @PassedCursor
WHILE @@FETCH_STATUS = 0
BEGIN
    IF @au_lname = 'Stringer'
    BEGIN
        FETCH RELATIVE 0 FROM @PassedCursor
        RETURN 99
    END
    FETCH NEXT FROM curAuthor INTO @au_id, @au_frame, @au_lname
    FETCH NEXT FROM @PassedCursor
END
```

We need to clarify a couple of assumptions here. First, @PassedCursor was opened by the calling procedure. We also have to assume that it has the following definition:

```
SET @PassedCursor = CURSOR FOR SELECT * FROM authors
```

Because of their definitions, both cursors contain the same number of rows, all the rows in the author table. Next, we need to note that we fetch from both our cursors using FETCH NEXT at the same time. In this manner, we keep both cursors in synchronization. When we do the relative fetch from the cursor variable, we instruct it to do a relative fetch using row 0, which is the current row. When we find the author named Stringer, we fetch his record into the output cursor and return to stop execution of the procedure. The output parameter is passed back to the calling procedure, and we can use the one row cursor there as we wish.

Closing and Deallocating Cursors

When you are finished with a cursor, you should close it. Use the following statement as a model for doing so:

```
CLOSE curAuthor
```

Even though you have closed the cursor, you have not destroyed it. You could reopen it if you wished, repopulating it with data. To completely remove the cursor from the database, you must deallocate it. The following statement undertakes this task:

```
DEALLOCATE curAuthor
```

If you fail to deallocate a cursor, cursors declared within a procedure will be destroyed when the procedure ends.

Note

Some databases, notably SQL Server, extend cursors to allow you to declare global cursors that are available to all procedures running on a database system. If you create a global cursor, you should be sure to deallocate it. If you don't, the resources created for it persist in the system tables until you do deallocate the cursor, or until your session is destroyed.

Cursors.sql

Project 15-1: Assemble a Stored Procedure

Let's assemble the stored procedure we have alluded to in this module. Create a procedure that will search for a record in the authors table (Pubs database) by author last name. It will return the record for that author as an output parameter.

Step-by-Step

1. Write your CREATE PROCEDURE statement.

2. Give the procedure two parameters, one for the cursor and one for the author's last name.

3. Mark the cursor as an output parameter.

4. Type in the statements in the previous sections that allow you to undertake the search.

5. Extend these statements to close and deallocate the cursor internal to the procedure before your procedure returns.

6. Write a procedure that calls this stored procedure to test it.

Ask the Expert

Question: Can you nest cursors?

Answer: Yes, you can, in a sense, nest cursors. That is, you can cycle through one cursor in a loop, and as a part of the processing of an individual row in this loop, you can use other cursors to undertake some work. For example, if you walk through the authors table using a cursor, within this loop you can use a cursor to retrieve all the books written by the author identified by the current row in the cursor.

Question: Can I test values in the current row and update the row based on what I find?

Answer: Yes, you can. Fetch the values you want to test into variables, and test the variables in any way that you need to. In a recent project involving nursing centers, I had to flag a nursing center as being in immediate jeopardy of being closed based on the values of four columns distributed in four separate tables. I built a cursor that brought all the columns together in a single recordset, and updated the column that flags this condition using WHERE CURRENT OF.

Question: What is the biggest argument against using cursors?

Answer: Performance is the biggest argument against using cursors. Cursors have higher overhead than queries. You need to remember, however, that many factors affect the performance of some procedures, and some procedures can easily be scheduled at off-peak times to ease the performance penalty. However, if I had a solution that was a SELECT that joined five tables versus a solution that used five cursors in loops, I would gravitate toward the former.

☑ *Mastery Check*

1. Which statement destroys a cursor?

2. What parameter should you check to walk through a cursor using a loop?

3. What option do you need to use in order to move through a cursor in reverse?

4. What code must you use to open a read-only cursor?

5. When do you need to use BEGIN and END with an IF statement?

6. Can you use multiple cursors in a single loop?

7. Can a cursor be a parameter?

8. What statement opens and populates a cursor?

9. What statement closes a cursor?

10. Are cursor implementations standard in all SQL databases?

Module 16

Building Unions

Goals

- Learn how to construct a union
- Learn about the constraints you must adhere to when using unions
- Learn how to work around union constraints
- Practice building practical unions

Sometimes joins simply do not return the results that you want. In the portfolio database, for example, we have stored several types of people in different tables. Teachers belong in the teacher table, and students in the student table. This arrangement is proper because we store different types of information about students and teachers. In the Pubs database as well, authors are stored in the author table, and employees in the employee table. Databases typically contain data that is very similar in nature, data about people, for example, but that is assigned to different tables because the people belong to different categories.

However, from time to time we may wish to list all the data that is similar in nature without respect to the categories. We may wish simply to know who has registered themselves to use the portfolio database, for example, both teachers and students. Or we might want to build a list of authors and employees so that we can invite everyone associated with our publishing enterprise to a party.

Getting such a list is not such an easy proposition. We cannot use the following syntax, for example:

```
SELECT fname, lname from authors, employee
```

This statement produces an error. First, you cannot list multiple tables following FROM. You must join the tables. Unfortunately, these two tables do not have a field on which the join can be created. Second, the columns for first name and last name are not named identically in the two tables. They are fname and lname in the employee table, but they are au_lname and au_fname in the authors table.

We could use two SELECT statements, like the following, to generate resultsets that contain the records we want:

```
SELECT fname, lname from employee
SELECT au_fname, au_lname from authors
```

With this solution, we wind up with two lists, which we can productively use to create invitations. If we would like them merged and sorted alphabetically, however, our options demand a great deal of work from us. We could print them, cut the printout apart, sort the names, and paste the list back together. Or we could write a program to receive the two resultsets and merge them together.

It would be useful to have a SQL statement that could perform the task of selecting and ordering the records for us. This statement would need to select the recordsets and merge them together. It would need to allow sorting and grouping. While there is no SQL statement proper that performs this operation, there is an operator that allows us to link multiple SQL statements to accomplish this task. This operator is the UNION operator.

Using the Union Operator

Using the UNION operator is very straightforward. First, write the individual SQL statements that will select records from the database and test them to make sure they pull the data correctly. We created two such statements in the previous section. Next join the two statements together using the UNION operator. The two statements we wrote look like this when so joined:

```
SELECT fname, lname from employee
UNION
SELECT au_fname, au_lname from authors
```

When you run this statement, the two recordsets appear as one recordset in the output (see Figure 16-1). The column names from the first statement appear at the top of the data.

If you want to sort the data, add the order by clause to the last query in the union, as follows:

```
SELECT fname, lname from employee
UNION
SELECT au_fname, au_lname from authors
ORDER BY lname
```

Hint

In using ORDER BY with unions, you should place the phrase only in the last query in the union. Placing it elsewhere only causes an error.

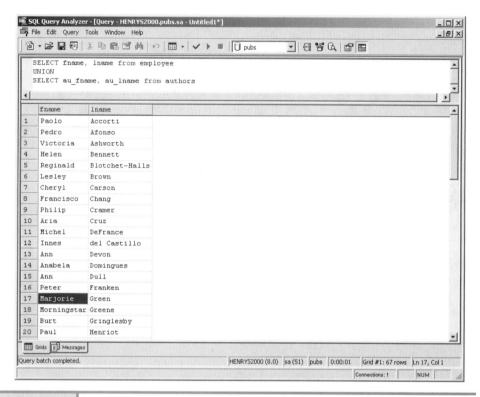

Figure 16-1 The output of the UNION operator

Adhering to Union Constraints

The UNION operator is far from perfect. One of the greatest failings that you will find is that UNION is not uniformly implemented across all databases, or even within recent versions of the same database. For example, SQL Server 7.0 does not allow you to use the UNION operator when you construct a view. SQL Server 2000 does allow you to use the UNION operator to construct a view. You may find that your database does not support the UNION operator at all.

If UNION is available to you, you need to keep these constraints in mind:

- You must refer to columns in the union using the column names used in the first query.

- Data types for the columns referenced in different queries need not be the same. The type for fname could be varchar(50), and the type for au_fname could be char(10). Data types will be converted to a mutually compatible type according to the precedence rules for converting data types that your database implements.

- You must reference the corresponding columns in the same order in each query. UNION uses position in the query to determine which columns to match. The first column in one query merges with the first column in any other query, the second column in one query merges with the second column in any other query, and so forth.

- Where corresponding columns are of different data types, you must make certain that a data type conversion is available. If your database does not supply the conversion for you in its precedence rules, you must supply the conversion explicitly in the queries you use to frame the union.

- All the queries in the union must have the same number of expressions between SELECT and FROM. By expressions, we mean column names, aggregate functions, subqueries, and so on—any element that you can place on this list according to the syntax of the SELECT statement.

- If you wish the results of a union to be stored in a table, place an INTO phrase in the first query in the union.

- You can use the UNION operator within the predicate of an INSERT statement.

- ORDER BY and COMPUTE may be used only within the last query of a union.

- GROUP BY and HAVING phrases apply only to the query in which they are used, and they can appear in any query in the union.

1-Minute Drill

- **What does a union do?**
- **Can you use a union to construct a view?**
- **Which query in a union defines the column names?**

Building Practical Unions

Our example of getting a list of names for all the people in the database is one example of how you might use a union. As an example, it is a bit contrived. Depending on your implementation of unions, you may have difficulty imagining practical uses for unions. Unions, however, are very useful. The trick to seeing how to use them is to see the union as a final result. The union query is the one that delivers a final product, a merged list of multiple recordsets. The real question at hand is how to use that product after it arrives.

One of the most critical factors in using a union is having a repository for the union that will allow you to use it. If you issue a query like our name union in the previous sections, you get the merged list of names. That list is of use to you only if you can manipulate it once you have it. One kind of repository might be a word processor that can attach the query to a mail merge, generating the invitations that we spoke of. Other possible repositories for a union query are external reporting packages that would attach the query to a report template, a spreadsheet that would merge the data into rows and columns to allow further manipulation, or a desktop database like Microsoft Access.

Most often, however, you do not want to move the data outside the confines of the SQL database. Databases like SQL Server 2000 offer the opportunity to materialize a union query as a view. Once you have the view, you can query the view to make further use of the data. The view option, as we have noted, is not universally supported. So what is a practical repository for the results of a union query? The most practical repository is a temporary table. Once the data is in the table, you can

- A union merges the results of two queries into a single recordset.
- You may be able to use a union in constructing a view. However, this depends on your database's implementation of both views and unions.
- The first query

query the table like any other table, join to the table, or use the union operator with other tables if you so desire.

You want to keep a few issues in mind. First, this table is temporary, even if you give it permanent existence in your database. The result of the union query will change as the data in the database is updated. Because you cannot count on the underlying data to remain stable, you must recreate the temporary table each time you use the union. You must truncate the table and repopulate it with each use to make sure that the union results reflect the status of the underlying data.

Second, you do not want to rely on data in this table over long periods of time. You must not rely on a table built from a union query an hour ago on a system that sustains hundreds of transactions per minute. You probably do not want to rely on a table built even a minute ago on a heavily transacted database system. You need to see whatever you do with this table as an operation of very short duration. You must also recognize that you are working with a snapshot. If you absolutely need to see the data exactly as it is right at this second, extracting a union into a temporary table and then querying the table is probably not the best solution.

Third, you need to remember that databases are multiuser entities. This table should be truly temporary. If you use a permanent table, some other user could attempt to run the same union query, starting with truncate table, and leave your query process looking at missing data at a critical moment. You should create this table on the fly and use a local table name. An example of such a table name is #MyTable. Local table names are prefixed with a single pound sign (#) and are visible only in your current session. No one else can grab your table and truncate it by accident, therefore.

Hint

You can create global temporary tables that are visible to any session by prefixing the table name with two pound signs.

Note

Check your database documentation to confirm how to name local and global tables. Implementations may vary.

Fourth, you want to remember to drop your temporary table when you are finished with it, so that you do explicit cleanup of your work and don't rely on default database procedures to do the cleanup. Explicit cleanup lowers the overhead for your work.

Having laid these ground rules, let's consider some suggestions for how to use unions. Let's look at a few scenarios. Any large database eventually hits the point where someone thinks of archiving some of the data. As a table hits several million rows, SELECT statements slow down because of the volume of data to scan. As data ages, it tends to be less likely to be queried. Sales from ten years ago usually have no bearing on quarterly or annual reports, for example. For this reason, some of the data can be moved to an archive table where it can be preserved, but it remains out of the way of the active SELECT statements.

Archiving data can improve performance. But archiving data also means that running a trend analysis over the last ten years becomes difficult. The data is now in two tables. A union allows you to resolve this problem. You can select the relevant data from both tables directly, especially if you are then going to hand the recordset off to a statistical analysis package to run the trend study. If you want to examine the trends directly with SQL statements, you can select the data from the two tables into a temporary table and work on the data in that table.

Building a product catalog is another situation in which a union can be necessary. Products, like the people in our earlier example, tend to fall into categories. Because of these categories, you may need to track different information about different types of products. Such categories typically are manifested as separate tables, one for each category. To get a recordset containing all the products and the standard information that you would display about any product in a catalog, you can use a union to link queries of each separate product category table.

Union.sql

Project 16-1: Build a Union

Having laid out the approach to building a union using a temporary table, let's build a union in this fashion. We will build on our name union, and add the logic necessary to create the temporary table using a SELECT . . . INTO statement. We will build the union as a stored procedure so that we can execute on the server from any calling client program. We will also try another method of populating the temporary table, and save the alternate as a stored procedure as well. You can use these two procedures as templates for working with unions.

Step-by-Step

1. Enter the name union query into the Query Analyzer.

2. Add INTO #temptable before the FROM keyword in the first query.

3. Add a SELECT statement to select all rows from the temporary table. (We are doing this just to prove the table was created. In place of this statement, you would include the queries that process the data in your union for a real working procedure.)

4. Add a DROP TABLE statement at the end of the procedure to drop the temporary table.

5. Test your query to make sure that you have access to the temporary table.

6. Add a CREATE PROCEDURE statement.

7. Run the CREATE PROCEDURE to create the stored procedure.

8. Now try an alternate methodology. Enter the following CREATE TABLE statement at the head of your SQL code:

```
CREATE TABLE #temptable (fname VARCHAR(50), lname VARCHAR(50))
```

9. Delete your SELECT statement.

10. Enter this INSERT INTO statement:

```
INSERT INTO #temptable
SELECT fname, lname from employee
UNION
SELECT au_fname, au_lname from authors
```

11. Keep the SELECT * statement and the DROP TABLE statement at the end of the procedure.

12. Test this query to make sure that you are creating and populating the table.

13. Use CREATE PROCEDURE to create this form of the union query as a stored procedure.

Ask the Expert

Question: You have emphasized the potential for conflict when unions are stored in temporary tables. Is this potential for conflict ever likely to be realized? Won't the database's locking strategy prevent conflicts?

Answer: Any time that you store data temporarily in a table that has permanent existence as a global object in the database, you have the potential for conflict. With unions in a multiuser setting, this potential is very real. Local temporary tables are just a simple method for guaranteeing you never experience such a conflict. Locking strategies alone will not prevent such conflicts, because locks get released as soon as it is practical to do so in order to improve performance. If during one of those releases another user truncates the table, one of your queries might return empty as a consequence. Local temporary tables are more effective.

Question: Is there an advantage of SELECT . . . INTO over using INSERT INTO with unions?

Answer: SELECT . . . INTO allows you to avoid the steps of creating the table and explicitly defining the data types for each column. If you are working in the query analyzer, this statement saves you some typing. If you are embedding the statement into a program, SELECT . . . INTO saves you some research into the exact nature of the data types. If you do not have permissions to view the data types in a tool like Enterprise Manager, this statement allows you to create the table without having to research the data types through a DBA.

Question: Are there any pitfalls in using unions?

Answer: As long as you stick to creating the temporary table locally, using the data, and dropping the table as a regular habit in working with unions, you should not experience any problems. You just need to remember that timing is the key. You are freezing a snapshot of the data in the union, and working with that snapshot. You need to refresh that snapshot when it is relevant to do so for your task. If you forget to do so, you may be working with outdated data.

Question: **Can views help out with this timing problem?**

Answer: If your database supports unions in a view, you can let the view handle the work of refreshing the data as you work with it, making your job just a little easier. However, not all databases will support the union operator in the query that defines a view.

☑ *Mastery Check*

1. Why use a temporary table to store the output of a union?

2. What defines the column names that appear in a union?

3. Where can you use ORDER BY in a union?

4. What is the scope of a WHERE clause in a union query?

5. Why use a local temporary table to store the results of a union?

6. Can the order of columns vary among the queries in a union?

7. What if the data type in one table varies from the data type in another table?

8. Why shouldn't you permanently create a temporary table for use with a union?

9. Why should you explicitly drop your temporary tables?

10. How are columns matched between two queries in a union?

Module 17

Winding Down the Portfolio Project

Goals

- Understand how to embed a client for the Portfolio database in the program
- Determine how to implement registration procedures for the Portfolio project
- Develop the SQL code to implement the Portfolio client
- Create the architecture for embedding a Portfolio client in any application

Throughout this book, we have worked on a Portfolio database and an administrative program for interacting with that database. Our goal in creating this project was to provide you with some real-world database experience. Specifically, we wanted to help you achieve the following:

- Experience defining a database concept
- Practice planning and normalizing tables
- Practice framing queries that represent common tasks relating to a database
- Experience converting queries to stored procedures
- Skill in creating embedded SQL in a program

In presenting the Portfolio project, we achieved the first two goals in Modules 6 and 7. In subsequent modules, we worked on the administrative program, which helped us to achieve the next three goals. The fifth goal was also the focus of the programming we did against the Pubs database in Modules 1 through 5. However, having achieved all these goals, we still have some loose ends in relation to the Portfolio project.

Note

In creating the embedded SQL that ran against both the Pubs database and the Portfolio database, our goal was to introduce you to common database programming methodologies and to introduce you to some of the common problems you have to solve when you are programming with embedded SQL. You may have noticed that we intentionally left bugs behind in creating our programs so that you would discover them and later resolve them. Our goal was to help you achieve some of the experience that you will inevitably get on the job in a nonproduction setting.

We have so far created the database and a simple utility for administrators. While this utility is more a prototype than a polished program, it serves to illustrate the basic technologies that you have to apply to provide a user-friendly front end to any database. You can perhaps easily imagine any number of enhancements that you would want to apply if you were using this program with real users. You would find this author in ready agreement with most of your suggestions. But enhancements beyond the basics are not our focus now. Those are not the loose ends to deal with here. Instead, we need to sketch how the registration process will work, since we said that we wanted both students and teachers to be able to enter themselves into the database with little administrator intervention. As we describe this process, we are not going to focus on the programming required to implement the requirement in Visual Basic or some other language. We are instead going to focus on the SQL required to do the job. We will also focus on the structure and architecture required for the client so that you have some sense of how you might be able to implement the registration process. Our goal in dealing with these loose ends is to give you one more chance to practice all the skills you have acquired. We want to help you integrate those skills into practical project planning and design, with a focus on the real world rather than the sample.

Note

The Portfolio project will actually become a real-world program about twelve months after this book appears. The author's company, Write Environment, Inc., plans to develop the system we planned together into an actual product that complements its educational software offering. You have actually participated in some of the ground-floor planning for this product as you have worked through this project.

The Client's Structure

In order to imagine students and teachers registering themselves to use the Portfolio database, we need to imagine them performing this activity from some kind of a client program. All sorts of clients are imaginable. We could write a teacher portfolio management tool that would allow teachers to review the contents of student portfolios. We could write a student portfolio management tool as well. We could write a portfolio management tool for each subject area, one for teachers of that subject and one for students of that subject. Any such program might be a valid approach to undertaking student and teacher registration in the Portfolio database. How would we undertake this decision? Would we use user-centered requirements analysis? Would we study the problem in usability laboratories?

Before you spend much time on this problem, we need to take a look at some research undertaken by Write Environment, Inc. Oddly enough, resolving this issue for educational software took fifteen years of trying out interfaces and failing in order to discover an appropriate interface for use with a project like the Portfolio project. What Write Environment, Inc., discovered is that users of such systems have preexisting priorities that govern their use of the software. Students who are learning to write see the production of text as the primary activity in which they are engaged. All other activities associated with writing, including the management of portfolios, are subordinated to this central priority. Because the word processor is the primary tool used in writing, students learning to write respond to tools that support subordinated processes better if those tools are attached to the word processor as extensions of the word processor. Therefore, the client piece for students interacting with a writing portfolio should be attached to a word processor.

Hint

If you want to read the research reports that document the priorities of students learning to write, visit http://www.writeenvironment.com/OnTeachingWriting.html. Although other learning processes are different in character, related research indicates that similar priorities are at work in other subject domains.

At least for students, the portfolio client ought to be an extension of the word processor. For other types of portfolios, the client ought to be the primary software tool that the students and teachers use to undertake the learning process for that subject matter. Because of the priorities that students apply when they learn to write, we are talking not about some sort of client application, but about some set of dialog boxes that can be attached to an application.

The actual form these dialog boxes take needs to depend on the requirements of the users. At the very least, to undertake orderly registration of a teacher or a student, we need to collect the uniquely identifying characteristics of such an entity for the database. What we have discussed so far is that the uniquely identifying characteristics would be first name, last name, and password. As a result, a minimal dialog box might look something like this:

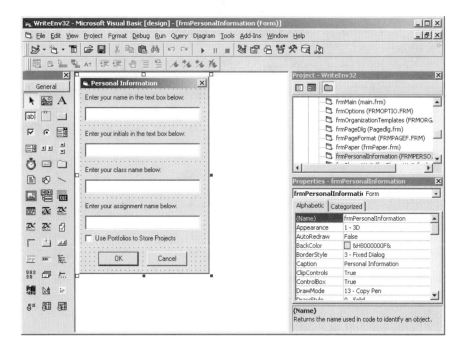

Without proceeding very far on the project, however, we might realize that several other kinds of events might need to take place. Students need to check work into a portfolio and check work out. They may choose to delete work, and they may choose to unregister themselves from the portfolio system. Because of these facts, we might need a more complex dialog box to handle all these options. Such a dialog box might look like this:

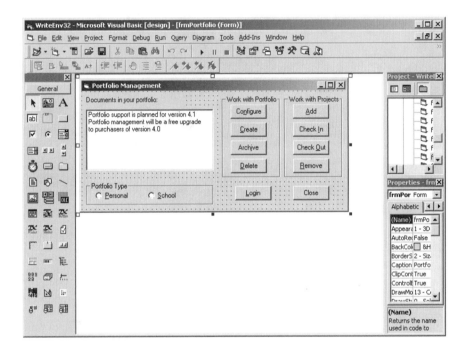

Having sketched the rough form that the program element that provides the portfolio functionality might look like, let's assume that we will be working with a dialog box that will attach to an application. That dialog box will contain input fields for first name, last name, and password. It will also contain buttons that, when clicked, invoke specific functions, like registering a student. We don't want to get lost in the programming side of such a dialog box. Instead, we want to focus on the SQL involved. So let's assume that we are working with a dialog box, and we need to write the stored procedures that will accomplish the following specific tasks:

- Register a student to use the Portfolio database

- Register a teacher to use the Portfolio database

- Allow an existing user, teacher or student, to unregister from using the Portfolio database

- Check work into a portfolio

- Check work out of a portfolio

- Delete work from a portfolio

Ask the Expert

Question: How do you research the interface design for such a project?

Answer: In educational products, designing an interface requires lots of trial and error effort. In many cases, students cannot tell you what they need as learners. Teachers can help, but they often lack the theoretical perspective to fill in all the details necessary. Theory also helps, but in many cases the learning theory on record is incomplete or misses the point entirely.

For an example of popular learning theory that is incomplete, consider phonics as a method of learning to read. Phonics arises from the theory that there are letter to sound correspondences that beginning readers must master in order to learn to read. This theory arises from the perception that if you can pronounce a word, you can read it. The idea seems to work well on the face of it, and phonics enjoys wide political popularity these days.

But if you want to design software that improves reading, especially reading comprehension, you need go no farther than the T-shirt "hukt on foniks werkt for me" to see the limitations of the theory. There are lots of letter to sound correspondences that are not right. And being able to pronounce a sentence does not mean that you can comprehend its meaning. (Read a few sentences aloud from Immanuel Kant's *Critique of Pure Reason* if you are in doubt.)

Designing the interface for the Portfolio project has, actually, required fifteen years of effort. Over that time, we took the best that we could glean from students, teachers, and theories. We designed an interface based on those parameters. We tried the interface out on students and teachers, and we learned from seven years of miserable failure how to get an interface that was at least usable, if not intuitive.

One of our first failures arose from the belief that having a conversation with a computer would be the best way to stimulate writing. We gave the computer a voice, and it talked with you as you worked, asking questions and providing hints. The first user request for that system was an off switch for the voice.

Question: Okay, so that was a really complex problem to solve. What about interfaces to more straightforward databases?

Answer: All interfaces have evolved over time, and you need to review the results of that experience industry wide to see how the results might apply to your interface. For example, the first word processors had a blank screen onto which you typed. WordPerfect's blue screen was probably the most famous. The idea was to simulate typing on a page. That would make using a word processor just like using a typewriter.

However, word processors are not like typewriters. Early word processors included hundreds of commands for manipulating text. WordStar used control key combinations for these commands, and there were so many of them that each command sequence required three key presses. WordPerfect took advantage of the function keys, but there were different meanings for CTRL+F1 and ALT+F1. Third-party products to help make these interfaces usable were key templates or key caps that had the commands printed on them for easy reference.

It took quite a while before the value of menus became apparent. It also took a while before dialog boxes became accepted as a way of interacting with a program. All of these changes took considerable trial and error to work out. Look at interfaces for similar programs to see what solutions they apply. Then ask yourself how you can make that interface better.

For databases, the interface needs both to accept and to display information. It needs to allow you to set up an insert or an update, it needs to allow you to confirm the action, and it needs to supply an elegant way of recovering if the change fails. Keep in mind that simpler interfaces are always valued over complex interfaces. Your constant question should be "How can we make this more intuitive and simpler?" Your main guide is going to be the failure side of the trial and error process, no matter how much research and forethought you put into planning the interface to your database. So plan to build prototypes. Plan to put the prototype in front of some actual users. Learn from what the users do. Plan at least three iterations of this process into your project's life cycle. And always keep in mind what a difference the invention of the Wizard made in dealing with software configuration. Stay focused on making your interface perform such wizardry.

The Registration Process

In order to prepare to implement registration and related processes, we need to understand what will be required. To add an individual to the database, we need to know the following:

- First name
- Last name
- Password

We are going to assume that once the program collects these items, it stores them in temporary variables for reuse. Because of such storage, once a user identifies herself to the system, she won't have to identify herself again for that session. Registration officially is adding the user to the database for the first time. However, it can also be seen as the processing of "logging on" to the database to be able to use the portfolio. In actuality, the user is not logging in to the SQL database. The user is just providing credentials to the client system that allow the client to identify the user's records in the database properly.

When a user registers, therefore, our program collects a first name, last name, and password from the user. The system also inquires whether the user is a teacher or a student, and whether the user is a new user or an existing user. Once in possession of this information, the client needs to look to see whether the user is already in the system. We will therefore need lookup procedures for both teachers and students. If the user is not in the system, regardless of whether the user identifies himself as new, the user gets added to the system. As a part of the process of adding a student, we need to add teacher and class information to the database. As a part of adding a teacher to the database, we need to add class information and optional school information. Once we have done so, we have registered a new user.

If the user already exists and the user identifies herself as an existing user, we only need to to store the first name, last name, and password in client program variables for future use. We have verified the user's identity and she can continue work. If a new user lookup finds that an existing user already has that first name, last name, and password combination, our client program needs to return a value that so indicates and then the client can prompt the user to enter a different password. Once a new user has identified a unique combination of first name, last name, and password, the new user gets inserted into the database, and registration is complete.

In order to undertake registration, therefore, we need a lookup procedure for both teachers and students. The lookup procedure needs to receive first name, last name, and password as parameters, and to return a code that indicates a failure to find this 3-tuple in the database or the existence of the 3-tuple in the database. Let's undertake building this procedure now.

Lookups.sql

Project 17-1: Write the Lookups

We are going to build two procedures, but they each have the same form. The only difference is the table that each procedure hits. Both are SELECT statements. Both must check @@ROWCOUNT to determine the number of rows affected by the SELECT statement. Follow these steps:

Step-by-Step

1. For each procedure, write a CREATE PROCEDURE statement.

2. Give each procedure three parameters, @FirstName, @LastName, and @Password.

3. Write a select statement for each procedure that selects all rows from the appropriate database table (Teacher or Student) where the appropriate fields equal the values of the parameters.

4. Return the value of @@ROWCOUNT as the return value for the stored procedure.

Hint

We are assuming that you have the skills now to look up appropriate data types for each parameter or variable you are required to use in the database table definitions.

Planning Required Insert Procedures

If we must insert a new user, the steps for inserting the user depend on whether we are inserting a student or a teacher. For a student, we follow this procedure:

1. The client program asks which class or classes the student is taking.

2. The client program inserts the student's first name, last name, and password into the Student Table.

3. The client program inserts one record into the Class_Student table for each class the student is taking.

For a teacher, we follow this procedure:

1. The client program asks which school the teacher is associated with.

2. The client program asks which classes the teacher teaches.

3. The client program inserts the Teacher's first name, last name, password, and school ID into the Teacher table.

4. The client program inserts one record into the Class_Teacher table for each class the teacher is teaching.

In all of these procedures, we have to assume that the list of schools and the list of classes are up to date. If they are not up to date, an administrator will have to update the records in the database using the administrative tool that we created. Let's build the insert procedures required now.

RegistrationInserts.sql

Project 17-2: Write the INSERTS

To insert a student, we need two procedures. One of these takes first name, last name, and password as parameters and undertakes an insert operation against the Student table. The other takes ClassID and StudentID as parameters and undertakes an insert operation against the Class_Student table.

To insert a teacher, you need two similar procedures. The first takes first name, last name, password, and school ID as parameters and executes an insert operation against the Teacher table. The other takes ClassID and TeacherID as parameters and undertakes an insert operation against the Class_Student table.

In each of these procedures, we are going to assume that the ID values are available to the client program. In the case of inserting information into the Teacher or Student table, we will return the ID values from the stored procedure that executed the INSERT. In the case of class ID values, we will assume that these are picked from a list box in the client program.

Step-by-Step

1. Create four CREATE PROCEDURE statements.

2. For one, create the parameters @FirstName, @LastName, and @Password.

3. Write an INSERT for this procedure that inserts these values into the Student table.

4. Define a variable in this procedure called @StudentID.

5. SELECT StudentID into this variable where First_Name, Last_Name, and Password match the parameter values.

6. Return @StudentID as the return value.

7. For the second procedure, create the parameters @FirstName, @LastName, @SchoolID, and @Password.

8. Write an INSERT for this procedure that inserts these values into the Teacher table.

17

9. Define a variable in this procedure called @TeacherID.

10. SELECT TeacherID into this variable where First_Name, Last_Name, SchoolID, and Password match the parameter values.

11. Return @TeacherID as the return value.

12. For the third procedure, create the parameters ClassID and StudentID.

13. Write an INSERT for this procedure that inserts these values into the Class_Student table.

14. Check the value of @@ERROR. If this value is not zero, return @@ERROR as the error code. This value will indicate that you attempted to insert a duplicate record. Otherwise, return zero as the return value.

Hint

To be able to rely on @@ERROR in this way, you need to create an index for the Class_Student table that is a multicolumn index, including both columns, of course. This index needs to be a unique index. Only unique pairings of StudentID and ClassID will be allowed in the table with such an index in place.

15. For the fourth procedure, create the parameters ClassID and TeacherID.

16. Write an INSERT for this procedure that inserts these values into the Class_Teacher table.

17. Check the value of @@ERROR. If this value is not zero, return @@ERROR as the error code. This value will indicate that you attempted to insert a duplicate record. Otherwise, return zero as the return value.

Hint

You need a multicolumn unique index on the Class_Teacher table as well.

Planning Required Unregister Procedures

As we have noted throughout discussion of the Portfolio project, we want to have users do as much administration as possible. Therefore, we are wise to have our client dialog box include an Unregister button, so that users can declare that they wish to stop using the Portfolio database. This option, of course, must be different for teachers and for students.

For teachers, we need only to change the Active column in the teacher table from its default value of 1 to the value 0. We don't need to mark anything else inactive for a teacher. We also don't want to delete any other entries for that teacher, because we want to be able to reactivate a teacher at will.

For students, we want to do the same for the Active column in the student table. We don't wish to make other changes, because we will want to be able to un-unregister the student at will.

Now comes an issue for debate. Do we mark student records relating to portfolio contents for deletion when we unregister a student? On the one hand, we might want to say yes, because the student's work is no longer relevant within the portfolio system. This is one approach. If we reregister the student, we can mark any items within the system as not deletable, assuming they still exist.

However, what do we do if a student writes nine months after leaving the school system and asks for the portfolio contents on CD? This is a very likely scenario. Will we say "Gosh, we hope that stuff is still around"? The better solution is to have the stuff still around, archived to CD if necessary, but still around. An archiving solution goes well beyond the scope of this discussion, so we will leave our decision as not to mark any student work for deletion at this time. Besides, we would need to distinguish between a work a student marked for deletion and a work that unregistering a student marked for deletion, and that issue is one that is more complex than the scope of this exercise allows for as well.

Hint

If we leave unregistered student work marked as active, we can tell by checking the student's Active bit and the work's Active bit whether the student marked the work for deletion. If the student is active and the work is marked for deletion, we can delete it, because an active student obviously intended to delete the work from the portfolio. If the student is inactive and the work is active, we should not delete the work, because the student never expressed an intention to delete the work. Some theoretical administrative DeleteStudentWork routine could check these fields and make appropriate decisions about what to do. However, such a routine should only be run well in arrears, because students are very likely to change their mind about whether to destroy work stored in a portfolio. You want maximally to protect changes of mind, as well as to protect your ability to send work to students who have departed the school system.

Unregister.sql

Project 17-3: Write the Unregister Procedures

Having examined all the issues, we need two unregister routines for our Portfolio project. They are remarkably similar, and their only difference is the tables they work on.

Step-by-Step

1. Write two CREATE PROCEDURE statements.

2. Give each parameters that receive the first name, last name, and password.

3. For one, write an UPDATE statement that updates the Active column in the Teacher table to zero where the first name, last name, and password match the parameters.

4. For the other, write an UPDATE statement that updates the Active column in the Student table to zero where the first name, last name, and password match the parameters.

5. Return the value of @@ERROR from each procedure so that we can tell whether an error has occurred with the update and take appropriate action in the client program if necessary.

1-Minute Drill

● **Is it wise to discard data from a database?**

● **What does @@ERROR tell you?**

● **What does @@ROWCOUNT tell you?**

Planning Required Checkout Procedures

When students have created a work and stored it in the portfolio, they will want to work on it again or just to view it. The Portfolio database supplies a mechanism that prevents accidental changes, which is to support checking out the work from the Portfolio system. Actually, all this checkout procedure entails is setting the InUse flag on the work's entry in the Portfolio_Contents table. Any client program working with the Portfolio database therefore has the obligation to check the In_Use field for the work's record, and to deny access to any user for whom this bit field is set to a value of 1.

The checkout procedure itself is simply an UPDATE statement that sets this bit field. The WHERE criterion for the UPDATE is the Content_Path column being equal to a value passed to the procedure. We are assuming that the file open dialog being used by the application obtains its contents from the Content_Path column, and that the value of Content_Path being passed in as a parameter is therefore identical to a path actually stored in the database. Let's create the checkout procedure.

● **No. Often you will need data that has been marked as inactive or for deletion even though it has been so marked.**

● **The error number for the last statement that executed**

● **The number of rows affected by the last SQL statement that executed**

CheckOut.sql

Project 17-4: Write the Checkout Procedure

Now that we have examined how to convert a select query to a stored procedure, it is time to convert all of the queries we have used so far to stored procedures. We need to find all the SELECT queries in the program and convert them. Take the following steps.

Step-by-Step

1. Write a CREATE PROCEDURE statement.

2. Add a parameter to receive a path value.

3. Write the UPDATE statement to set In_Use equal to 1 where the column Content_Path equals the parameter.

4. Return @@ERROR so that we can check for success in the client program.

Planning Required Check-In Procedures

If we can check work out, we obviously must be able to check it back in. This procedure is simply the reverse of the checkout procedure. We know the content path of the item checked out because we have the item in hand. All we need do to check it in is to set the In_Use field back to 0 in the database (as well as save the file). Let's write the check-in procedure.

CheckIn.sql

Project 17-5: Write the Check-In Procedure

Now that we have examined how to convert a select query to a stored procedure, it is time to convert all of the queries we have used so far to stored procedures. We need to find all the SELECT queries in the program and convert them. Take the following steps.

Step-by-Step

1. Write a CREATE PROCEDURE statement.

2. Add a parameter to receive a path value.

3. Write the UPDATE statement to set In_Use equal to 0 where the column Content_Path equals the parameter.

4. Return @@ERROR so that we can check for success in the client program.

Planning Required Delete Procedures

Deleting an item from a portfolio is a little like unregistering a student or a teacher. Because students may change their minds, we would like not to delete an item from storage until we are absolutely certain that there is no need for the item in the future. Because of this requirement, deleting is a matter of setting the Deleted field to 1 in the record for any item stored in the Portfolio_Contents table.

Hint

We are assuming that Content_Path will always be unique for any given item stored in the Portfolio system. Under some circumstances, this assumption may not be valid. Much depends on how the client system organizes the storage for student portfolios. Our preference would be to create storage folders based on the teacher's name, the student's name, the PortfolioID, and the student's StudentID value in order to guarantee this uniqueness. However, if some storage schema that does not guarantee uniqueness is in place, you might want to pass the PortfolioID as a parameter as well to guarantee that you uniquely identify the record to be updated.

A delete operation is therefore much like a checkout procedure in that it involves an UPDATE statement. The procedure must accept a Content_Path value as the single parameter. Let's create the procedure.

Project 17-6: Write the Delete Procedure

PortfolioDelete.sql Now that we have examined how to convert a select query to a stored procedure, it is time to convert all of the queries we have used so far to stored procedures. We need to find all the SELECT queries in the program and convert them. Take the following steps.

Step-by-Step

1. Write a CREATE PROCEDURE statement.

2. Add a parameter to receive a path value.

3. Write the UPDATE statement to set Deleted equal to 1 where the column Content_Path equals the parameter.

4. Return @@ERROR so that we can check for success in the client program.

A Client Architecture

We have talked a lot about the client program that should support students and teachers using the Portfolio database. We have suggested what its look and feel should be, and we have made several comments about what we assume it should do. How should we attach this program to software that might interact with the portfolio database?

We have two approaches that we can use. One is to program the functionality into each and every program that has to use the Portfolio database. This would mean creating the dialog boxes, functions, and subroutines required, storing these in a set of files that can easily be included in any program, and copying the functionality into place in any program that we see as a portfolio client.

While this approach gets the job done, it creates many problems for the deployment of our product. What if we need to fix a bug in the client piece? Well, we fix it in every place that we included the client. Even if we compiled it into a C language link library or its equivalent, we would need to recompile and relink each program that uses the client. What if we want to modify an off-the-shelf program to use the Portfolio database? We would need the source code for that application. What if we cannot afford lots of connections to the Portfolio database, either because of licensing costs or poor performance?

The solution to all of these problems is to write the code once and compile it separately from the applications that use it. Then we need to expose an interface to the program to all the programs that we intend to use it. The only requirement for a potential client program would then be that the potential client support the interface to our client software. Fortunately, for virtually any operating system, there are methods for doing so.

In the Microsoft arena, we would write the client as a COM component. Applications written for the Microsoft Windows operating system would need a macro language that supports instantiating and using a COM object in order to use the Portfolio system. (Most off-the-shelf programs support this functionality.) Or we would need to program the application ourselves to use a COM object. The object itself could be installed on the local system, or it could be installed in the Microsoft Transaction Server. The Transaction Server solution makes the object available to all client computers on the network, and it adds the advantage of reducing the number of connections required by the database, because the Transaction Server pools connections at the database end to reduce the overall number required.

If we are working outside the Microsoft arena, as the release of Corel's office suite for Linux suggests might be possible, we would be using CORBA objects instead of COM objects. The goal would be the same: to have written and compiled the client package once, and to enable any program that supports its interface to become a client of the Portfolio system using our client package to undertake the communication.

Moving to this type of architecture for the client package means that, if we were writing the software in Visual Basic, we would build a class that contains the functions necessary to do the work. We would then expose the member functions of the class as methods, and the essential variables as properties. Any application that instantiates our object can see these properties and methods, and use them to undertake client communication with the database. This option gives us a maintainable and reusable client package.

Ask the Expert

Question: OK, author, this is my last crack at you. Where do I go from here?

Answer: We have tried in this book to acquaint you with SQL from the perspective of the way the average programmer has to learn it. This hasn't been an introduction to SQL for database administrators, obviously. This has been SQL for the majority of the people who have to use SQL to take a look at data.

As a result, we have focused on statements and their utility. We have looked quite a bit at how to use embedded SQL. We have avoided issues strictly related to database administration, and we have soft-pedaled a number of theory issues.

To get acquainted with the theory we have avoided, turn to Appendix B of this book. It is a good starting place for understanding how SQL is organized. When you are ready to move on to get more background about SQL, you should look for a book that addresses database administration if you need to understand more about how to plan and build databases. If you are looking for advanced SQL programming, you should look for a book that discusses tips, tricks, and techniques, which are just code words for esoteric stuff about SQL programming. "Secrets" is a similar code word, as are "mastering," "unleashed," "expert," and "maximizing." One project I worked on used "ultimate" to designate this sense of expertise.

So much for tips about how to spot your next book by title. The best way to find your next book to help you work with SQL is to examine your questions. When you outgrow this *Beginner's Guide*—and all involved expect that you will—make a list of the questions you have that this book does not answer. Go to the bookstore with that list of questions, and look at the SQL books on the shelf. Don't look at the table of contents, because you won't find answers to your questions there. Look instead at the index. Look up answers to your questions. Buy the book that answers your questions according to what you find in the index.

Two other tips. First, if you like this book, check for other series by this publisher. A publisher that has met your needs once is likely to do it again. It's like finding the right vineyard, if you like wine. Vintages come and go. What you are looking for is a vineyard whose wine maker has roughly the same taste you do. Second, if you find an author whose work you like, look for other books by the same person. The same principle applies. Like minds think in like ways, and you can learn more from someone who organizes things your way than you can from someone who doesn't organize things your way.

Question: **If I want to advance my career as a programmer, which database should I learn?**

Answer: This is a tough question, because fashions come and go. Seven years ago, I would have said Oracle or Informix, and that you should learn these on a UNIX platform. Now the operating system preferences have changed, as have the allegiances of those who use and consume databases.

You certainly cannot go wrong by learning Oracle. It is, if not an industry standard, the database that everyone has to reference if you are migrating to their database. Oracle has been around a long time, and it is almost the reference standard.

SQL Server is very popular right now, because of Microsoft's penetration into the software market. However, SQL Server still has issues relating to scalability, and it runs on only one operating system, and that operating system still has yet to mature as far as UNIX has.

Probably the best advice along these lines is not to pick a database, but to get more training in standard SQL. You can apply the standardized language to any database, and you can always pick up the implementation details as you need to. I have worked with several companies that have multiple databases in deployment at the same time. Does this make sense as a corporate strategy? In my opinion, no. In fact, this strategy obscures corporate goals. But they did it anyway, and your goal is to fit into what exists so that you remain employable.

Question: If I want to move toward database administration, which database should I learn?

Answer: Popular databases right now in client/server environments are Sybase, SQL Server, and Oracle. Borland's InterBase may have a strong impact, largely because they are offering it free with source code. The best way to tell what database to focus on as a DBA is to go to http://www.dice.com, and to search for DBA jobs. You will get a very strong sense of the skill sets in demand in your area. You should also read the trade press to keep abreast of apparent trends. *Computer World, InfoWorld,* and similar publications cover the broad spectrum of the industry, as do several online news services. Keep abreast of who is using what in this fashion, and you can keep your career plans on track.

☑Mastery Check

1. Find a column in the Portfolio database that should be deleted or redefined.

2. Under what circumstances should you delete data from the database?

3. What is the best architecture for the client piece for the Portfolio database?

4. What do check-in and checkout procedures actually do?

5. What does the delete procedure actually do?

6. What critical field do the register and unregister procedures modify?

7. When a teacher registers, what two tables need to be updated?

8. When a student registers, what two tables need to be updated?

9. What fields uniquely identify a student?

10. What uniquely identifies a content item in a portfolio?

Appendix A

Answers to Mastery Checks

Module 1: Accessing the Database

1. When should you use a User DSN to create an ODBC database connection?

Use a User DSN when you want only a given user to be able to use it while logged into the machine.

2. When is ADO the best database object technology to use for making connections?

ADO is the best technology to use when you are planning to move forward with Microsoft's data access technology. While DAO is currently being maintained, ADO is the object technology most likely to be supported in the future. It is receiving all the XML features, for example, while DAO is not.

3. Which methods can be used to create connections to SQL databases?

A. Data Access Objects

4. Give the practical use for a tool like Microsoft's Query Analyzer for programmers who are developing SQL database programs.

The Query Analyzer allows you to develop and test queries outside a programming environment. It gives you feedback about what might be wrong, such as the line number on which the error occurred. If you try to frame SQL entirely from within a program, you must debug your queries blind. You can always pull a problem query into Query Analyzer and work on it directly, and then place it back in your database program.

Module 2: Retrieving Data

1. A SELECT statement can have the following parts:

D. ORDER BY, HAVING, GROUP BY

2. Use a join to accomplish which of the following tasks:

A. Linking two tables so that rows return from both tables for a query

3. Explain what embedded SQL is.

SQL used inside a computer program not written in SQL

4. What is the older syntax for creating an outer join?

A plus sign after the table name that should return all rows

5. What is the concatenation operator?

The plus sign

6. Explain what the AS keyword does.

AS allows you to rename any element you select from the database, so that the element appears as a new column in the resultset with the name that follows AS in the SQL statement.

7. What type of join returns the fewest rows?

An inner join

8. The distinguishing characteristic of an outer join is:

A. It returns at least all the rows from one of the joined tables.

9. What is a join that does not rely on an equality in the WHERE or ON clause called?

A non-equijoin

10. What does GROUP BY do?

GROUP BY creates groups within the dataset according to the values of the column name you choose to group by. If you group by sex, your rows are grouped into two sets of rows, one where sex = male and one where sex = female. If you compute an aggregate for another column, you will get an aggregate value for males and an aggregate value for females.

Module 3: Inserting Data

1. An INSERT statement can have the following parts:

D. Both A and C

2. A SELECT INTO statement can have the following parts:

A. Table name, list of columns, list of joins

3. Explain when to use SELECT INTO.

Use SELECT INTO when you want the result of the operation to be a new table containing the columns and values you specify in the statement.

4. Explain when to use a SELECT inside an INSERT.

Use a SELECT with an INSERT when you want to insert data into a temporary table that contains columns stored primarily in multiple tables elsewhere in the database, or when you want to create a view.

5. How can constraints cause problems for an INSERT?

Constraints can prevent an INSERT from succeeding if you attempt to insert a value that must appear in another table before it can appear in the target table.

6. Can you insert NULL into a key value?

No

7. How do you check to see whether constraints operate on a table?

Right-click the table title bar in a database diagram and select Check Constraints from the context menu.

8. What does the GetDate( ) function do?

GetDate( ) returns the current date and time at the database server.

9. If you modify a table after some programmer has been working with the table for some time, what should you take care to do?

If you must modify an existing table against which programs insert data, you should either make the column nullable or design it to insert a default value if it is not included in an INSERT statement.

10. If you use a key column in multiple tables, what should you take care to do?

You should name key columns by the same name no matter where an instance of the key appears in the database.

Module 4: Updating Data

1. An UPDATE statement can have the following parts:

C. UPDATE, SET, SELECT

2. A SET phrase can have the following parts:

D. Column name, assignment operator, value

3. Explain what happens if you do not use WHERE or HAVING.

You update every row in the table.

4. Explain how to use LIKE to search for a zip code that begins with 40 and then has any single character followed by 2 followed by another character.

LIKE '40_2_'

5. What mathematical and logical operators can be used in a WHERE clause?

You may use any mathematical or logical operator in a WHERE clause.

6. Can you do math in a WHERE clause?

Of course you can do math in a WHERE clause, just as we described for the SELECT statement.

7. What keyword allows you to use multiple tables in an UPDATE statement?

FROM

8. What does the DATEPART() function do?

DATEPART() returns the part of the datetime value you specify in the first argument from the value identified by the second argument, which may be a column containing datetime values or a single datetime value itself.

9. What must you do to include a HAVING or a JOIN in an UPDATE statement?

You must use a FROM phrase with a SELECT statement.

10. How many tables can you update at once?

One

Module 5: Deleting Data

1. Which two statements can delete data?

D. TRUNCATE TABLE and DELETE

2. A DELETE statement should have which one of the following elements:

A. A WHERE Clause, because disaster happens if you don't have a WHERE clause. The table name is something you must have.

3. Explain what happens if you do not use WHERE in a DELETE statement.

You delete every row in the table.

4. How can you make a quick copy of your data to protect against DELETE errors?

Use a SELECT INTO statement just before your DELETE statement.

5. How do you start a transaction?

Use the BEGIN TRANSACTION statement.

6. How do you roll back a transaction?

Use a ROLLBACK TRANSACTION statement.

7. How do you complete a successful transaction?

Use a COMMIT TRANSACTION statement.

8. What prompting does SQL provide to prevent you from making errors with the DELETE statement?

Joins are not permitted in a DELETE statement. However, a join may appear in a subquery used in the WHERE clause.

9. Can you use a join in a delete statement?

Yes, one

10. How many tables can you delete at once?

One

Module 6: Creating Tables

1. A multipart key is also called:

D. All of the above

2. ALTER TABLE can have the following parts:

D. All of the above

3. Explain what happens when you use ON UPDATE CASCADE.

The UPDATE also changes data in the table where the primary key reference by the foreign key resides.

4. How would you add a column named Here with data type char(6) to a table named Places?

ALTER TABLE Places ADD COLUMN Here char(6)

5. What is the best data type for an integer column?

Tinyint, if the values range from 0 to 255, smallint for the typical integer, int if you need to store larger numbers.

6. You need to store the computer name in a column, and you know that NetBIOS names have been extended to 255 characters for Windows 2000. What is the best data type, char, nchar, varchar, or nvarchar?

In the United States, the best data type is varchar. First, you probably won't be using Unicode characters in computer names. Second, few organizations are using 255-character computer names. If you are working in a language that requires a Unicode character set, the answer is still varchar. The text boxes that accept NetBIOS names do not allow for easy Unicode character entry.

7. Do you think it is better to use float, decimal, or money for monetary values?

Money, because it is optimized to store monetary values. Float requires more overhead to handle an unknown number of decimal fractions. Decimal is not optimized to handle monetary values as efficiently.

8. How do you delete a table?

DROP TABLE *tablename*

9. How do you delete a column?

DROP COLUMN *columnname*

10. Can a DROP take place within an ALTER TABLE?

Yes

Module 7: Creating Databases

1. When you are ready to create a database, you must:

A. Check the documentation to confirm which statements to use.

2. To import an operating system user, use the following procedure:

A. sp_grantlogin

3. What is a key clue that you must use bridge tables?

One to many relationships between two entities

4. How do you locate the primary entities in any given database?

Primary entities typically have larger numbers of relationships to other entities. They are also the "one" side of the equation in one to many relationships.

5. Why didn't you need to include a Student_Portfolio table?

The Portfolio table itself already contained the necessary functionality.

6. Why use the bit data type for the columns named Active?

Bit requires less storage overhead for values that are essentially on or off.

7. What is an entity-relationship diagram?

Entity relationship diagrams show relationships among the entities that make up the tables you design in a database and the constraints that apply to them.

8. Why use the data type varchar for names?

You cannot predict the length of someone's name. Varchar does not pad the field with blank spaces in order to have a fixed-length string represented by the data type. It stores only the number of characters necessary.

9. Why include a Delete field in Portfolio_Contents?

The Delete field allows you to implement an undelete feature for portfolios.

10. What procedure adds a database login?

sp_addlogin

Module 8: Using Operators

1. When you want to select one item from a list returned by a subquery, you must:

C. Use IN

2. To pattern-match in strings, you use:

A. The % wildcard

3. Assume that you have set up a table of book chapters. For each chapter record, you store book_ID, chapter_number, chapter_title, and page_count. If the author has not yet assigned a chapter title, you want to display "Title not yet assigned" in any query results. How could you do this?

Make chapter_title a nullable field and use ISNULL to return the string when a NULL is encountered.

4. If you want to match the values A, B, and C in one position in a string, how would you do it?

LIKE 'restofstring[A,B,C]restofstring'

5. What is the crucial trick in using EXISTS?

Make sure that you include a field from the main query in the WHERE clause of the subquery.

6. Does IN require a subquery?

IN does not require a subquery. It can use a comma-separated list instead.

7. What does *WHERE city = ANY (SELECT city FROM publishers)* match?

It matches city from the main query to any city returned from the subquery. If there is one or more matches, the expression returns true. If there are no matches, it returns false.

8. What does *WHERE city = ALL (SELECT city FROM publishers)* match?

The field city in the main query must match all of the cities returned by the subquery. If there is a failure to match on even one of the returned cities, the expression returns false. If there is a match on all the cities, the expression returns true.

9. What is the truth value of *NOT 1 = 2*?

True

10. What is the truth value of *NOT 3 = 4 AND NOT 1 = 1*?

False

Module 9: Using Functions

1. When you want to count the number of records that match a specific criterion, which function do you use?

C. COUNT

2. To pattern match in strings, you use:

D. Either a or b

3. To get the length of a string, which function do you use?

LEN

4. To make certain that you are viewing an angle's measurement in degrees, which function do you use?

DEGREES

5. In SQL, what is the default measurement system for angles?

Radians

6. Which function returns the sine of an angle?

SIN

7. Which functions return the upper and lower bounds of a measurement?

FLOOR and CEILING

8. What function do you use to get a square root of a number?

SQRT

9. How do you make certain that the value returned from column1 has no padding?

RTRIM(LTRIM(column1))

10. How do you get the date at the database server?

GETDATE()

Module 10: Building Subqueries

1. Give the purpose of a subquery.

To return a value or a recordset for use in another query

2. What are the two most common locations for a subquery?

In the list of values to select and in the WHERE clause

3. Can you use a subquery in a HAVING clause?

Yes, but only if you have grouped your data

4. Where do you place the subquery in a DELETE statement?

In the WHERE or HAVING clause

5. Where do you place a subquery in an INSERT statement?

In the SELECT list or in the WHERE clause

6. How do you use a subquery to check to see whether a recordset has been returned?

Use the EXISTS keyword.

7. How do you tell if the subquery has returned a specific value?

Use the IN keyword.

8. What does the ANY keyword achieve in relation to a subquery?

You can tell whether any value returned from the subquery has a specific relation to a value.

9. How do you debug queries containing subqueries?

Break the queries apart and determine whether the separate queries seem to return the appropriate results. Then assemble the complete query and imagine the circumstances that would yield the incorrect results.

10. How do you prevent a grouping in a subquery from affecting the grouping in the main query?

Make certain that values in the subquery do not determine the critical grouping in the main query.

Module 11: Building Views

1. Give the purpose of a view.

To provide protected access to a set of records

2. Why might you use an updateable view?

To allow users to insert data into a limited portion of a table

3. In an updateable view, what does using WITH CHECK OPTION accomplish?

It forces the check of any INSERT or UPDATE against the WHERE conditions used to create the view. Violations of these conditions produce an error.

4. Can you use a UNION in a view?

UNION statements are typically not supported in views.

5. In the SQL Server view builder, what happens if you end your query with a semicolon?

You get an error when you try to save the view. Semicolons are not supported in the view builder tool.

6. Can you use a CASE in a view?

CASE is not supported in views in most databases.

7. What happens if you do not provide a column list in a view?

The view uses the column names in the underlying table.

8. How many subqueries can you use in a view?

Theoretically, there is not a limit on the use of subqueries. Your database may have a practical limit on the number it can handle.

9. Is it wise to create views that reference other views?

You should avoid referencing views from other views. You can create serious performance problems quickly using views that reference other views.

10. What restriction characterizes updateable views?

Updateable views must be based on one and only one table.

Module 12: Building Stored Procedures

1. Give the purpose of a stored procedure.

A stored procedure executes SQL statements at the database server, taking advantage of server resources.

2. Under what circumstances might it be preferable to execute as much SQL processing on the client side as possible?

Where resources on the database server are extremely taxed. No server can provide a performance boost if it does not have the resources to allocate to executing the procedure.

3. What SQL statement cannot be used in a stored procedure?

All data manipulation statements are legal. We focused only on SELECTS in this module because we wanted to introduce the core concepts related to stored procedures.

4. With what tools should you create the query for the stored procedure?

You need to use a tool like Query Analyzer. While you can create procedures in minimalist editors like Notepad, it's nice to have color-coded syntax and immediate run capabilities while you work on the query.

5. What SQL statement actually creates a stored procedure?

CREATE PROCEDURE

6. What do you gain if you include numbers in stored procedure names?

The ability to drop a set of procedures by dropping the root name without any number attached to it.

7. Is GO always preferred over RETURN to end a stored procedure?

No. If you want a value passed back to the calling program, you must use RETURN.

8. How do you invoke a stored procedure?

EXEC *storedProcedureName*

9. How should you name stored procedures?

You can name procedures any way you wish, but you are wise to include links to the program that uses the procedure and the specific code in the program that uses the procedure in the procedure name.

A

10. What is the white space used for in laying out a stored procedure in the editor?

White space provides redundant ways of signaling where syntax elements begin and end. Creative use of white space helps you to spot errors quickly.

Module 13: Programming in Stored Procedures

1. What flow control options do you have in SQL?

IF . . . ELSE and loops.

2. What kinds of loops does SQL provide?

The loop structures implemented by the database vendor.

3. What statement raises an error?

RAISEERROR

4. What global variable holds the last error?

@@error

5. How do you get a value out of a stored procedure?

Use RETURN.

6. What must you include in a RAISEERROR statement?

The keyword, the error number or error message, the severity level, and the state number.

7. What value does RETURN return by default?

0

8. How do you obtain the return value from a stored procedure?

EXEC @*SomeVariable* = *storedProcedureName*

9. What does %d mean in an error string?

Substitute a signed integer value here.

10. How are substitution parameters matched with substitution codes in an error string?

The first value in the comma-separated list of values is substituted for the first code, the second value for the second code, and so forth.

Module 14: Using Parameters

1. What happens if you pass two parameter values to a stored procedure that has three input parameters and default values specified for all parameters?

The stored procedure runs. It uses the two values that you provided, and it uses the default value for the third parameter.

2. What happens if you pass two parameter values to a stored procedure that has three input parameters and no default values specified for the parameters?

The stored procedure will encounter an error and fail.

3. How do you add a parameter to the parameters collection?

Use the command's CreateParameter method to create the parameter, and then append the parameter created to the parameters collection using the collection's append method.

4. How do you collect a return value from a stored procedure using SQL?

Include a variable to collect the value in the EXECUTE statement.

5. How do you specify that a parameter is an output parameter in SQL?

Use the OUTPUT keyword in the parameter list when you declare the parameter.

6. What happens if you create a parameter using the command object and you provide none of the optional arguments for CreateParameter?

You create a parameter with default values for the five attributes. Its direction will be adParamUnknown, for example, and you must access the parameter using the index value rather than a name.

A

7. How do you create an output parameter using CreateParameter?

Provide the direction adParamOutput when you call CreateParameter.

8. Under ADO, when are parameter values made available to your program?

After the recordset has completely returned.

9. Is there a disadvantage to not naming parameters under ADO?

Yes. You must access parameters by index values, which have no inherent meaning. You must always make certain that the index value matches the parameter you intend to use.

10. How are parameters matched between the ADO Parameters collection and the actual stored procedure?

Parameters are matched by index number. The input or output parameter with the lowest index value matches the first parameter in the stored procedures parameter list, the input or output parameter with the next higher index matches the second parameter in the stored procedures parameter list, and so forth.

Module 15: Using Cursors

1. Which statement destroys a cursor?

DEALLOCATE

2. What parameter should you check to walk through a cursor using a loop?

@@FETCH_STATUS

3. What option do you need to use in order to move through a cursor in reverse?

SCROLL

4. What code must you use to open a read-only cursor?

FOR READ ONLY

5. When do you need to use BEGIN and END with an IF statement?

When you want to conditionally execute more than one statement.

6. Can you use multiple cursors in a single loop?

Yes

7. Can a cursor be a parameter?

A cursor can be a parameter if you use a cursor variable to pass it.

8. What statement opens and populates a cursor?

OPEN

9. What statement closes a cursor?

CLOSE

10. Are cursor implementations standard in all SQL databases?

No. Most databases extend cursor functionality in some way.

Module 16: Building Unions

1. Why use a temporary table to store the output of a union?

So that you can query the resultset created by the union.

2. What defines the column names that appear in a union?

The column names used in the first query

3. Where can you use ORDER BY in a union?

After the last query.

4. What is the scope of a WHERE clause in a union query?

WHERE applies only to the query it is in. It does not apply to the entire set of queries in the union.

5. Why use a local temporary table to store the results of a union?

The local temporary table is visible only to your session on the database. You prevent other users from truncating the table while you use it.

6. Can the order of columns vary among the queries in a union?

No. Each query must specify the corresponding columns in the same order in order for the union to work.

7. What if the data type in one table varies from the data type in another table?

Your database will attempt to resolve the conflict in data types by using default data type conversion. However, if your database cannot resolve the conflict between data types, it will give an error. You can always explicitly perform the conversion in your queries.

8. Why shouldn't you permanently create a temporary table for use with a union?

In a multi-user database, a permanent table (or a global temporary table) can be accessed by any user that knows the table name. You run the risk of having one user's work overwrite another user's work as they work with the union.

9. Why should you explicitly drop your temporary tables?

To avoid incurring the overhead of the database having to clean up the table after as the session closes. An explicit drop is more efficient, and it guarantees that you know when the table is destroyed.

10. How are columns matched between two queries in a union?

Columns in the same position in the list that follows the SELECT keyword are matched in the union. Column 3 in query 1 goes with column 3 in query 2, for example.

Module 17: Winding Down the Portfolio Project

1. Find a column in the Portfolio database that should be deleted or redefined.

The ClassID field in the Student table. One student may take many classes, and including a single ClassID field in the Student record makes little sense. Either the name of this field should be changed to reflect its actual role, or the field should be deleted.

2. Under what circumstances should you delete data from the database?

Only under the circumstance where you are absolutely and irrevocably sure that you never need to see the data again.

3. What is the best architecture for the client piece for the Portfolio database?

A reusable object, a COM object on a Windows system or a CORBA object on Linux.

4. What do check in and check out procedures actually do?

Change the value of the In_Use field for the item checked in or out.

5. What does the delete procedure actually do?

Change the value of the Deleted field rather than actually deleting records.

6. What critical field do the register and unregister procedures modify?

The Active field in either the Student or the Teacher table.

7. When a teacher registers, what two tables need updated?

The Teacher table and the Class_Teacher table.

8. When a student registers, what two tables need to be updated?

The Student table and the Class_Student table.

9. What fields uniquely identify a student?

First_Name, Last_Name, and Password

10. What uniquely identifies a content item in a portfolio?

The Content_Path column.

Appendix B

A Little SQL Theory

The view of SQL that we have taken is the view from a programmer's perspective, not the view from a database designer's perspective. As a result, we have focused on what you do with SQL rather than how it is formulated, structured, and thought of as a programming language. The purpose of this appendix is to introduce you to the other point of view. Our goal here is a quick tour of SQL theory.

Declarative, Not Procedural

Probably the biggest difference you might have noticed between the Visual Basic code that we examined and the SQL code that we wrote is that SQL is not terribly procedural in nature. Visual Basic, like C, FORTRAN, COBOL, Pascal, Algol, PL/1, and other computer languages, focuses on telling the computer what to do. Statements describe actions in a process. You declare a variable, and then you tell the program to put a value in that variable. Then you instruct the computer to loop three times and add 20 to the value of the variable. After compilation, each statement involves an explanation of what the computer should do with memory, processor registers, the mathematical unit on the CPU, and the logical unit on the CPU.

SQL, in contrast, is called a declarative language. Declarative languages allow you to describe to the computer something you would like to accomplish. The computer examines your description and then determines how to achieve an appropriate result. You tell your database, for example, that you would like to have a two-column output of first names and last names where the last names all begin with "S." The database takes this description and translates it into a process for returning the table. You have given the database no hint about how to undertake collecting the data and returning the result. The database has to formulate its own plan of action.

When you think about it, making a database query language declarative makes sense. Each database is going to have its own methods of retrieving data, and vendors are not interested in sharing their query optimization strategies with other vendors. The goal in building a database as a product is to outperform the competition. In designing the product, you have to make choices about operating systems, query plan generation, methods for scanning tables, and so forth. Since we see these choices as proprietary intellectual property, we don't want to share them by creating a procedural language that exposes them. We would much prefer to translate SELECT into a series of procedures ourselves, and let the next company do so as well. Such methodology allows users to have a common database language while each database can have its own method of selecting data. Every vendor implements SELECT; as users, we do not need to know what procedures are used to accomplish the SELECT. In addition, vendors can change their implementations of methods at will without having to revise the language used to invoke those methods.

A Relational Model

SQL assumes a relational database model. Before explaining that remark, we need to point out that databases need not be relational in structure. A ready example of a nonrelational database is the Windows Registry. Data is not organized into rows and columns. Instead, data is organized into a tree-like structure, with nodes and leafs. To find data, you traverse the nodes in search of a leaf that contains the appropriate value. Search instructions are formulated as paths. HKEY_LOCAL_MACHINE\ Software represents all we need to know to find the software settings in the Registry efficiently. We know our entry point node into the tree, HKEY_LOCAL_MACHINE. We then walk through the child nodes immediately below the entry point and match for node name. When we have found Software, we have found our location. Notice that we do not need to search every value in the database. We needed only to search the nodes immediately below HKEY_LOCAL_MACHINE. This hierarchical structure allows for very efficient retrieval of data so long as you know the path to the value. If you don't have the path, searching is very slow. (Just try searching your Registry for a value using the Registry Editor to prove the point.)

A relational model is based on other premises. First, we are assuming that we will not know the path to the value we are looking for. Node-based searching is therefore inefficient. Second, we are assuming that the data in the database is somehow self-organizing; that is, there are relations among the data elements themselves. Hence the name relational database.

Relations among the data are expressed formally as mathematical sets. A set, for all practical purposes, is a collection of objects that belong together for a reason. The reason is the relation that binds the data. The items could be the attributes belonging to a person, in which case there is an inclusive relationship among the data items. Items are included in the set because they describe one member of the set. Sets can also be based on exclusive relations, as in the set of all numbers that are not multiples of three. Items are included in the set because they are not some other item.

In relational databases, sets are expressed as tables. To take a simple example, all the numbers that are not multiples of three, the table would be organized as follows: one column represents the set, and the individual members of the set each have their own row in the table.

Sets, however, can have complex structures in relational databases. Each item in a set may have its own set of attributes that are common across all items in the set. Addresses, for example, have parts, and we can choose to break the parts out into separate columns in order to refer conveniently to the parts, as well as to the whole address. For example, if I ask you what your address is, you are going to give me a street number, city, state, and zip code. I can write all of this into one column in the table. However, I might later want to know what your zip code is. I can find your address in the table and read the zip code at the end. This approach works. But then I might realize that I want to find addresses of people who live near you. Then breaking the zip code into a separate column allows me to sort the table by zip codes and find the collection of people who live near you. Generally, in relational databases, you want to break as many attributes of an item off as separate columns as you can. You then have a means of examining your data by subparts so that you can answer interesting questions using queries that search for subparts. You gain flexibility in examining your data by doing so.

A row in a relational database table is, therefore, a representation of a set member. Whatever comprises the row represents the attributes of a single member of the set. The list of rows represents a list of the set members. Columns represent attributes of set members. Each row is called a record.

How tables are actually stored on disk is a vendor-specific issue. SQL Server typically uses a single file to store all tables. (You can optionally use multiple files.) Other databases, Quadbase, for example, use one file per table. Others use complex data structures that are written to disk in files that do not match the table structure we perceive when we work with the database. The exact implementation is up to the vendor, and the implementation does not matter as long as we can work with the data using the familiar table, column, and row structure.

The Structure of the Language

SQL consists of three languages, each with its own purpose. In general, this structure reflects a reality. We can talk about databases in at least these three ways, and they are three common ways that we have to talk about the database. The next three sections describe these three ways of talking about a database.

Data Definition Language

We need to be able to describe the data that goes into a database. If we are going to store addresses, for example, we need to describe what an address is and what its parts are. When we do so, we are in a very real sense defining the nature of our data. The statements that we make to define our data are collectively known as the Data Definition Language, or DDL.

How do we describe data? First, we have to be able to create the tables that store the data. In our address example, we know that we need a table that contains street number, street name, unit number, city, state, and zip code. These fields usually describe an address in the United States. The CREATE TABLE statement that builds the table describes the data to the database, right down to the data types for each column that make up the table. If we discover that we need to include addresses from other countries, we need to add new fields and perhaps to change the names of other fields. (It is polite to refer to the zip code column as the postal code, for example.) An ALTER TABLE statement allows us to describe this change. If we ever need to delete the table, the DROP TABLE statement we use describes the change.

Data Definition Language includes the statements we use to create, alter, and drop objects in the database. We say "objects" here because data definition can go beyond tables. It includes views and stored procedures, as well as the users who will interact with the data. All of these fall under the rubric of DDL.

Data Manipulation Language

For most of this book, we have worked with Data Manipulation Language, or DML. The statements that allow you to select, insert, update, and delete make up this language. In addition, the statements and predicates that allow you to format and display the results of queries belong to the realm of Data Manipulation Language.

Data Manipulation Language is the part of SQL that programmers use most. Its power derives from its ability to allow you to declare the structure of the data as you want it. When you issue a DML statement, you have no knowledge of how the data is currently ordered and stored, nor do you need to care. You simply describe to the database the results you want to achieve. The database's job is to reformulate the data to match the plan described by the DML statement.

Data Control Language

Data Control Language allows you to describe who may have access to the data. We have not focused on this language as a part of this book, mainly because programmers typically do not have administrative rights over their databases. Data Control Language is the province of the database administrator, not the programmer, and well it should be. Data control is successful if and only if a limited number of highly trusted individuals control access to the data. If anyone can set access to the data, you have no security and privacy associated with your database at all.

Two SQL statements form the core of DCL, GRANT and REVOKE. Using GRANT, you grant access to the data. Using REVOKE, you limit access to the data. Two kinds of objects are involved in DCL, users and roles. You can create database users using special stored procedures for this purpose. In SQL Server, for example, sp_addlogin allows you to create a user account. Roles are typically defined by the database, and they are ways of using the database to which users can be added. Every user you create is a member of the public role. Whatever permissions you grant to public, every user has. Databases typically define other roles. SQL Server has db_datareader and db_datawriter, for example.

Note

There are three statements for permission in SQL 2000, Grant, Deny, and Revoke. Revoke removes a previously granted or denied permission, leaving other permissions intact.

The permissions that you can grant are to select, insert, update, delete, or execute. These permissions are related to the main query verbs. Execute is for stored procedures, allowing users who hold the permission to run the stored procedure.

To take complete advantage of your Data Control Language, you need to dig into the details of your database's implementation. Each database extends the DCL to meet its own implementation goals, so the exact details of the DCL you will use depend on the vendor.

Dependence on Transactions

Working with a relational database would be a waste of time if you were not certain that the data would remain safe and protected in the database. If you go to the trouble of storing the data in the first place, you want to be able to retrieve it when you need it. Relational databases rely on the concept of transactions to protect your data.

Transactions are groups of statements, usually Data Manipulation Language statements, of which all must succeed together or all must fail together. If the group of statements succeeds, the database is left in a consistent state. If the statements all fail, the database is left in the same consistent state that it was in before the transaction started. Transactions are designed to protect the consistency of the data.

In practical terms, each SQL statement is its own transaction. If you attempt an INSERT and it fails, you are not left with a couple of columns that made it into the database and a few that didn't. The database cleans up after the failure, leaving the table you attempted to insert into in the same state it was in before you made the attempt.

When you run a group of statements, each succeeds or fails, and the cleanup routines take care of each statement. However, SQL and your database cannot tell what your intentions are for a group of statements. You can define a batch of statements using GO, but you may not care whether they all succeed as a group if an error occurs. To indicate that you do care, you wrap the statements with a BEGIN TRANSACTION . . . COMMIT TRANSACTION block. You check for errors and explicitly execute a ROLLBACK TRANSACTION statement if an error occurs. When you use a transaction, if a catastrophic failure of some kind occurs, such that you cannot even get to the point where you check for errors, the database engine has enough information to clean up after the failed transaction. Transactions, therefore, keep your database in a consistent and predictable state.

Focus on Integrity

Relational databases also need to focus on the integrity of the data. They rely on several strategies to protect data integrity. The definition of data types is one such strategy. For example, if you define a column's data type as money, then the database engine makes sure that the values that go into the column are values that reasonably represent monetary values. You have to use numbers, and the numbers have to have no more than four decimal places. If the data being inserted does not meet these expectations, you receive a data type mismatch error that you must deal with. Declaring whether a column can accept a null value is another way of protecting data integrity.

The more important form of integrity associated with relational databases is referential integrity. This concept recognizes that we may have multiple references to data in our database. We used the example of shipping zones tied to zip codes in this book. To implement a table of shipping zones successfully, you need to tie the zones to zip codes. The zone is a calculation based on the distances between two zip codes. In the zone table, we have a reference to a zip code and the zone calculation, two columns. In the address table, we have a zip code column. We can look up the zone for an address by joining the two tables on zip code.

We now have two tables that contain zip codes. Because zip codes are stored in two locations, it is possible for the two columns in the two tables to be out of synchronization. In order to join the tables effectively, we need at least one entry in the zone table for each zip code in the address table; otherwise, we would never be able to look up the zone for any given address. Referential integrity is the theoretical construct that allows us to guarantee that such consistency is enforced.

This theoretical construct is implemented as a set of constraints. The constraint rules cause the database engine to check to see whether the zip code for the address is present in the zone table before the address is entered into the database. If the constraint cannot be satisfied, the address table cannot be updated. As we worked with constraints, we noted that there are several types that can be implemented. Foreign key constraints make sure that the foreign key is a primary key somewhere else before it is added to a table as a foreign key. Check constraints make sure that a column entry meets an expected format or pattern. Primary key constraints force each row in a table to have a unique identifier. Each of these types of rules enforces a certain kind of data integrity.

Referential integrity rules guarantee that multiple references in multiple tables to the same data item are consistent. In our zip code example, references to the same zip code in the two tables have to be consistent. Referential integrity also requires that if we remove one reference to a data item, we remove all other references. Since we guarantee that a zip code in the address table must appear in the zone table, if we remove an entry from the zone table, we need to remove all entries for that zip code from the address table. Imagine a situation where a zip code is decommissioned. (It's not likely to happen, but it could.) When we remove the entry from the zone table, we need to be sure that all the address entries are corrected to the correct zip code, whatever codes they happened to be merged into after the decommissioning. If we have not done so, we will have an orphaned zip code in our data and we cannot look up the shipping zone for it. Referential integrity constraints guarantee that we cannot remove the zip from the zone table until all the references to it in the address table are corrected.

Conclusion

These basic theoretical constructs inform the design of any SQL database. They also inform the design of any SQL implementation, and the design of the SQL standards. Like normalization rules, you can find much more about SQL standards in the body of literature published on database design. This appendix has sought to give you the basic grounding so that you can investigate that literature further if you so desire.

Index